Southern Biography Series
Bertram Wyatt-Brown, Editor

HENRY HUGHES

AND

PROSLAVERY THOUGHT IN THE

OLD SOUTH

HENRY HUGHES

AND

PROSLAVERY THOUGHT IN THE

OLD SOUTH

DOUGLAS AMBROSE

LOUISIANA STATE UNIVERSITY PRESS

BATON ROUGE AND LONDON

Copyright © 1996 by Louisiana State University Press

All rights reserved

Manufactured in the United States of America

First printing

05 04 03 02 01 00 99 98 97 96   5 4 3 2 1

Designer: Amanda McDonald Key

Typeface Granjon

Typesetter: Impressions Book and Journal Services, Inc.

Printer and binder: Thomson–Shore, Inc.

Library of Congress Cataloging-in-Publication Data

Ambrose, Douglas, 1957–

    Henry Hughes and proslavery thought in the Old South / Douglas
Ambrose.

       p.   cm. — (Southern biography series)

    Includes bibliographical references and index.

    ISBN 0-8071-2080-4 (cl : alk. paper)

    1. Hughes, Henry, d. 1862.   2. Sociology—Southern States.
3. Slavery—Southern States.   4. Southern States—Race relations.
I. Title. II. Series.

HM22.A-Z.U6H843   1997

301'.0975—dc20   96-30214
                                               CIP

The paper in this book meets the guidelines for perma-
nence and durability of the Committee on Production
Guidelines for Book Longevity of the Council on Library
Resources. ⊖

For my parents,
James and Elsa Ambrose, with love and gratitude

I feel like I am the man for times coming.

　　　　　　　　　　　—Henry Hughes, 1852

CONTENTS

ACKNOWLEDGMENTS

Like all authors, I have accumulated a number of debts over the years. Although formal acknowledgments cannot begin to satisfy those debts, they nonetheless permit me to offer heartfelt thanks. My greatest debt is to my parents, whose love and support have nourished me all my life. My sisters and brothers have remained constant sources of love and encouragement, even when they wondered just what it was I was doing.

I owe enormous intellectual debts to my teachers. At Rutgers University, many years ago, Thomas Forstenzer helped me understand why and how we study those with whom we disagree. At Binghamton University, Charles Freedeman, Charles Forcey, Bernard Mason, W. Warren Wagar, and Thomas Dublin forced me to sharpen my thinking and refine my analytical framework. Professor Forcey deserves special thanks for his valiant efforts to make me clarify both my ideas and my expression of them. I also learned much from my fellow graduate students, who made Binghamton in the 1980s a wonderful place to study history.

The Mississippi Department of Archives and History provided a most congenial environment for research. I am most grateful to the friendly and professional staff, especially Hank Holmes and Mickey Hennen, Jr., for their invaluable assistance. Michelle Hudson and Charlie Brenner of the Eudora Welty Library of the Jackson-Hinds Public Library System deserve special thanks for making my time in Jackson, Port Gibson, and Natchez so enjoyable and rewarding. Binghamton University provided the financial support that I needed to conduct much of my research. Thanks also to the administration of Hamilton College for its generous junior faculty leave policy, which permitted me to devote the last year to the writing of this book. My colleagues, especially Robert L. Paquette, and students at Hamilton also deserve appreciation for the patience and support they have shown me over the past six years.

The professional and personable staff at Louisiana State University

Press skillfully guided the manuscript through its final stages. Margaret Dalrymple initially oversaw the process and, after her departure, John Easterly and Catherine Landry smoothly completed it. Trudie Calvert proved to be a wonderful copy editor; her sharp and insightful eye caught many errors, and she helped tighten my argument and presentation.

Several dear friends merit special gratitude. Thomas Wermuth and Joe McCartin have listened to and read my thoughts about Henry Hughes, proslavery thought, and innumerable other topics for over ten years. Their criticism, encouragement, and support have sustained me and have made me a better historian. Thea Arnold has also listened, read, and in many other ways helped shepherd this project from a rough initial proposal to its final incarnation. Her valuable criticism and equally valuable support over the years have contributed mightily to the progress of this work.

I am grateful to William K. Scarborough for his careful reading of the original manuscript. Bertram Wyatt-Brown, the editor of the Southern Biography Series, read the manuscript and provided helpful advice and encouragement. I am especially indebted to Michael O'Brien for his characteristically close and penetrating readings of this manuscript. His detailed and thoughtful comments have strengthened the final book.

I owe far more than thanks to Elizabeth Fox-Genovese and Eugene D. Genovese for the ways in which they have influenced me and improved this book. As scholars they provided models of academic excellence; as teachers they generously shared their passion for and knowledge of the South; as friends they have encouraged and supported me as I have developed my own understanding of southern history. Neither they nor anyone other than myself is responsible for the shortcomings of this work. They are, however, largely responsible for whatever strengths it might have.

Sheila O'Connor has witnessed only the final stages of this book's preparation, but her acute editorial eye and probing questions have improved its final form. More important, her love and faith promise that life "after the book" will be filled with joy and grace.

HENRY HUGHES

AND

PROSLAVERY THOUGHT IN THE

OLD SOUTH

INTRODUCTION

During the early decades of the nineteenth century, the political, religious, and intellectual leaders of southern society moved from a defense of slavery as a necessary evil to the defense of slavery as a positive good. The leading proslavery ideologues differed in the emphasis they placed on the various positive attributes of slavery as a social system, but most concurred both in defending their own specific social relations and in attempting to abstract from those social relations general rules of social order. Henry Hughes of Port Gibson, Mississippi, formulated a distinct view of the future of southern social and political development. He envisioned a southern social order that was centered around and grounded in a powerful, authoritarian state. His embrace of state power as the means for both the preservation and extension of unfree labor distinguished him from most antebellum southern intellectuals. More important, his statism forcefully demonstrated his rejection of the principles of individual rights, personal liberty, and the efficacy and morality of the market as the basis of economic and social life.

The intellectual history of the Old South, of which the proslavery argument formed an important but by no means exclusive part, has recently become the subject of much historical inquiry. Reversing a long-standing tendency to regard the antebellum South as an intellectual desert incapable, primarily because of slavery, of supporting the life of the mind, a growing number of historians have persuasively demonstrated the vitality of southern intellectual endeavors.[1] Yet, as rich as this literature has been, it has focused mainly on individuals from the eastern seaboard states and has neglected those, like Hughes, who lived in the hinterland of the

---

1. The field of southern intellectual history has grown tremendously in the past two decades. For some of the most important developments in the field, see the works of Lewis P. Simpson, Drew Gilpin Faust, Michael O'Brien, Elizabeth Fox-Genovese, Eugene D. Genovese, and Bertram Wyatt-Brown listed in the bibliography.

Old Southwest. The study of Hughes's life suggests that by broadening the scope of southern intellectual history to include less developed regions than Charleston and tidewater Virginia and figures other than Hugh Swinton Legaré and George Frederick Holmes we can better appreciate the breadth of intellectual activity in the Old South and the depth of the proslavery sentiment that accompanied much of that activity.

Hughes was a product of small-town Mississippi. The son of a minor cotton factor and merchant, Hughes acquired and nurtured his intellectual interests in Port Gibson, which was located on the Bayou Pierre about forty-two miles north of Natchez. The county seat of Claiborne County, Port Gibson resembled many small but important towns within the cotton belt of the Southwest that served as economic, political, and cultural centers for the surrounding countryside.[2] Born, raised, and educated in and around Port Gibson, Hughes emerged as an intellectual of wide-ranging interests, but one who concentrated on defending and promoting the unfree labor system on which that town and its larger society was based.

The chapters that follow explore the relation between Hughes's intellectual interests and his proslavery convictions. Like most southern thinkers, Hughes was not consumed by the issue of slavery.[3] His interests ranged from science to art to language. But if he was not obsessed with

2. On southern towns, see E. Brooks Holifield, *The Gentlemen Theologians: American Theology in Southern Culture, 1795–1860* (Durham, 1978), esp. Chap. 1; James C. Bonner, *Milledgeville, Georgia's Antebellum Capital* (Athens, Ga., 1978); Ulrich Bonnell Phillips, "Historical Notes of Milledgeville, Georgia," in Phillips, *The Slave Economy of the Old South: Selected Essays in Economic and Social History,* ed. Eugene D. Genovese (Baton Rouge, 1968); John Hebron Moore, *The Emergence of the Cotton Kingdom in the Old Southwest: Mississippi, 1770–1860* (Baton Rouge, 1988); Walter C. Hearn, "Towns in Antebellum Mississippi" (Ph.D. dissertation, University of Mississippi, 1969).

3. Michael O'Brien has perhaps been most adamant among southern historians in rejecting the notion of "the obsession of the Southern mind with slavery." In a survey of the contents of leading antebellum southern literary periodicals, O'Brien found that only 10 to 20 percent of articles addressed either slavery or politics. Although heated political times, such as 1851, drove the percentage up to 35, these percentages make it clear that southern intellectuals found much more to write about than slavery and political issues. See O'Brien, "On the Mind of the Old South and Its Accessibility," in *All Clever Men Who Make Their Way: Critical Discourse in the Old South* (Fayetteville, 1982), 1–25. This essay, with minor changes, is also included in O'Brien's *Rethinking the South: Essays in Intellectual History* (Baltimore, 1988), 19–37.

slavery to the exclusion of all other intellectual pursuits, he nonetheless
wrote far more in the defense of slavery than on all other topics combined.
This focus is hardly surprising given the period during which Hughes
reached maturity and began publishing his writings. His first major
work, *Treatise on Sociology: Theoretical and Practical,* appeared in 1854,
just as the sectional crisis moved into its most heated phase.[4] Hughes died
during the Civil War, and his publications all appeared before 1861.
Unlike Legaré, who began publishing in the 1820s and who died in 1843,
or Holmes, who began publishing in 1839 and did not stop until the mid-
1880s, Hughes had a literary life that was narrowly concentrated into six
of the most politicized years in American history.

The turmoil of the times did not alone account for the intellectual
energy Hughes devoted to the slavery question. He recognized the crisis
between slavery and free labor as the great issue of the day—one that
deserved all the attention and effort he could offer. Although other matters interested him, he subordinated them to the paramount problem that
contemporaries referred to as the "social question" posed not only to the
South but to all of Western civilization. For Hughes, slavery, or, more
properly, unfree labor, was not a narrow political or economic issue but
one that cut to the heart of all aspects of social order and human progress.
Hughes did not fixate on slavery; he was deeply concerned about the
relations between social organization and social development in general
and about the struggle between southern slavery and northern free labor
in particular.

Hughes's desire to defend unfree labor and attack free labor led him
to develop his own unique vision of the model social order. This vision,
which Hughes termed "warranteeism," employed elements he acquired
from his reading of contemporary European and American social theorists and critics. Like most southern thinkers, Hughes actively participated in the intellectual developments of the Atlantic world.[5] In the diary

4. Henry Hughes, *Treatise on Sociology, Theoretical and Practical* (1854; rpr. New
York, 1968).

5. The idea that the Old South was cut off from the intellectual innovations and
developments of Europe and elsewhere is difficult to sustain in light of much of the
literature listed in note 1 above. In fields such as theology, political economy, and medicine, southern intellectuals displayed sophisticated familiarity with contemporary issues.
For a critique of the notion that the South was out of touch with the intellectual currents

he kept from January, 1848, to May, 1853, he meticulously recorded the classic and contemporary works he read. But Ronald Takaki errs when he states that Hughes read European and American writers "only because he wanted to use their ideas and methods to refute the charges that slavery was 'morally and civilly inexpedient.'"[6] Hughes's diary shows that his interest in those "ideas and methods" was well established before he turned to the defense of slavery. Nonetheless, his interpretation and application of the knowledge he garnered through his readings and his tour of Europe in 1853–1854 ultimately resulted in an attempt to incorporate elements of Western social thought into a defense of the unfree labor that was the basis of his society. This book delineates the ways in which his life and thought reflected a particular variant of the proslavery movement, a variant that sought to anchor the defense of unfree labor on new, modern grounds. Hughes's proslavery argument relied on neither property rights nor fears of racial chaos; rather it urged southerners to recognize that only a sweeping expansion of state power, planning, and control could save their society and the values it represented.

Hughes, of course, shared much with his fellow proslavery advocates, most obviously a firm conviction that southern unfree labor had to be preserved. But unanimity did not distinguish southern thought, even within the proslavery argument.[7] No individual can fully represent that argument, and this work makes no such claim for Hughes. But his thought does not simply attest to the diversity of southern proslavery arguments. His vision of the proper social order constituted a bold and original attempt to strengthen both the southern social system and its formal defense in the face of the increasingly powerful material and

---

of the day, see O'Brien, "On the Mind of the Old South and Its Accessibility," in *All Clever Men Who Make Their Way.*

6. Ronald T. Takaki, *A Pro-Slavery Crusade: The Agitation to Reopen the African Slave Trade* (New York, 1971), 98.

7. The diversity of and conflict within southern thought have been much studied. For debates among political economists see Eugene D. Genovese and Elizabeth Fox-Genovese, "Slavery, Economic Development, and the Law: the Dilemma of the Southern Political Economists, 1800–1860," *Washington and Lee Law Review,* XLI (1981), 1–29; for the often vicious discussions on the nature of people of African descent, see William Stanton, *The Leopard's Spots: Scientific Attitudes Toward Race in America, 1815–1859* (Chicago, 1960); and for the intense debate over the proposal to reopen the African slave trade, in which Hughes participated vigorously, see Takaki, *Pro-Slavery Crusade.*

ideological forces of free labor. Although this vision incorporated many elements that other proslavery ideologues also held dear, it departed in significant ways from their main arguments.

Hughes most closely resembled George Fitzhugh in his uncompromising advocacy of unfree labor as the only proper basis for social organization. Like Fitzhugh, Hughes urged the abolition of free labor wherever it ruled and its replacement with unfree labor. Fitzhugh, however, displayed a Burkean conservative appreciation for tradition and distrusted science and philosophy.[8] In stark contrast, Hughes emphatically rejected the past, including the South's, as a guide for present and future actions and enthusiastically embraced science, reason, and especially the notion of progress, which he understood as the spread of unfree labor and the destruction of free labor through the use of state power. He maintained, in fact, that slavery no longer existed in the South but had evolved into "warranteeism." Warranteeism differed from slavery most notably in that the "warrantor" or master did not own the "warrantee" or servant but instead, as "an agent of the State," enforced the "civil obligation" of warrantees to labor.[9] Hughes's concept of a vast, authoritative state as the vehicle by which progress would be achieved and order preserved stands as his most distinctive and significant contribution to proslavery thought. This fundamental aspect of his work strongly supports Bertram Wyatt-Brown's observation that Hughes was "the most forward-looking of the proslavery zealots."[10] He was, indeed, the foremost proponent of statism in the antebellum South.

The state, as Hughes understood it, would not only provide a fundamentally different basis for unfree labor than one person's ownership of another, but it would also prevent the market from being the central organizing principle of society. Like Fitzhugh, Holmes, and other proslavery figures in the 1850s, Hughes rejected contemporary political econ-

---

8. On Fitzhugh see Harvey Wish, *George Fitzhugh: Propagandist of the Old South* (New York, 1941), and Eugene D. Genovese, *The World the Slaveholders Made: Two Essays in Interpretation* (New York, 1969), Pt. 2.

9. Hughes's concept of warranteeism and the ways it differed from slavery are discussed fully in Chapter 3.

10. Bertram Wyatt-Brown, "Modernizing Southern Slavery: The Proslavery Argument Reinterpreted," in *Region, Race, and Reconstruction: Essays in Honor of C. Vann Woodward,* ed. J. Morgan Kousser and James M. McPherson (New York, 1982), 40.

omy as a science on which society ought to be based. Instead, he developed a "science of societary organization" or "sociology" that forcefully subordinated economics to politics and focused less on economic development than on what he saw as the proper relations between society's members. While many proslavery advocates, including Louisa S. McCord, James D. B. De Bow, and Jacob Cardozo, did attempt to reconcile political economy and the defense of slavery, Hughes recognized the incompatibility of contemporary political economy and his notion of proper social organization. He consequently attempted to construct a more "scientific" and thus more powerful defense of unfree labor in the abstract. That attempt led him to articulate a vision of the future in which neither slavery—understood as one person's ownership of another—nor free labor predominated. Rather, society would be organized according to principles developed and implemented by a state that commanded the obedience of all. Yet, as the chapters below make clear, Hughes was unable to reconcile the contradictions within southern society. Even as his theory sought to eliminate or severely restrict the role of market forces, especially in social relations, his more immediate need to defend the South from external attack led him, at times, to claim that market forces encouraged benevolent treatment of slaves by masters. Hughes's inconsistencies reveal the difficulties he encountered in his attempts both to formulate an abstract vision of the model social order and to defend an existing society that was inextricably embedded in the capitalist world market.

During his life Hughes was neither powerful nor widely influential. The future that he pointed to remained beyond the ability of the slave South to realize before it sought its independence. Much of what he recommended could be only partially implemented under the stresses of war.[11] Yet the marginal position of Hughes and his ideas in southern life should not lead us to conclude that he and they were somehow foreign to southern society. Hughes and his thought expressed genuine tendencies

---

11. For more on the expansion of state power in the Confederacy during the Civil War see the Conclusion of this book. The most recent, and extensive, discussion of how the war affected state development can be found in the work of Richard F. Bensel. See his "Southern Leviathan: The Development of Central State Authority in the Confederate States of America," in *Studies in American Political Development,* Vol. II, ed. Karen Orren and Stephen Skowronek (New Haven, 1987), 68–136, and *Yankee Leviathan: The Origins of Central State Authority in America, 1859–1877* (New York, 1990), esp. Chap. 3.

in southern cultural and intellectual life. He recognized the crisis unfree labor faced in the mid-nineteenth century; as well, he recognized the crisis the "social question" posed to all societies. He boldly proposed both to save unfree labor and solve the social question by employing modern notions of science and state planning and control in an effort to create a hierarchical social order wherein an authoritarian state regulated all aspects of social activity.

Like many proslavery advocates, Hughes urged the reform of southern slavery. But unlike those who, for example, called for Christian respect for slave families, he proposed a fundamental alteration of southern social relations. Only such an alteration, he believed, could ensure order, stability, and progress in a world rapidly becoming dominated by the chaos, anarchy, and decadence produced by free labor society and ideology. Although Hughes died at the age of thirty-three in 1862 in a war that ended his dream of southern warranteeism, the idea of an authoritarian state regulating a multiclass, hierarchical society has continued to appeal to others who have looked at equality and have seen disorder, and at freedom and have seen license. Hughes, as southerner and American, reflects a tendency in our history that we have too often ignored or too quickly dismissed as aberrant. In fact, he embodied a persistent reaction against the rule of the market and claims of liberal individualism that have accompanied capitalism's triumphant march through American history. Although this reaction surfaced throughout the antebellum United States, only in the South did it both constitute the expression of the dominant class in society and grow out of the material basis of unfree labor.[12] In Hughes's thought and writings, the antebellum southern alternative to a social vision based on freedom and equality found its most forceful and comprehensive expression.

12. Larry E. Tise, in his provocative book *Proslavery: A History of the Defense of Slavery in America, 1701–1840* (Athens, Ga., 1987), argues that proslavery thought, which he loosely defines as "the general attitude of favoring slavery," "was a mode of thinking, a concatenation of ideas, and a system of symbols that expressed the social cultural, and moral values of a large portion of the population of America in the first half of the nineteenth century" (xv). Although Tise's study helps us understand the persistence of conservative and even proslavery elements in northern thought, he fails to emphasize adequately the enormous differences in the social and material contexts of the North and South that determined, to a large extent, the marginal, defensive nature of proslavery thought in the North and its dominant, offensive nature in the South.

1

THE ORIGINS OF THE SOCIOLOGIST
1829–1848

Henry Hughes prided himself on being a Mississippian. Although he lived in New Orleans for a short time and traveled to the North and Europe, Mississippi was always home. Born, educated, and buried in Claiborne County, Hughes was nothing if not a product of the culture and society of antebellum Mississippi.

His family background typified in many ways that of middling sorts who settled in Mississippi during the early decades of the nineteenth century. His father, Benjamin Hughes, born in Kentucky in 1789, served as assistant deputy quartermaster general under General William Henry Harrison in the War of 1812. He remained in Kentucky after the war and in 1818 married Nancy Brashear in Senecatown, Kentucky.[1] Benjamin Hughes married well. The Brashears, Huguenots who had settled in Virginia in the mid-seventeenth century, had been, like the Hugheses, in central Kentucky since the early 1780s.[2] The Brashears already had well-established and successful kin in Claiborne County, Mississippi, when Benjamin and Nancy Hughes and their three-year-old daughter Mary Ann migrated there in 1824.[3]

1. Brashear Genealogy, Folder 2, Box 22, and Benjamin Hughes Materials, Folder 6, Box 11, in Smith Coffee Daniell IV Collection, Mississippi Department of Archives and History, Jackson (hereinafter cited as MDAH).

2. Brashear Materials, Folder 5, Box 18, *ibid.*

3. Early Family Correspondence, Folder 1, Box 11, Brashear Genealogy, Folder 2, Box 20, and Hughes Family Genealogy Materials, Folder 4, Box 22, *ibid.*

In migrating to Mississippi, which had just become a state in 1817, the Hughes family joined thousands of others who flocked to the cheap and fertile lands of the Old Southwest. Although the area around Natchez had been settled as far back as 1716, settlement in the Mississippi Territory before 1815 generally remained confined to the greater Natchez district. But the War of 1812 and the worldwide demand for cotton combined to transform the sparsely inhabited territory into a bustling frontier. The war devastated the indigenous tribes of Alabama and Mississippi, most notably the Creeks, and although the Choctaw and Chickasaw tribes remained in the northern two-thirds of Mississippi until the 1830s, the southern third of the state was wide open after the war. The rage for cotton, which had slowed appreciably during the war, took off in the years immediately following the Treaty of Ghent. Although the Panic of 1819 and the subsequent depression tempered the demand for and price of cotton, by the early 1820s Mississippi cotton production reached new highs and continued to climb. New disease-resistant breeds bolstered farmers' confidence and helped make cotton the crop of choice among Mississippi agriculturists.[4]

As popular as cotton cultivation was, Benjamin Hughes did not come to Mississippi to become a planter. Instead, the Hughes family settled in Port Gibson, and Benjamin set himself up as a merchant in nearby Grand Gulf. In 1824 Port Gibson was one of the largest towns in Mississippi, although it numbered fewer than five hundred inhabitants.[5] Port Gibson was the center of a rapidly expanding agricultural region, and men like Benjamin Hughes serviced the cotton planters who dominated the surrounding countryside. But the town was more than a simple appendage to the sprawling plantations in Claiborne County. Although dependent

4. For the early development of the area that became the state of Mississippi, see Lewis Cecil Gray, *History of Agriculture in the Southern United States to 1860* (2 vols.; 1933; rpr. Gloucester, 1958), II, 687–88, 893–901; John Hebron Moore, *Agriculture in Ante-Bellum Mississippi* (New York, 1958), 13–68; and Moore, *Emergence of the Cotton Kingdom,* 1–18.

5. Neither the 1820 nor 1830 federal censuses recorded the populations of Mississippi towns other than Natchez. The earliest recorded population of Port Gibson is from 1829, when the town had 592 inhabitants, black and white. This figure is from an article taken from the Port Gibson *Correspondent,* August 15, 1829, and included in "Early Days of Claiborne County," Port Gibson *Reveille,* August 19, 1926, quoted in Katy McCaleb Headley, comp., *Claiborne County, Mississippi: The Promised Land* (Port Gibson, Miss., 1976), 57.

on cotton for its existence, Port Gibson developed a society that set it apart from the rural isolation of the plantation. In many ways, the town served as the cultural and intellectual center of a predominantly frontier area. It imparted to its citizens a style of life characterized by a degree of sophistication and worldliness not known in most of Mississippi.

Founded in 1788 by Samuel Gibson, Port Gibson had slowly evolved into a significant inland town by the first decade of the nineteenth century. The early history of the town, located on the Bayou Pierre, a small tributary of the Mississippi, resembled that of many outposts in the thinly populated Mississippi Territory. In 1809 Fortesque Cumings traveled down the Ohio and Mississippi rivers and on his return trip passed through Port Gibson. His record of the journey reveals a town still caught up in the early throes of settlement. Port Gibson had already assumed an important place in the economy of the area. It was, Cumings related, "esteemed the most thriving place in the territory." He noted that the town prospered most "when the waters are up and the Bayou is navigable for the large craft," for the storekeepers would import goods and export cotton. While impressed by the economic activity in Port Gibson, Cumings also found much to his moral distaste in the new town: "Gambling is carried to the greatest excess, particularly horse racing, cards, and betting—a wager always deciding every difference of opinion. On the whole, Port Gibson and its neighborhood is perhaps the most dissolute as well as the most thriving part of the territory."[6] Another account of the town in 1822 states that "there were but few families, few children, and but one young lady, but plenty of bachelors."[7] These "vegetating nondescripts" contributed to Port Gibson's reputation as a wild settlement, just barely above barbarism.

This portrait of Port Gibson as a dynamic yet decadent town gradually changed as it became less a seasonal center of exchange and more a permanent home to merchants, lawyers, and others. In 1818 Port Gibson established the first library in the new state of Mississippi. In the same year it acquired a newspaper, making it only the second town in the state,

6. Fortesque Cumings, *Sketches of a Tour of the Western Country* (Pittsburgh, 1810), 286, 319–21, quoted *ibid.,* 54–55.

7. "Port Gibson and Vicinity Forty-Five Years Ago," Port Gibson *Standard,* July 17, 1874, quoted *ibid.,* 57. The article described Port Gibson in 1829, but this sentence refers to the town "seven years since," or in 1822.

after Natchez, to have one. Both the Methodists and the Presbyterians erected churches in Port Gibson during the 1820s, conducted Sunday schools, and established organized religion as a prominent aspect of town life. In 1826 the state legislature incorporated the Presbyterians' Clinton Academy, which served about fifty students in 1829.[8] As its economic growth continued, Port Gibson in the 1820s emerged as one of the most stable and cultivated towns in Mississippi.

Port Gibson impressed many who passed through it in the late 1820s and early 1830s, including Joseph Ingraham, a northerner who traveled through Mississippi during the early 1830s and published *The South-West, by a Yankee* in 1835. Ingraham criticized some of what he saw, especially the relentless, single-minded pursuit of land, cotton, and slaves that characterized Mississippi during the period known by contemporaries and historians since as the "flush times." But Ingraham had little but praise for what he encountered in Port Gibson. He extolled it as "one of the most flourishing and beautiful towns in the south. It is second only to Natchez in the beauty of its location, the regularity of its streets, the neatness of its dwellings, and the number and excellence of its public buildings." More than the physical condition of Port Gibson struck Ingraham. Clearly aware of the town's early reputation, he marveled at its moral evolution: "The citizens were once distinguished for their dissipation, if not profligacy; but they are now more distinguished for their intelligence and morality as a community. There is no town in the south which possesses so high a standard of morals as Port Gibson."[9]

Ingraham did not limit his portrait of Port Gibson to its moral character. He understood well the basic function of antebellum southern towns, and Port Gibson certainly supported his observation that "a county seat, and a cotton mart, are all that an agricultural country requires."[10]

---

8. *Ibid.*, 53, 121–25, 129–34, 57, 159–61. The school changed its name to the Port Gibson Academy in 1830, and in 1854 it was incorporated and chartered as the Port Gibson Female Collegiate Academy. For more on antebellum academies see Aubrey Keith Lucas, "Education in Mississippi to 1860," in *A History of Mississippi*, ed. Richard A. McLemore (2 vols.; Jackson, 1973), I, 352–58.

9. [Joseph H. Ingraham], *The South-West, by a Yankee* (2 vols.; 1835; rpr. New York, 1968), II, 164–65. The term "flush times" was popularized by Joseph G. Baldwin in his *The Flush Times of Alabama and Mississippi: A Series of Sketches* (1853; rpr. Baton Rouge, 1987).

10. [Ingraham], *The South-West*, II, 205.

Although an antebellum town may have developed a culture distinct from that of the countryside, the supremacy of the latter in economic and ideological terms never wavered. The plantation remained the dominant institution in southern life. Ulrich Bonnell Phillips cogently summed up the relation between town and plantation in his brief 1903 article on Milledgeville, Georgia: "Except for the great export staple there would have been little use for merchants or towns." As cotton culture spread through the Southwest, towns followed, providing the support services cotton demanded: credit institutions, supply stores, legal aid, and social activities. Port Gibson provided all of these. An 1829 article in the Port Gibson *Correspondent* that listed the various occupations in the town reveals the dependence of the townspeople on agricultural activity. The list included physicians, lawyers, merchants, grocers, apothecaries, tavern keepers, mechanics, a printer, as well as millinery and fancy storekeepers. All these men and women relied on the countryside for their livelihoods. Ingraham noted the dual function of southern towns, to provide economic and social needs to surrounding planters: "In these towns are the banks, the merchants, the post offices, and the several places of resort for business or pleasure that draw the planter and his family from his estate. Each town is the centre of a circle which extends many miles around it into the country, and daily attracts all within its influence. The ladies come in their carriages 'to shop,' the gentlemen, on horseback, to do business with their commission merchants, visit the banks, hear the news, dine together at hotels, and ride back in the evening. The southern town is properly the 'Exchange' for the neighbouring planters, and the 'Broadway' for their wives and daughters."[11]

Port Gibson served as both "exchange" and "broadway" for the planters of Claiborne County. As residence of the county government and courthouse, of merchants and lawyers, of the local newspaper and theater, the town provided essential services for the scattered surrounding settlers. Although it lacked the frenzied activity of a major river port, its links

11. Phillips, "Historical Notes of Milledgeville, Georgia," in Phillips, *The Slave Economy of the Old South,* ed. Genovese, 177; "Early Days of Claiborne County," Port Gibson *Reveille,* August 19, 1926, from the Port Gibson *Correspondent,* August 15, 1829, quoted in Headley, comp., *Claiborne County,* 56–57. For more on the relation between town shopkeepers and the countryside see Moore, *Emergence of the Cotton Kingdom,* 255–56; [Ingraham], *The South-West,* II, 205–206.

through the Bayou Pierre with the Mississippi River town of Grand Gulf tied it closely to the flow of cotton to the busiest port in the South, New Orleans. Of all Mississippi towns in 1835, Grand Gulf ranked behind only Natchez in volume of trade.[12] Port Gibson provided many of the facilities found in Natchez and Grand Gulf so planters could conduct their business locally. These planters and cotton farmers relied on the experience of Port Gibson's commission merchants or factors to facilitate the movement of cotton from farm to market as well as the return flow of credit and supplies to the plantation. Factors represented in many ways the primary function of the town itself: they served the needs of the countryside, becoming in the words of historian Harold Woodman, "King Cotton's retainers ... the cotton planter's commercial alter ego, his personal representative in the marketplace."[13] Benjamin Hughes made his name in Port Gibson as one of these "retainers."

Harold Woodman, Lewis Atherton, John Hebron Moore, and others have closely examined the role of the factor in southern society.[14] Woodman's study remains the definitive analysis of the nature and function of these critical players in cotton's rise and dominance in American commerce during the antebellum period. Woodman finds factors, like the towns they resided in, to be indispensable to cotton's regime, yet they were subordinated both socially and ideologically to the planter and the plantation.[15] Although Rosser Howard Taylor has argued that "factorage was the one branch of trade which was not regarded as derogatory to social standing," factors rarely assumed the status held by planters in southern society.[16] As Woodman argues, the factor who did attain social equality with the planter was usually a slaveholder and planter himself. Only factors who employed their wealth in socially acceptable ways, in-

12. Moore, *Emergence of the Cotton Kingdom*, 195.

13. Harold D. Woodman, *King Cotton and His Retainers: Financing and Marketing the Cotton Crop of the South, 1800–1925* (Lexington, Ky., 1968), 14.

14. *Ibid., passim;* Lewis E. Atherton, *The Southern Country Store, 1800–1860* (Baton Rouge, 1949), esp. Chap. 2; Moore, *Emergence of the Cotton Kingdom,* esp. Chap. 10.

15. Woodman, *King Cotton and His Retainers,* 47–48, 193–95. Also see Phillips, "Historical Notes of Milledgeville, Georgia," in Phillips, *The Slave Economy of the Old South,* ed. Genovese, 177.

16. Rosser Howard Taylor, "The Gentry of Ante-Bellum South Carolina," *North Carolina Historical Review,* XVII (1940), 117.

vestment in land and slaves, were respected as leaders of the community.[17] Yet southerners did not reject as disreputable any line of work outside of farming. Towns did not earn the wrath of southern ideologues who condemned the decadence and corruption of large cities, both northern and southern.[18] Southerners viewed towns as valuable complements to the agricultural order, and they recognized townspeople's instrumental roles in that order.[19]

Benjamin Hughes operated his merchant business in both Port Gibson and the neighboring Mississippi River town of Grand Gulf. Although we know little about the nature of his business, what has survived suggests that as a businessman he earned the respect of his peers and benefited from them. Like many merchants, Benjamin Hughes played a prominent role in town affairs. In 1826 he acted as a trustee of Clinton Academy, and in 1829 he was listed as a director of the Port Gibson branch of the Bank of the State of Mississippi.[20] Hughes's interest and participation in the town's cultural life culminated in 1839 when the Port Gibson Theatre Company elected him its president.[21] An article in the December 15, 1854, Port Gibson *Herald and Correspondent* reminded its readers that Benjamin Hughes had been "one of the most devoted promoters of the interests of our town."[22]

We do not know much about Benjamin Hughes's thoughts regarding

17. Woodman, *King Cotton and His Retainers,* 47–48, 150; Phillips, "Historical Notes of Milledgeville, Georgia," in Phillips, *The Slave Economy of the Old South,* ed. Genovese, 177. Also see Clement Eaton, *The Growth of Southern Civilization, 1790–1860* (New York, 1961), 221. For an antebellum southerner's account of the shopkeeper made respectable by purchasing a farm, see Daniel R. Hundley, *Social Relations in Our Southern States,* ed. William J. Cooper, Jr. (1860; rpr. Baton Rouge, 1979), 115.

18. See, for example, Henry Hughes's contrasting impressions of Port Gibson and New Orleans in Henry Hughes Diary, July 11, 1852, Henry Hughes Papers, MDAH.

19. Atherton, *Southern Country Store,* Chap. 8; Woodman, *King Cotton and His Retainers,* 43–48 and *passim;* Hundley, *Social Relations,* 112–15.

20. Headley, comp., *Claiborne County,* 159, 57.

21. Claiborne County Land Deeds, Box 42, 1839, Book S, 229, MDAH. This deed conveyed a lot of land from R. J. Bland to Benjamin Hughes (who was elected president of the Port Gibson Theatre Company) so that the company could become incorporated. For more on the theater in Port Gibson, see James J. Pillar, "Religious and Cultural Life, 1817–1860," in *History of Mississippi,* ed. McLemore, 414–15.

22. Port Gibson *Herald and Correspondent,* December 15, 1854, clipping in Henry Hughes Scrapbook, Hughes Papers.

his dealings in land, but we do know that he speculated in it from the late 1820s until his death in 1842. In so doing he fit well into Mississippi's "flush times." Both contemporary and historical literature describe the veritable explosion of land speculation in Mississippi, especially during the 1830s, when major land cessions from the Choctaw and Chickasaw tribes, skyrocketing cotton prices, and cheap credit combined to make Mississippi a haven for immigrants seeking quick fortunes. By the end of the 1830s Mississippi had become the leading producer of cotton in the United States. Joseph Ingraham, the Maine traveler, commented on this process of settlement and production in 1835: "Not until every acre is purchased and cultivated—not til Mississippi becomes one vast cotton field, will this mania, which has entered into the very marrow, bone, and sinew of a Mississippian's system, pass away." The most famous contemporary chronicler of this period and place was Joseph Baldwin, whose *Flush Times of Alabama and Mississippi* first appeared in 1853. Mississippi in the 1830s, he related, "seemed to be a reservoir, and every road leading to it a vagrant stream of enterprise and adventure." In Mississippi during the 1830s it seemed as if "nearly every man was a speculator."[23] For Benjamin Hughes, speculation became a part-time but serious undertaking.

Between 1827 and 1840 in Claiborne County alone, Benjamin Hughes bought land thirty-two times and sold land twenty-seven times. Often the purchased lands were resold in a matter of months, and Hughes turned sizable profits during this period of rapidly rising land prices. Slaves also figured in some of Hughes's dealings, and he apparently bought and then resold them with but one intent: to make a profit.[24] Unlike many southerners engaged in mercantile activity, Benjamin Hughes apparently did not desire to become a planter. Through his speculative dealings he several times acquired the possessions necessary to be a full-fledged planter; in 1831 one of his purchases included 640 acres of land and 21 slaves. But he would not turn these possessions into

23. [Ingraham], *The South-West,* 86; Baldwin, *Flush Times,* 83.

24. For Hughes's land dealings in Claiborne County, see Claiborne County Land Deeds, Box 38 (for 1827–31), Box 39 (for 1831–35), Box 40 (for 1835–38), Box 41 (for 1838), and Box 42 (for 1838–39). For Hughes's dealings in out-of-county lands, see Benjamin Hughes Materials, Folder 6, Box 11, Daniell IV Collection.

a profession; in the following year Hughes sold not only these valuable assets but also over 400 additional acres and 29 more slaves.[25]

The personal tax rolls from these years further illustrate that Hughes was more involved in dealing in land and slaves than in permanently acquiring them and the position in southern society they conferred. The tax records of 1835 reveal that he owned only eight slaves and that his land was valued at $10,000. In 1836 Hughes owned but four slaves, and his land value remained at $10,000.[26] Hughes's decision to remain a merchant and factor instead of becoming a planter cannot be definitively explained, but it does appear that while he recognized the value of land and slaves in southern society, he maintained an allegiance to town over country and to mercantile activity over farming. That neither of his sons became planters but instead found their livelihoods in town professions as well (William became a merchant and Henry a lawyer) testifies to the value and respect Benjamin Hughes accorded nonplanting pursuits. As a factor, Hughes participated in but remained outside of the direct operation of plantation slavery. His activities facilitated the expansion and consolidation of the slave economy and society of Mississippi, yet Hughes himself remained, like the town he lived in, a peripheral participant in that slave system.

Benjamin Hughes's speculations in land and slaves took an ominous turn in 1836. Efforts by the federal government to restrain the wild pace of land sales through such measures as President Andrew Jackson's specie circular seriously affected the pace and profits of land speculation. For Benjamin Hughes, like many in the Southwest, the situation became acute when banks began calling in their loans. Credit, which had been plentiful in the immediately preceding years, quickly dried up. Land prices tumbled as demand dropped. Hughes went into a selling frenzy in 1836, making eight sales and only one purchase. Included in the sales were his commercial properties in both Port Gibson and Grand Gulf. He had owned the downtown Port Gibson lot since 1828. The eight sales and one purchase in 1836 yielded Hughes over $32,000, but this money clearly went to creditors because Hughes made no purchases in 1837 or 1838. His tax records from 1837 also indicate a changed fortune. He

25. For Hughes's purchase see Claiborne County Land Deeds, Box 39, Book M, 174; for the sale see *ibid.,* 179.

26. Personal Tax Rolls for 1835, 1836, MDAH.

owned no town lots in 1837, compared to the three in 1836 that had been valued at nearly $11,000. Although he had six slaves in 1837, his total state and county tax totaled only $5.62 1/2, whereas in 1836 his combined tax was more than ten times that amount, $57.96 3/4.[27] Clearly, hard times had hit the Hughes family.

The Panic of 1837 and subsequent depression ruined many who had sought a quick fortune in the Southwest during the flush times of the early and mid-1830s. The reckless expansion of credit, the rapid clearing and cultivation of newly purchased lands, and the obsessive emphasis on cotton combined with international financial and market conditions to send the American economy into a tailspin such as the country had never previously experienced. The depression lasted well into the 1840s, and cotton prices did not return to their predepression levels during the entire antebellum period. The depression hit Mississippi especially hard. Fortunes made overnight crashed just as quickly. As Joseph Baldwin noted, "Men worth a million were insolvent for two millions. . . . The frolic was ended, and what headaches, and what feverish limbs the next morning!"[28]

Benjamin Hughes never recovered from the setback he experienced in the wake of the Panic of 1837. Although by 1839 he had reacquired a lot in Port Gibson valued at $5,000 and held on to his six slaves, he did not begin to approach his earlier financial position.[29] Hughes died in Port Gibson in 1842. He was fifty-three years old. Hughes's son-in-law, Bushrod W. Morehead, who had married his eldest child, Mary Ann, acted as the administrator of his estate. At the November, 1842, term of the Probate Court of Claiborne County, the court found Hughes's estate to be insolvent. The court then received and recorded Morehead's inventory and appraisal of the estate, which amounted to $501. Morehead then

27. Jackson's specie circular required that only specie be accepted for federal land sales. Banks with specie reserves lower than the amount of notes they had issued soon found themselves unable to redeem their notes, and, consequently, their notes rapidly lost their value. For a brief, general discussion of the economic crisis in the late 1830s, see Douglass C. North, *The Economic Growth of the United States, 1790–1860* (Englewood Cliffs, N.J., 1961), 194–203. For Hughes's land sales see Claiborne County Land Deeds, Box 40, Book P, 168, 252, 335, 430, 576, 626, 632, and Book Q, 88, 404; Personal Tax Rolls for 1836 and 1837.

28. For cotton prices see Gray, *History of Agriculture*, 696–700; Baldwin, *Flush Times*, 90.

29. Personal Tax Rolls for 1839.

petitioned the court to "respectfully showeth unto your honor that the said Hughes died greatly indebted and leaving assets to an amount far less than the amount of his indebtedness." Morehead had a gift for understatement. Hughes owed more than $93,229—$48,468 to the Bank of the United States and the rest to the Planters Bank of Port Gibson. Morehead then concluded that he "has knowledge of other debts . . . [totaling] at least twenty five thousand dollars." In addition to the appraised $501 personal estate, Morehead estimated that Hughes had debts and judgments in his favor of about $15,000 and "other old debts and judgments to the amount probably $10,000 all of which are desperate."[30]

The condition of the Hughes family when Benjamin died certainly seemed bleak. At the time of his death he left a wife, two daughters, Mary Ann, age twenty-one, and Maria Jane, age ten, and two sons, William, age seventeen, and Henry, age thirteen. But the family had more than Nancy Brashear Hughes's family connections to support them. During the December, 1842, term of the Claiborne County Probate Court, the court ordered to Nancy Hughes "for her dower, one third part in the lands and tenements of her husband." This action resulted from an 1839 Mississippi statute, commonly known as the Married Women's Property Act, which preserved for a widow one-third of her husband's property. This third could not be claimed by creditors and thus whatever debts Benjamin Hughes had contracted during his life were not the legal obligation of his widow. Like many antebellum southern women widowed in their forties, Nancy Hughes never remarried.[31] Instead, with her dower and her family's support, she began raising her three minor children on her own.

We know little about Nancy Hughes. Her antebellum tax records suggest that she maintained a comfortable living standard; the main item on which she paid state tax was slaves. Although she and her children

30. Probate Court Records, November, 1842, Term, Roll 11, 373–74, Roll 12, 127, 128, 129, MDAH.

31. Probate Court Records, December, 1842, Term, Roll 12, 131–32. On laws concerning married women's property, see Suzanne Lebsock, *The Free Women of Petersburg: Status and Culture in a Southern Town, 1784–1860* (New York, 1984), 84–86. For the infrequency of middle-aged southern women remarrying, see Catherine Clinton, *The Plantation Mistress: Woman's World in the Old South* (New York, 1982), 78; Lebsock, *Free Women of Petersburg*, 26–27.

lived throughout the 1840s and 1850s in the small house her husband had built in the suburbs of Port Gibson, her tax records reveal that she owned more than a dozen slaves throughout those decades. These slaves may have resided on land that Nancy owned but did not occupy. The 1860 census schedule for Claiborne County lists the value of Nancy Hughes's real estate at $10,000—far more than the house lot in Port Gibson was worth. She also might have leased her slaves to neighbors or local planters and supported herself and her family with the revenues. Henry Hughes mentions a family slave only once in his entire diary, and that is in an anecdote about himself as a very young boy.[32] Nancy Hughes owned slaves, but it appears that she did not manage them or rear her children in a household in which they played a prominent role.

Nancy Hughes raised her children much as she and her husband had before his death. Although she apparently had the resources to farm and raise her sons to be planters and her daughters to be wives of planters, she instead cultivated in them an appreciation of professional town life. All but her youngest daughter pursued nonplanting interests. The eldest child, Mary Ann, had married a doctor, Bushrod Morehead, by the time of Benjamin Hughes's death. Morehead died in 1844, and fifteen years later Mary Ann married another doctor, Robert Harper. William soon succeeded his father as a merchant in Port Gibson. Henry became a lawyer. Only Maria Jane departed from this family tendency. In 1851 she married a childhood friend of her brothers, William Thomas Magruder, a struggling planter.[33]

Nancy's preparation of her sons for professional life included giving them a college education. Higher education in antebellum Mississippi was by no means confined to the children of townspeople, but as Joseph Ingraham observed in 1835, "Many planters are opposed to giving their sons, whom they destine to succeed them as farmers, a classical education. A common practical education they consider sufficient for young gentlemen who are to bury themselves for life in the retirement of a plantation."[34] Ingraham found town children to be better educated than their

32. Personal Tax Rolls for 1849, 1859, 1860; Hughes Diary, August 8, 1852.
33. Hughes Family Genealogy Materials, Folder 4, Box 22, Daniell IV Collection; Hughes Diary, April 22, 1848, March 23, 1851.
34. [Ingraham], *The South-West,* 208. For a similar conclusion see Moore, *Emergence of the Cotton Kingdom,* 242.

plantation counterparts. Ingraham may have exaggerated the differences between town and plantation children's education, but he correctly saw the different emphasis placed on education by townspeople and planters. For male children who lived in towns, the only socially respectable options other than planting—law, medicine, mercantile pursuits, and the clergy—all required proper education. William and Henry Hughes obtained this proper training at the local institution of higher education: Oakland College.

That a respected college was located in Claiborne County should come as no surprise. Founded in 1830, Oakland College, like the library, theater, and Clinton Academy, reflected the interests of the citizens of Claiborne County in general, and of Port Gibson in particular, in developing a cultured and enlightened community. As historian E. Brooks Holifield has suggested, southern colleges, to a large extent, "were an extension of urban ambitions and tokens of local enterprise. Until well into the 1850s, local communities were far more active than religious denominations or state governments in the formation of colleges. Promoters usually located a college in a specific community in return for pledges of support; the churches initially provided little more than sanction and encouragement."[35] A list of the major financial subscribers to the college in the 1830s testifies to the strong support the local elites provided it.[36]

Yet while Oakland did reflect the "ambitions" of the middle and upper classes of Claiborne County, it also received more than just "sanction and encouragement" from its Presbyterian affiliation. Like many other southern Presbyterian colleges, Oakland, under its first president, the Princeton-trained Reverend Jeremiah Chamberlain, stressed both "the principles of the Reformation of the sixteenth century" and "the usual branches of Science and Literature taught in the colleges of the country."[37] It sought both to enlighten its students in the ways of the world and to inculcate in them the values of Christianity. The secular and religious founders of Oakland College thus envisioned an institution that would enhance the cultural and social life of the region, educate ministers of the

35. Holifield, *Gentleman Theologians,* 45.

36. Headley, comp., *Claiborne County,* 174.

37. Melvin Kellogg Bruss, "History of Oakland College, Mississippi, 1830–1871" (M.A. thesis, Louisiana State University, 1965), 40; J. W. Kennedy, "A History of Oakland College" (n.p., n.d.), quoted in Headley, comp., *Claiborne County,* 170.

gospel to serve the rapidly expanding population, and provide educated lawyers, doctors, and teachers for the middle and upper classes—and accomplish these goals locally. As Aubrey Keith Lucas has noted, the founders of Oakland hoped that the college would "stop the flow of [southern] students to northern schools."[38]

Oakland College's many functions illustrate the desire of Claiborne County's elite to stabilize society and to develop an intellectual and cultural center of Mississippi and the nation. Local youths, including a number from nearby Louisiana, would emerge from Oakland with a high-quality education and occupy positions of respect and authority. The 1856 records of Oakland's alumni suggest that the college served its functions well. Of a total of 155 graduates, 65 came from Mississippi and 45 from Louisiana. Thirty-nine graduates became lawyers or students of law; 21 became ministers or students of theology; and 19 became physicians or students of medicine.[39] Although Oakland may not have earned a reputation throughout the South, it clearly earned the respect of people in the Southwest because its enrollments remained stable until the outbreak of the Civil War.

Henry Hughes entered Oakland College in 1845. During his years there the curriculum stressed the classics, especially Greek and Latin language and literature. Oakland, however, exposed the young Hughes to more than just the classics. Other required courses included Natural Philosophy, Logic, Natural Theology and Evidences of Christianity, Political Economy, Mathematics, Chemistry, Astronomy, Hebrew, and History.[40] This curriculum did not differentiate Oakland from other southern colleges of the period.[41] Although "Natural Theology and Evidences of Christianity" might suggest a religious orientation, Oakland attempted to strike a balance between religion and reason. As Holifield has argued, courses on the "evidences" were part of the southern theological attempt

38. Lucas, "Education in Mississippi to 1860," in *History of Mississippi*, ed. McLemore, 363. For more on the motives for establishing denominational colleges, see Holifield, *Gentleman Theologians*, 45–47.

39. Headley, comp., *Claiborne County*, 172.

40. For Oakland's curriculum at the time of Hughes's attendance, see "Oakland College Catalog and Commencement Proceedings for 1845," Oakland College Papers, Box 4, MDAH.

41. For the classical emphasis of antebellum curricula, see E. Merton Coulter, *College Life in the Old South* (1928; rpr. Athens, Ga., 1983), 33–40.

to "puncture liberalism" by proving "that reason established the criteria for recognizing and validating . . . Biblical revelation." The major works read in these courses at Oakland were by the famous English anti-Deist William Paley and included his *Natural Theology* (1802) and *Evidences of Christianity* (1794). Both of these works enjoyed a wide and respected audience in southern colleges, not least because of their efforts to reconcile limited but nonetheless powerful human reason with divine revelation. Such efforts defended the scriptural authority of the Bible and the validity of miracles against the teachings of skeptics such as David Hume.[42] Thus the religious instruction at Oakland and other "rational orthodox" institutions emphasized thought and study rather than feeling and emotion. For these southern youth, religion was not "fire and brimstone" but a course of study that demanded the highest intellectual rigor.

We do not know the exact extent to which Oakland's curriculum and orientation affected Hughes or his ideas about religion. His diary, which he began keeping the year after he graduated, reveals a deep religious sensibility as well as an intense appreciation of Francis Bacon and the scientific method. The coexistence of both preoccupations suggests that his days at Oakland left a mark on his intellectual as well as spiritual development. Yet he did not seem to have reflected much on this process or its implications. His brief discussion in the diary of his days at Oakland concerns not his religious training, the "principles of the sixteenth century," or any other aspect of a "rational orthodox" education, but rather his place in his class and his membership in a collegiate society called the Adelphic Institute.[43]

Henry did well at Oakland, placing first in his class of seven. Although Oakland featured a four-year program of study, Hughes finished in just two years. The Reverend William D. Moore, his biographer and friend, commented on the youthful Hughes's intellectual performance, relating that during his college days "he fulfilled all the promise of his precocious childhood, and in a class of all of whom were his seniors in years, he early took the place of honor and held it undisputed to the end." But

42. Holifield, *Gentleman Theologians,* 85, 55, 83, 91–96; Theodore Dwight Bozeman, *Protestants in an Age of Science: The Baconian Ideal and Antebellum American Religious Thought* (Chapel Hill, 1977), 89–92, 206 n. 29.

43. The relation between these aspects of his personality will be discussed in more detail in subsequent chapters. See Hughes Diary, January 1, 1848.

even his placing first seems to have held less importance for Henry than his membership in the Adelphic Institute. Literary societies of antebellum southern colleges played an important role in a student's life. Student members, remarks E. Merton Coulter, "might in the great world outside forget their old professors, their classrooms, and textbooks, but few ever forgot their old society halls." This was certainly the case with Hughes. After matter-of-factly stating in his diary that he "Received the first honors in a class of Seven," he added that "Of this Class James Alexander and myself were the only two members of Adelphic Institute." Hughes did not elaborate on why his membership held such importance to him, but it might have been because of the select nature of the society. Hughes disdained mediocrity and craved public recognition. To belong to an elite literary society, which had its own building on campus as well as its own library, marked him off from the other students in a way that emphasized Hughes's intellectual distinction. In addition, because debating was the major function of these societies, Hughes could display his intellectual and oratorical skills publicly and thereby enhance his reputation among his colleagues.[44] Belonging to the Adelphic Institute brought Hughes some of what he longed for for the rest of his life: public acknowledgment of and respect for his superior intellect. Upon graduating from Oakland, he sought a profession in which he could continue this quest for recognition and respect and the one element that would guarantee both: power.

It did not take Henry Hughes long to decide upon the career that would best suit his aspirations and abilities. He noted in the first entry in his diary that he began reading law about the first of August, 1847, just months after completing his work at Oakland.[45] Hughes probably became a lawyer for no better reason than that it appeared the best available option. His brother had already assumed the family business and was a merchant in Port Gibson. Medicine could have provided a respectable livelihood, but it did not usually lead to public office. Law was a respected and proven starting place for many a public man. For an ambitious and talented man of eighteen, a career in law could lead to higher

---

44. William D. Moore, *The Life and Works of Col. Henry Hughes: A Funeral Sermon Preached in the Methodist Episcopal Church, Port Gibson, Miss., October 26th, 1862* (Mobile, 1863), 11; Coulter, *College Life,* 103–33; Hughes Diary, January 1, 1848. On debating within the societies see Coulter, *College Life,* 114–25.

45. Hughes Diary, January 1, 1848.

office in just a few years. Hughes wasted no time in aligning himself with those in the profession who could offer him not only excellent training but access to power.

Hughes began to read law with John B. Thrasher, a Port Gibson attorney prominent for both his legal abilities and his stature in local society. A practicing attorney in Port Gibson for nearly twenty years, Thrasher had amassed a small fortune by the time young Hughes came to study with him. According to the 1849 tax rolls, Thrasher owned 90 slaves. By 1859 he had increased that number to 162, one of the largest holdings in the county.[46] Active in "all matters of a public nature," Thrasher seemed to be an ideal mentor for Hughes.[47] But after only a few months, Hughes left. By January, 1848, he had relocated to New Orleans, where he resumed his studies under Thomas Jefferson Durant, United States district attorney for Louisiana.

As important as Port Gibson was to Claiborne County and the surrounding area, as sophisticated and refined as it was relative to other towns in Mississippi, Port Gibson could not match New Orleans as a social, economic, cultural, and intellectual center. By far the largest city in the Deep South, New Orleans served as the entrepôt of the cotton kingdom. It ranked second in the country behind New York City in the value of its exports. But the vitality of New Orleans' urban life was not confined to its economic activity. The city abounded with public lectures, theaters, literary and scientific societies, newspapers, journals, and countless other forms of cultural and intellectual expression. And though it could not yet equal Charleston, South Carolina, it nonetheless offered young intellectuals in the emerging Southwest excellent resources and facilities.[48]

These resources and facilities alone may have attracted Hughes to New Orleans, but there were family considerations as well. When he arrived there in late 1847, he took up residence with Dr. William B.

46. Personal Tax Rolls of 1849, 1859. Harris G. Warren has stated Thrasher's worth at $35,000 in 1860. See Warren, "People and Occupations in Port Gibson, 1860," *Journal of Mississippi History,* X (1948), 108.

47. *Biographical and Historical Memoirs of Mississippi* (2 vols.; Chicago, 1891), II, 912.

48. For a discussion of New Orleans at the time of Hughes's arrival and residence in the city, see Robert C. Reinders, *End of an Era: New Orleans, 1850–1860* (New Orleans, 1964).

Lindsay, who was married to his maternal aunt Ruth.[49] For the young law student, having family in New Orleans eased the transition from small-town Port Gibson to the enormous city. It also saved him the expense of room and board while he pursued his legal studies. Hughes was fortunate as well in being able to study under Durant. A slave-owning Democrat "recognized as an outstanding figure in local legal and political circles," Durant would not only provide Hughes with able training but would also be in a position to introduce him to the elite of New Orleans society.[50]

At 10:00 P.M. on January 1, 1848, the eighteen-year-old Henry Hughes began to keep a diary. He would write weekly for over five years. Although the initial entry consisted of the equivalent of one typed page, it covered his personal life history up to that night. He noted his parents' names, the size of his family, some personal habits, and some organizations he belonged to. He did not mention his father's business activities or the enormous debt he left when he died. He did not discuss the town of Port Gibson or its relation to the surrounding area. He mentioned his mother and siblings only briefly. His days at Oakland College occupied but five sentences. His desire to study law received no mention. He did not say why he left Port Gibson to study law in New Orleans. Yet all of these events and developments influenced him, helped make him the man he was.

That he chose not to go into much detail concerning these years further clouds our knowledge of their impact on him. Perhaps those years contained experiences that he did not want to remember or expose to others. He may have chosen not to dwell on his background but to concentrate on the dilemmas and exigencies that faced him at the time he wrote. Hughes wanted to establish himself in the world, to attain heights of power and fame beyond those of all public men before him. To spend his thoughts reliving days that at best were preparatory probably seemed not only inexpedient but distracting and wasteful. The business of his life lay before him, in the achievement and exercise of power. It was in life after college, life in the world beyond Port Gibson, that Hughes sought

49. Hughes Diary, January 1, 1848.
50. H. W. Howard Knott, "Durant, Thomas Jefferson," in Allen Johnson and Dumas Malone, eds., *Dictionary of American Biography* (20 vols.; New York, 1946), V, 543.

his fame and place. Childhood may have been both irrelevant to the task presently at hand and a period of life that he would rather not look at closely. Rather than focus on his past and what it had made of him, Hughes chose to focus on his future and what he would make of it.

Yet while Hughes may have wanted to get on with his life and the burning question of his destiny, his early life clearly left imprints on his character, even if he did not or would not recognize them. He grew up in the midst of a rapidly expanding slave society, and although his father never owned more than a handful of slaves, his work as a factor depended on slavery. Henry Hughes grew up in a small town but one that prided itself on its sophisticated and refined character and sought to impart to its citizens a rich cultural legacy. His father, although respected and active in local affairs, died deep in debt, leaving little behind to be remembered by. Henry excelled in college, earning a distinguished position among his peers, a position he remembered fondly. He chose a career that, more than any other, presented possibilities of public fame and power.

When Henry Hughes sat down to record his diary, the child, to a large extent, had already fathered the man. Ambitious, intelligent, eager to make the world take notice of his talents and his achievements, Hughes displayed characteristics that had their origin in the environments of his youth. Although he chose not to engage in prolonged discussions of that youth, it would play a vital role in his life, for Hughes took the characteristics forged in his childhood and adolescence into his adult life. The diary he kept for the next five years, as he sought to establish himself in the world, tellingly reveals the force and fate of those characteristics of his youth, as well as the new directions his life and thought would take as he and his society advanced into the 1850s.

2

THE MATURATION OF THE SOCIOLOGIST
1848–1853

This record is dedicated to my soul and to Fame. . . .
Learning these pages, the future biographer will read my thoughts, & learn my
history.

—Henry Hughes Diary, January 1, 1848

Diaries serve many functions. Some, like William Bryd's, are designed to be secret. Their contents, though not necessarily more revealing and honest than those of others, do not seek to project a public image of the diarist to an expected audience. Others, like Henry Hughes's, envision an audience from their inception and seek to impress upon it a particular image of their authors. The opening lines of Hughes's diary boldly establish his ambition by assuming that his life would merit a biographer. In truth, what Hughes left out of his diary may reveal as much as what he put in. And how he presented his thoughts may tell us as much as the thoughts themselves.

From January 1, 1848, until May 1, 1853, Hughes kept a weekly diary. Its form and function, the manner in which and the reasons for which he kept it, illuminate this period in his life and the ways these years influenced the man who in 1854 would emerge into the public eye with his most important work, *Treatise on Sociology*. The diary offers our only entry into Hughes's private life and inner thoughts. And though he may have conceived it as a public record of his ascent to fame and glory, what emerged is, more often than not, a private, painful account of a southern intellectual driven by ambition and the desire for power but torn by ambivalence and doubt. Alternately revealing and masking, Hughes's diary provides an incomplete yet intriguing insight into the mind of a not yet fully formed proslavery ideologue.

Hughes began keeping his diary about two months after his arrival in New Orleans. Eighteen years old, in a strange and large city, knowing no one except the aunt and uncle with whom he resided, and filled with ambitious thoughts, he had to express himself, and his diary allowed him to do so without restraint. He intended it to be more than a record of his doings and thoughts; it would, as he made clear in the opening entry, chart his "history," which he confidently expected to end in glory and fame. For a lonely eighteen-year-old who was just beginning his law studies, the diary would be his refuge, the place in which to reaffirm his ambitions and dreams of power. But mixed in among the yearnings for public recognition were many details of his personal, professional, and intellectual life. Although Hughes considered most of these details to be irrelevant to his primary purpose in life, they nonetheless provide important glimpses into his personality.

After recording the entry that began this chapter, Hughes entered a brief sketch of his family. Noting his father's death "while my life was in its Spring," he refrained from any further details about his family or his thoughts about them. He did thank Providence "for making me the Son of such parents, the brother of such sisters and of such a brother," but said no more of them.[1] This brevity, much like his discussion later in the entry concerning his college experience, suggests that Hughes did not credit his family background with much influence on his history, or, alternatively, found it too painful to discuss. Although he never went into much detail about his family, his few brief references fill out the picture of his family and his relation to it.

Of all the members of his immediate family, Hughes was closest to his elder sister, Mary Ann. Eight years older than he, the widowed Mary Ann received some of the warmest and highest praise he conferred on anyone. Of primary importance, in Henry's eyes, was her ability to under-

1. Hughes Diary, January 1, 1848.

stand and accept him and his ambitions. Although he did not state that
the rest of his family had rejected him, his praise of Mary Ann suggests
that he did not elsewhere receive the approval he needed. Mary Ann, he
wrote in 1848, was "almost the only one who appreciates my spirit &
sympathizes with my desires." Less than two months later, he again
exalted her: "On earth, of all whom I have ever known, My eldest Sister
Mary Ann Morehead had the powerful influence on me. Her soul is the
Sister of mine. She and one dear other seem alone to have *fully,* sympa-
thetically appreciated me. Others lavish their compliments upon me, but
for these two loved ones only, have I felt a kindred, a unison of mind."
The "one dear other" to whom Hughes referred remains a mystery
throughout the diary, and Mary Ann maintained pride of place in Henry's family relations.[2] In 1852 he again revealed the intimate connection
he had with her alone. After stating that his letters contained his "best
history," he continued: "I write regularly to no one but my elder sister.
She is a wise, pure, earnest woman; she is heroic, and knows it not. Her
spirit is an angel; an angel is with her and she knows it not." Mary Ann
furnished Henry with financial support and, no less important to him,
books.[3] But even more important than this material support, she provided
him with familial love and encouragement from which he derived confidence and strength.

Although Mary Ann occupied a favored position in Hughes's heart,
he did grant the other members of his family some attention. Hughes
never criticized any relative directly in his diary, and even though he had
political differences with his Whig brother William, he never commented
on them extensively. Hughes clearly loved his mother, who supported
him and housed him throughout much of his adult life. With his father
dead since he was thirteen, Hughes relied on his mother for parental
guidance and support, and she filled both maternal and paternal roles.

2. *Ibid.,* March 26, May 14, 1848. Hughes provided no clue to the identity of the "one
dear other." One is tempted to speculate that it may have been his brother-in-law William
Thomas Magruder, who alone received praise similar to that which he bestowed on Mary
Ann. But Hughes did not mention Magruder until 1851, almost three years after the "one
dear other" reference. I suspect that the "one dear other" was Hughes's mother.

3. *Ibid.,* June 20, 1852. In the entry for April 13, 1852, Hughes noted that Mary Ann
"presented me the 'History of the Course of Human Philosophy,' by Cousin." The letters
to Mary Ann to which Hughes refers have been lost.

"How my mother loves me," he wrote in September, 1850, and although he never meditated on that love as he did on Mary Ann's, he acknowledged his debt and gratitude a number of times.[4] Recognizing his dependence on her in 1851 at the age of twenty-two, when he was "so poor" that he did not have "money to buy a pair of shoes," he thought of teaching in the "Public Night School" in order "to make me independent of the assistance of my mother & sister."[5]

Nevertheless, Hughes remained dependent on his mother until the Civil War. The census of 1860 lists him as still residing in his mother's house, and the tax rolls of that year indicate that he owned almost no property.[6] Yet the effect of this dependence on his personality remains unclear, for he did not detail the nature of his relation to her, nor do his entries in which he mentioned her seem to mask any latent resentment or hostility. Accordingly, it is difficult to determine whether his decision to return to Port Gibson rather than remain in New Orleans was dictated by practical considerations or by emotional ties. In short, Hughes, raised through adolescence by his widowed mother, came to rely on her, especially financially, in a way that occasionally extended to his choices in life. Hughes mentioned only one instance in which his mother offered him advice. After he had nearly completed the text for a speech for a Democratic party barbecue in nearby Grand Gulf in August, 1851, he "received my mother's & sister's—elder—most peremptory wishes to abandon it." Although exceptionally eager to make a name for himself in local politics, Hughes acceded to his mother's—and sister's—request: "I honor my mother & forego the effort."[7]

4. *Ibid.,* September 8, 1850. For other expressions of indebtedness and gratitude, see entries for October 20, 1850, December 7, 1851, and February 8, 1852.

5. *Ibid.,* November 9, 1851. Earlier in 1851 Hughes had lamented, "I am so poor that I have not without borrowing, money to buy a pair of shoes. Rather than borrow money, I wear a worn-out pair. Feet now not dry." Whether the "borrowing" here referred to was from his mother is not clear, but, given the other passages, likely. See *Ibid.,* February 2, 1851. Hughes's poverty was particularly acute late in 1851. In addition to the November 9 entry, those of November 30 and December 7, 1851, also comment on his lack of money. These lean times continued into 1852; on March 7, Hughes again declared: "I am very poor. I have not money with which to buy books or other necessaries."

6. 1860 Census Population Schedules, Claiborne County, Mississippi, Roll 580; the personal tax rolls of 1860 list the following for Henry Hughes: "Amount of state tax: $.65."

7. Hughes Diary, August 4, 1851. Mary Ann also advised Henry on the preparation of an obituary he wrote for publication. See *ibid.,* August 15, 1852.

This episode, though confirming Hughes's respect for his older sister, also suggests that Nancy Hughes took an active role in his public life. Although this episode is the only example of that activity in his diary, it would be surprising if it had remained the only one in his life. He did not seem to interpret his mother's advice as excessively controlling, and his choice to remain with her throughout his active public years suggests that he did not find her intrusive. Willing to respect her wishes, grateful for her support through the years, and comfortable enough to live with her throughout his adult life, Hughes obtained from his relation with his mother an anchor that enabled him to indulge his studies and further his ambitions. And if the emotional weight of that anchor kept him from giving speeches or remaining in New Orleans, he did not seem to mind.

Hughes mentioned his father only infrequently. What few remarks he did make contain none of the love or emotion that can be found in his references to his elder sister and mother. In fact, both males of Hughes's family receive similar treatment. Benjamin Hughes, dead less than six years when Henry began his diary, and William, four years older than Henry, are spoken of with respect but little else. Hughes appears to have been much more emotionally distant from his father and brother than from his female family members. Although this may at first appear simply as a different way of speaking about males and females, Hughes could be quite emotional about males. Rather, it seems clear that Henry found nothing to say about his father or brother that entailed love or something resembling it.

This silence does not mean that Hughes harbored no feelings for his father. A father-son relation, even, perhaps especially, one cut short, entails an entire gamut of emotions, both positive and negative. What emerges in Henry's diary hardly exhausts the feelings he had toward his father. The pain of his death and absence may have led Henry to discuss him as a noble, respectable "public man." In fact, Henry discussed his father and brother almost exclusively as businessmen, rather than as family. In January, 1852, he wrote of his brother: "My brother William has sold his store in Port Gibson Mi. As a merchant, he was popular, prudent & successful." A few months later, in June, Henry entered the longest passage about his father. It expresses a child's love as well as regret over his death but focuses on his public reputation: "Of my Father who died when I was old enough only to love but not appreciate him; the more I hear, the more I venerate him. He attempted to reform the dishonesties of cotton factorage; he would have succeed[ed] but death came. He was 'of the early breed of Athens.'"[8] Hughes thus attributed his "veneration" to what he heard rather to what he felt. His image of his father came largely from without, and his respect came from his public, professional activities, not his role in the household. This may have been a result of Benjamin's financial troubles and Henry's need to hear that his father was an honest man who sought to reform corrupt practices. But it remained the public persona, not the parental figure, in which Henry expressed interest. He received love and affection from his sister and mother; he looked to his dead father to provide, posthumously, someone to venerate and respect, someone who achieved some public acclaim and recognition. By 1852, it appears, Benjamin had achieved his role, and, fittingly, Henry placed him in a noble, but distant, historical dimension.

Hughes wrote very little about his younger sister, Maria Jane. He expressed fondness for her on one occasion, but his other brief references to her contain no sense of emotion.[9] He seemed detached from his younger sister but not from her husband, William Thomas Magruder.

No other person mentioned in the diary received so thorough a description as did Magruder. In March, 1851, Hughes entered the news that Maria Jane would marry in early April and followed with a character sketch that reveals the interest he already had taken in Magruder: "His mind is well educated & by nature of an influential cast. Of its elements, intellect of the practical sort, industry and that quality of the moral principle which implies a consciousness of God's being balanced strong desires, imagination and Southern inertness." Soon after the marriage, Hughes indicated that Magruder's relation to him would be more than familial: "He is one fitted to change the current of events."[10]

During the next three years, Magruder would be Hughes's closest family member, adviser, and trusted supporter. Magruder evoked a strong emotional response, and at times Henry's love for his brother-in-law approached the limits of social respectability. Recognizing this, Hughes made a revealing but characteristically vague reference about male love. On May 11, 1851, after asking his brother William and Ma-

8. *Ibid.,* January 25, June 7, 1852.

9. See his references to her, *ibid.,* March 23, 1851, January 25, 1852, and February 8, 1853.

10. *Ibid.,* March 23, April 6, 1851.

gruder to inquire about the availability of a Port Gibson newspaper's editorial chair, he received from Magruder the news that none was available. In the midst of his regret over not becoming an editor, Hughes included a declaration about his feelings toward Magruder: "My brother-in-law, whom I so much—so much love—for man can love man—& I will test socially the dear fact!" Hughes never explained what he meant or how he intended to "test socially the dear fact," and his intriguing language, here and throughout the diary, suggests that Hughes may have been sexually ambivalent.[11] Yet the diary as a whole more strongly suggests that Hughes employed the language of love and sensuality to describe a wide variety of personal relations, including, for instance, those with his brother-in-law, with certain authors, and especially with God.[12] Regarding Hughes's relation with Magruder, what emerges from this and subsequent entries is not a sexual relation but a nonetheless powerful, unique bond between them that Hughes at least believed could only be characterized as "love."

Magruder became Hughes's chief adviser within months of his mar-

11. *Ibid.,* May 11, 1851. The question of Hughes's sexual orientation and behavior will never be satisfactorily answered because the evidence is so ambiguous. As I argue below, however, his use of intimate language to describe all sorts of relations weakens but does not eliminate the possibility that he was homosexual.

12. The most interesting passage in which Hughes uses the language of love in reference to an author concerns Tennyson. On August 1, 1852, after noting that he had read from Tennyson, Hughes wrote: "Oh Woman Tennyson, Sweet Tennyson; darling dearest. My love, you are not a—a man. Are you? Say 'no.' But you are wild-eyed, tender, tipsy girl. You are half drunk of Apollo,—Bacchus never. The lovely God is in you[.] The sleepy, dreamy, sunny God.——" Stanford M. Lyman, in his introduction to *Selected Writings of Henry Hughes,* quotes selectively from this entry in his discussion of Hughes's "amatory feelings towards other men" [Lyman, ed., *Selected Writings of Henry Hughes, Antebellum Southerner, Slavocrat, Sociologist* (Jackson, 1985), 41]. I would argue, however, that in this case Hughes found it difficult to admit that a man's poems could touch him in the way that Tennyson's did. This reaction may well indicate a confused notion of sexuality, but I believe it more clearly demonstrates Hughes's tendency to attribute certain traits to specific sexes. Thus Tennyson's poems, to Hughes, reflected the expression of a "wild-eyed, tender, tipsy girl," not that of a man. Hughes loved the feminine character of Tennyson, not the man himself. Hughes also declared on October 26, 1851, after reading Hugh Garland's *Life of John Randolph,* that "I love John Randolph." Again, the word *love* here could express any of a number of deeper feelings. I discuss Hughes's use of similar language in reference to God later in this chapter.

riage to Maria Jane. On July 27, 1851, Hughes wrote that Magruder had "advised me to prepare myself to occupy the rostrum in behalf of ours the Democratic party." The speech Hughes prepared was the one his mother and elder sister ultimately advised him against giving. Although in this instance Hughes's immediate family won out over Magruder, he would remain, especially in political matters, a significant influence in Hughes's life. When in August, 1852, Magruder presented Hughes with a copy of "Calhoun on Government," Hughes had dropped the formal "brother-in-law" for the more intimate and heartfelt "My darling, wise brother Tom." [13] Magruder earned such affection from Hughes with more than advice. His interest in Henry's future, his support and encouragement of his public life, and his love for him provided Henry with confidence and gave him direction. For all these things, Henry was grateful.

Hughes did not find much love and support outside his family. His diary indicates that he had few close friends, certainly none who approached Mary Ann or Tom in significance. Strong feelings of social isolation plagued him throughout the five years of the diary, but he did little to alleviate them. In fact, he seemed, at times, to have enjoyed and cultivated his isolation. In some ways, he saw his being an outsider as an intellectual advantage; by remaining "above" society, he was better able to understand, analyze, and control it. Hughes would not allow social attachments to deter him from his goals of power and fame.

The conflict Hughes felt between his social and intellectual worlds emerged early in his diary. On February 20, 1848, he expressed the tensions he experienced at social functions: "However I may seem animated in society by the forced enthusiasm of the moment, however my face may be wreathed with smiles; yet I still have but little pleas[ure] in the ordinary conviviality of company." Yet Hughes's lack of "pleasure" was not caused by simple misanthropy; quite the contrary. "My nature is social. If I had founded my continued gratification in the society of the World, I could be as happy as is usually permitted. Amidst festive recreations, the memory of my ambitions will rise, and interrupt the flow of [illegible]. In the

13. *Ibid.*, July 27, 1851, August 8, 1852. Hughes especially liked to use the word *darling* when expressing feelings of intense love. He employed the word frequently in reference to God. Hughes occasionally referred to himself as God's "darling." See *ibid.*, July 2, 1848, July 28, 1850, December 21, 1851, March 14 and July 4, 1852.

throng of pleasure, I often feel a bitter contempt for the frivoties [sic] of the World, and gladly turn to the lettered manuscript, open page, & solitary lamp." Just one week later Hughes complained of his inability to resist the "throng of pleasure." He recognized that only constant vigilance could prevent him from succumbing to the temptations of social encounters: "But what I most lament is a disposition which is so naturally convivial that in the gentle but unguarded excitement of a Society in which are many gay female friends,—I descend from the grave seriousness which should characterize my demeanor, and participate in their levities. May Age remedy this fault."[14]

Hughes's desire to resist the pleasures of social intercourse competed with his "social nature" and with his accompanying interest in social activities. But rather than withdrawing totally from social intercourse, he attempted to turn it into an activity that better served his ambition. In June, 1848, he wrote: "I observe the conversation of others in preference to participation." Participation entailed losing oneself in "levities." But observation was a scientific exercise requiring a degree of detachment. Hughes could maintain "grave seriousness" while observing conversations and could thereby prevent descent into "the ordinary conviviality of company." In March, 1849, he again revealed the higher purpose of socializing: "I prefer female conversation, except when men can give me knowledge. From all, it is my rule to gain knowledge."[15] Social activities could be frivolous and make Hughes contemptuous. But if they provided him with knowledge, they could be beneficial. Hughes's inability to enjoy relaxed, casual conversation was part of a larger conflict between personal happiness and personal ambition. He could justify socializing only if it could aid his ambition. The extent to which any activity served that ambition became Hughes's yardstick by which he measured nearly all his actions.

The one person outside his family with whom Hughes did develop a friendship was his legal preceptor, Thomas J. Durant. Durant became more than just another teacher. He emerges from the diary as one of the only people Hughes considered worthy of praise, although not exclusively for his legal acumen. On September 23, 1849, he pointed out the special significance Durant held for him: "His character is such that when I have

14. *Ibid.,* February 20, 27, 1848.
15. *Ibid.,* June 18, 1848, March 11, 1849.

been Sceptical & soul-sick at human dishonesty & unfaithfulness; it almost alone, preserved me from despairing of my species. For I could not know his esoteric history, and believe all men villains." More than two years later, Hughes reiterated his admiration of Durant: "I love Mr. Durant, & respect him. Of whom else can I say this?"[16]

Hughes wrote of Durant as if he were a surrogate father. Not only did his upright character impress Hughes, but Durant stimulated his ideas, especially those concerning social issues. On April 8, 1849, just nine days before his twentieth birthday, Hughes wrote: "Although I have not commenced the Study of Social organization, it attracts my observation. Mr. Durant has, I think, adopted opinions favorable to Social reformation. Let it not be supposed that he can, or any one, influence my opinions. Whenever truth is offered, I accept it. In every thing, *I* judge. It matters not who propounds."[17] In this passage Hughes simultaneously reveals Durant's influence on his thought and his determination to deny it. This denial can be read as an attempt on Hughes's part to stand apart from Durant, to emerge as a distinct individual independent of parental—or any external—control. Durant served as a moral model for Hughes and as a source of knowledge, two roles his dead father could not play. And like an ambitious son, Hughes desired to establish his reputation outside the shadow of his father. Durant could have influenced Hughes, but for Hughes to have admitted such influence would have, in his mind, suggested dependence. Thus the influence had to be denied to preserve and foster the idea that Hughes alone produced his thought. Hughes's fear of and hostility toward dependence, especially in intellectual matters, run throughout his diary. But with Durant that fear and hostility combined with love and respect. This combination points to the paternal character and function that Durant furnished the young Hughes. Like a father, Durant provided Hughes with a model of adulthood. Like a son, Hughes loved, respected, and distanced himself from Durant.

Hughes's relation with Durant remained one of respect and distance. Hughes never suggested that he and Durant established anything more than a professional friendship, one marked by inequality and deference. Yet Durant emerges as the only significant figure in Hughes's life during his years in New Orleans, when he maintained what can only be char-

16. *Ibid.,* September 23, 1849, November 2, 1851.
17. *Ibid.,* April 8, 1849.

acterized as a lonely existence. "I converse but little," he wrote in March,
1849, "This from necessity, for at the office, I read; here [at home], I read
or think." On December 28, 1851, he wrote: "Nobody ever talks to me.
In every conversation, I lead or nothing or little is addressed to me. The
little-boy in our office talks to me; that is, if we are by ourselves." Although he occasionally attended social functions, Hughes spent most of
his time reading and otherwise preparing himself for his destiny. He
usually felt little but contempt for the social world: "Glory holds me to
an earth hated, to the company of men for whom I have no sympathy
or reverence." Perhaps it was this contempt along with the conflict he
saw between social "frivolity" and his life's goal that prevented him from
feeling anything but lonely. "I have friends, but feel friendless; am loved,
yet feel loveless."[18] Hughes found himself torn between a desire for loving
friends and a desire to rise above such "faults" to achieve power and
glory. This conflict was nowhere more pronounced than in his relations
with women.

In March, 1848, Hughes recorded his thoughts about love. "I have
never had many to love me. From my childhood have been esteemed,
honored,—flattered, admired. Yet there were no spirits with whom I
could feel a sympathy." This feeling of isolation, of being unable to "feel
a sympathy" with another, plagued Hughes throughout the five years of
the diary. But it was not the lack of a partner that plagued him so much
as his own profound reluctance to enter into relations that he believed
might thwart his destiny. He continued in the same entry: "I found at
length a soul which could mingle with my own. A year Since then has
passed. After a protracted absence I have met her again. I love,—she tells
me that she loves me.—Here while the pale sorrowing stars look down
upon me for a little while & sink into darkness, while one by one, pleasure
after pleasure has receded; I renounce the pure joys which marriage
would bestow until jealous Glory which I woo shall give her Consent. I
love, but I tear down the idol from the altar where a sublimer divinity
is placed. . . . O my God I have now no other support but Thee."[19]
Hughes would find that this process of denial would require more than
a declaration. For the next five years his longing for a human companion

18. *Ibid.,* March 11, 1849, December 28, 1851, March 5, 1848, August 4, 1851.
19. *Ibid.,* March 19, 1848.

provoked the jealousy of his dream of glory. It proved to be a difficult struggle.

Some passages in the diary indicate that Hughes, in fact, enjoyed the company of women more than men. On May 19, 1850, he commented: "In conversation, improving. With ladies, more agreeable than with men. I am with the ladies more." Women provided Hughes with the few pleasures he seems to have gained through social activity. Near the end of his diary, he reflected on the association of women and pleasure in his life: "Have I ever had a pleasure in which woman was not an element.— Since my eighteenth year, I have not been unloved. And so again and— still—clasped hands, embracing arms, kissed lips and pillowing bosoms." But even the pleasures of women could not be separated from his other passion. The next line in this entry reads: "Ambition and Love, these are my life." [20]

Since Hughes proved unable to avoid the pleasures of women, he attempted to use his social activities to sharpen the skills he thought necessary for his future. As in all his social relations, he tried to extract from his contact with women such knowledge as would contribute to the attainment of power and glory—that would teach him about human nature. Thus any encounter with women, sexual or not, became an opportunity for the ambitious and inquisitive Hughes to discover some new facet of humanity. "From woman," he wrote on May 26, 1850, "I have and am gathering a large & opulent experience. My principles in oratory, I illustrate in Love." Hughes also used women to help him establish the boundaries of morality. At times, these episodes approached the passionlessness of scientific experiments. On June 27, 1852, he wrote: "Kissed a young lady—this was gallantry only—on my part. Talked immodestly to another one; she liked it; I was as usual learning; during the talk, reflected what was most immodest, so as to utter it over her chair & in her ear. Was this bad?" [21]

In early January, 1848, Hughes conducted an even more calculated "experiment." This episode reveals both Hughes's recognition of sexual urges and his desire to control them for more than carnal ends. "Unhallowed desires have filled & delighted my mind. . . . My thoughts seek diversion, and imagine forbidden things. Deeds may hereafter realize

20. *Ibid.,* May 19, 1850, January 9, 1853.
21. *Ibid.,* May 26, 1850, June 27, 1852.

them." His desire to "realize" these unnamed "forbidden things" resulted not from base cravings but from calculated reasoning. "For I esteem it necessary that I should stir up even the sediment of pleasure, and taste the dregs of every cup. Will it not be required that I shall feel every variety of Woe and enjoyment, in order to stimulate and control with certain and resistless power, the emotions of the multitude." Although all humans had emotions, Hughes saw his as serving a higher purpose: "May my Guardian Select for it [his soul] such sensual gratification as will best adapt it to the task of the orator,—the animation and government of human passions."[22] Passion became something to control, for by controlling it Hughes would be better able to understand and govern humanity. Although he found "the emotions of the multitude" tempting, by rising above and mastering them Hughes would prepare himself for the ultimate responsibility of exercising power over others.

Hughes soon "realized" the "forbidden things" he had imagined. A week after experiencing his "unhallowed desires," he excitedly recorded the results of his deeds. "The past week has been fraught with invaluable experience. I have learned the vanity of Sensual & forbidden enjoyments, from experiments purposely tried." Although seemingly aware of the "vanity" of physical passion, Hughes felt the need to conduct more "experiments" during the following week. On January 16, he wrote: "I have reaped a little of the whirlwind of experience; have fully tested the insufficiency of carnal enjoyments."[23] Hughes's language here of "experiments" and "tests" reveals his intense desire to devise "scientific" means of controlling his own "human passions" so that he would eventually be able to "control with certain and resistless power, the emotions of the multitude." His sense of relief at the "insufficiency of carnal enjoyments" expresses his need to believe that his own self-control was critical to the realization of his social and political ambitions.

Yet, although sex may have been insufficient, the desire for love continued to tempt him. Just a few months after conducting the "experiments" noted above, he wrote the entry in which he renounced "the pure joys which marriage would bestow" in favor of "Glory." But neither the insufficiency of sex nor the desire for glory could quell the longing for love. On January 20, 1850, Hughes reflected on the nature of his relations

22. *Ibid.,* January 2, 1848.
23. *Ibid.,* January 9, 16, 1848.

with women. Again noting his larger objective and the use of women to obtain it, Hughes acknowledged the strong emotional impact women continued to have on him: "My first amatory engagement is dissolved. 'T'was bright, t'was Heavenly, but tis past.' I dissolved it. There now remains one avowed engagement, and two tacit ones. Since previous by a few months my eighteenth birthday, I have never been disengaged." As if to dispel any notion among his readers, or himself, that such "engagements" reflected amorous desires that might have interfered with his ambition, he continued: "But I have conscientiously acted. These engagements, that is, the latter ones, I contracted with a view to oratory, human nature, that is a knowledge of it, and composition." Yet even with this disclaimer, he could not deny the emotional significance of the "engagements." "Of my life," he entreated, "blot out any other portion, but not that, not that, no,—no—not that. It has been my liquor, cards, Otherwise I never gambled, never drank. For me, there was some excuse, some palliation to be pleaded. I never trifled, was never rejected." He concluded the passage with a vow to "woman," although it is not clear if by "woman" he meant an individual or the sex itself. "Woman, dear, dearest, woman, if the exertions of the loving Aspirant can accomplish it, you shall be advanced towards, shall attain your deserved dignity." [24] Whether the "woman" was a specific person or the female sex, Hughes saw himself as responsible for the attainment of her "dignity."

The tension evident in this passage surfaces throughout the diary. Hughes could not remain aloof from the stirrings of passion, although he did his best to deny them. In addition to denial, Hughes tried to substitute "glory" or "power" for women as the object of his love. Just two weeks after dissolving one of his "amatory engagements," Hughes wrote: "She who watches me, believes beloved and rejected. I never where

24. *Ibid.,* January 20, 1850. Hughes's reference to himself here as the "Aspirant" recurs occasionally throughout the diary. He even contemplated writing a "tragedy" entitled "The Aspirant." See, for example, *ibid.,* February 25, 1849, January 27, 1850, January 26, May 11, 1851, March 6, 13, 1853, in which he states that he had "begun the 'Aspirant.' I do not mean it to be a novel, but an announcement, real, earnest, practical, truthful and in faith." Hughes mentions the tragedy in the entry for November 18, 1849. Whether Hughes ever completed the "Aspirant" is unknown, but the probate court's inventory and appraisal of his possessions, filed on January 27, 1863, three months after his death, lists "one unpublished novel," which, unfortunately, has never been located. See Claiborne County Probate Court Records, February, 1863, Term, Roll 16, 433–34.

I set my amorous hopes was successful." But rather than continue with melancholic regret over his lack of success in human relations, Hughes projected his love onto what he hoped would be a more successful partner: "But I love Glory, Power, Fame, Energy." He reached levels of praise never approached in his descriptions of women: "What is her name. She is my Soul's idol. To her, I, with a lover's hot devotion, kneel. She is my sweet." Searching for literary and historical parallels, he chose ones with tragic connotations, as if he recognized the ominous nature of his relation to "Glory, Power, [and] Fame." "Romeo never more truly loved. I am her Antony. In her soft arms, on her fair bosom, beneath her warm eyes and balmy breath, I forget all joys & pains. To me, she is Cleopatra. But for her, I will not lose but gain a world. Come Caesar, Come Lepidus. Glory is mine, or death."[25]

Hughes tried to make his love of glory surpass and suppress his continued attraction to and interest in women. He did not succeed. Through the period covered by the diary two women, Emma Caffery and Martha Parker, tested his devotion to glory.[26] Although he ultimately married neither, this outcome was never certain. Hughes's feelings about these two women reveal the ambivalence and fear that characterized his relations with women in particular and humankind in general.

Although Hughes wrote sparingly and enigmatically of both Caffery and Parker, various references establish their importance to him. His 1848 remark about finding "a soul which could mingle with my own" remains oblique, as do two strange entries in December, 1849, in which Hughes quoted passages from love letters he had received. He neither commented on the letters nor offered any explanation for inserting them in the diary.[27]

25. Hughes Diary, February 10, 1850.

26. On February 24, 1850, Hughes noted that he "Saw the actress Miss Charlotte Cushman; benefited." He again mentioned Cushman in the March 10, 1850, entry: "Saw Miss Cushman (Charlotte), From her, I learned." Although these references are found among entries that speak of love—for instance on March 17, 1850, Hughes asks "Am I heart-broken?"—I do not believe that Hughes was romantically linked to Cushman. Both references speak of "seeing" Cushman, but it is unclear whether she was performing when Hughes saw her. His language in these references differs from that used when referring to Emma Caffery and Martha Parker. Hughes may well have been romantically interested in Cushman, but the evidence, unlike that for Caffery and Parker, is thin and ambiguous.

27. The first excerpt appears in the entry for December 24, 1849, and is dated Sep-

Less than a month later, he mentioned that his "first amatory engagement is dissolved," but he did not connect this event with the letters. The rest of 1850 seemed to have been an uneventful year in Hughes's relations with women. But in March, 1851, he again began to suffer the pain of unrealized love. "I love; still, still, I love." Yet with the love came doubt: "And she who subjugates my soul, is she fair? Is she constant, 'pure & sacred?' Rambling Spirits loving her, would esteem her a burning seraph; and seeing her, an angel." Such emotion pushed Hughes's thought to other concerns that illustrate the effect of his feelings of love. The next line in the entry reads: "Thoughts of Suicide & fame."[28] Hughes's post-adolescent penchant for melodramatic depictions of his troubled emotional life is surely evident here, as it is throughout the diary. Yet such excesses should not prevent us from recognizing that romantic love prompted feelings in Hughes which he felt he could suppress only by suicide or by thinking of the fame that he so loved and desired. For the time being, he chose thoughts of fame. But the person who elicited these feelings continued to cause him distress, and that distress contributed to both his private life and his understanding of the world around him.

On his twenty-second birthday, April 17, 1851, Hughes reflected on the past year of his life. While looking back, his first thoughts turned to his personal life. "I esteemed myself, Godguided. If such it is, my delusion was so great that I thought [that] He had caused a beautiful woman to love me. I parted with her but yesterday and discovered What? I cannot say that she loves me; or that she is indifferent. I know not what!"[29] Hughes's exasperation illustrated, in part, ambivalence about his own feelings, as well as those of the woman he wrote about. He had always wanted to be in control of his emotions, as he made clear during his "experiments" with "carnal enjoyments." Women were sources of "experience" for him, aids for his ascent to glory. But now they had become much more than that; they threatened to distract him from his goal.

His irritation resulted both from the woman's vague signals and his own inability to control the situation. This inability was tied to his conflicting desires, to his belief that he could have but one "mistress." Several

tember 24, 1849. Although the second excerpt follows, it is entered on December 23, 1849, and is dated April 23, 1847.

28. *Ibid.,* March 16, 1851.
29. *Ibid.,* April 17, 1851.

months after this episode, Hughes acknowledged his dilemma. On June 8, 1851, he pondered: "Power, knowledge, Love: you three divinities; which is fairer?" The passage that follows this query reveals Hughes's use of sensual language to convey the intensity of his desire for all three of these "divinities": "I will be your Paris. Strip to me. Be naked. Let me possess that I may decide your beauties."[30] Hughes's use of sexual metaphors to describe his desire for power or glory was not new here. He used such language early in the diary when he "wooed" "jealous Glory." Hughes sought to channel his sexual energy and passion in directions that would benefit his life's goal. And though feelings for women competed for that energy and passion, he kept trying to maintain his course for glory.

Whether the woman Hughes refers to in these passages is Emma Caffery or Martha Parker remains a mystery. But the tension and anxiety Hughes evidenced in these examples also marked his relations with both of them. On January 1, 1852, Hughes affirmed his "oath and Consecration," first recorded on January 1, 1851, although apparently declared earlier since he was on this earlier date "renewing" it. The oath reads: "Now my Father, I consecrate to Glory, myself. By our long loves; by your omnipotence, and omniscience: I swear it." But on January 1, 1852, when Hughes again recorded his oath, he added this passage before it: "This oath was first taken after he loosed his soul from Emma Caffery."[31] When, why, and how he "loosed his soul" is not known, but that the break with Caffery led to the "oath and Consecration" reveals the conflict between his relation with a woman and his devotion to glory. His language, notably the word *soul,* further suggests that he saw his relation with Caffery as total, all-encompassing. He had to sever the relation with Caffery to pursue glory; compromise was not possible.

Hughes had "loosed" himself from Caffery but not from his feelings toward her. On July 25, 1852, he noted: "Heard to day that Miss E. C. had arrived. Now, now my soul." Caffery clearly affected Hughes, but he never detailed their relationship. His first mention of her by her full name is the January 1, 1852, entry. But his contact with her seems to have gone back several years. In a fascinating passage from September 29, 1850, Hughes described a personal revelation in terms that suggest an intimate

30. *Ibid.,* June 8, 1851.
31. *Ibid.,* January 1, 1851, January 1, 1852.

relation with Caffery: "A revolution, an advance has in my mind, onward & upward wheeled. I have hitherto nursed for, my profession a regard of which its utility was the cold sire. But a new, warm and ruby-cheeked affection leaps, like a father's prattler to my arms. It is the child of my soul's own bosom. I recognize, I welcome it. Young & rose-lipped cherub: you shall be dandled. I will give you nectar. It shall be as sweet as that of Emma's breast."[32]

Hughes's invocation of "Emma's breast" as a source of sweet nectar shows that he associated her with pleasure. But he also pointed out that what he would give to "the child of my soul's own bosom" would be as sweet as what Emma gave him. Hughes's "child" was an idea; yet he used a human metaphor and a sexual reference within it to describe how he would nurture and love this thought. He took Caffery's love and gave it to his thoughts and plans, much as he tried to channel passion for women into passion for glory. Although unable to stifle all feelings for her, he could not develop a lasting, loving relation. His desire for glory, for fame and power, prevented him from accepting feelings of love, which he believed could only detract from and conflict with his ultimate destiny.

Hughes's conflicted feelings toward women, most clearly evidenced in his relations with Emma Caffery, also marked his references to Martha Parker. He first mentioned her on January 25, 1852, merely stating that "Miss Martha Parker is now in the City [New Orleans]." Although he did not mention her again by name until July 25, 1852, during the intervening months he did write of a woman who caused him suffering. On July 4, he penned a long and emotional entry: "Oh, Angel's heart!—Why should it be thus? Tears, now are in my eyes; hereafter it will not be so, for the bosom which was flesh to love, must be marble to forget!—How did she apprehend all! how bowed to fate." Hughes did not specify the precise nature of this passage. But three weeks later, on July 25, he hinted that the woman in question was Parker. "Saw Miss M. P.; the Fate seemed coming. How now it shall [be] is with God. My Faith shook never for a moment, and now I still can smile." One week later he again mentioned an unnamed woman: "She of my thoughts did not come. A mistake of women to fright me from my stool." As in the previous two passages, Hughes continued this entry with a reference to a "Fate" that

32. *Ibid.*, July 25, 1852, September 29, 1850.

remained unexplained: "The love-scheme moves well God loves me, the Fate, the long Bliss comes."[33] The "long Bliss," which he likened to the "Fate," could refer to either a continued relation with a woman or the end of such a relation.

Hughes's own ambivalence toward women and his relations with them prevents us from definitively concluding whether "Bliss" meant happiness with a woman or a "loosening" of himself from a woman. Clearly the ambivalence ran deep. He never, at least in the course of the diary, resolved the tension between his longings for love and his desire for glory. Emma Caffery and Martha Parker forced Hughes to confront this tension, yet even at the end of the diary it remained unresolved. On March 6, 1853, Hughes noted, with characteristic uneasiness, that "Miss M. R. P. and Miss E. C. are both in town.—Is there providence; What is this life?" His queries about "providence" and the meaning of life reflect his inability to act and his related hope that some other force would decide for him and thus end his dilemma. His entry the next week further illustrates this reliance on something outside himself to end his vacillation: "What of Love? They were here, and one is gone. The coming of Time is heavy, and swelling; let it break and disgorge.—Come what come may." Hughes's fatalistic attitude at the end of this passage continued in the weeks ahead. Caffery had left, for the next week Hughes wrote: "Tomorrow, call on Miss M. R. P.—'There is a tide'—." One week later Hughes penned the last reference to a woman in his diary. The previous week's call on Parker received no comment. Instead, Hughes simply recorded that "M. R. P. . . . is still here." He then quoted a poem that illustrates his melancholic state: "'Dim Hour, that sleepst on pillowing clouds afar / Oh Rise and yoke the turtles to thy car.'"[34]

Women aroused in Hughes feelings of love and pleasure and of fear and doubt. His personality was torn between his dreams of glory and his conflicting desire for a conventional life of love and family. Although other men had both glory and love, for Hughes the two remained mutually exclusive, even locked in perpetual struggle. He depicted this struggle as part of a larger, more comprehensive conflict between the powers of knowledge and will and those of the senses. Although his diary, like so many antebellum diaries, focuses a good deal of attention on his

33. *Ibid.,* January 25, July 4, 25, August 1, 1852.
34. *Ibid.,* March 6, 13, 20, 27, 1853.

(usually ill) health, Hughes tended to link feelings toward women with his health because both of them disturbed his paramount desire for power. His health, like his sexual urges, threatened to limit him, to prevent him from realizing his destiny. And this threat, like sex, often paralyzed him. On July 31, 1848, he wrote: "My eyes are still very weak. Can it be that those failing organs & members are to control my actions. Can I not free myself from them, & commune with Nature & spirits undisturbed by the pangs of the flesh?"[35] His "freeing" himself from his senses parallels his "loosening" his soul from Emma Caffery. Just as that "loosening" would have allowed him to consecrate himself to glory, so "freeing" himself from the senses would have permitted him to "commune with Nature." In both cases he sought to transcend the material, sensual world and proceed with his more important responsibilities. His unsettling fear that "failing organs," like his sexual longings, might "control [his] actions" strengthened his conviction that only by escaping such control could he realize his ambition to control himself and his world.

At times, however, Hughes felt drawn toward the simplicity and ease that sensual and material pleasures could provide. "Across my mind," he wrote on September 17, 1848, "there sometimes flits a temptation to abandon the high career which God & myself have marked out for me, and seek happiness in the amassment of wealth, & possession of wedded beatitude." Such moments did not last long. He continued, "My contempt for these enjoyments soon urges me with keener desire to power and glory."[36] Hughes viewed every and any pleasure as somehow opposed to his higher duty. On October 7, 1849, he exhibited a pathetic compulsion to avoid pleasure, even when it was not sensual or material: "I will, if I have leisure take a full course of medicine. It would give pleasure, but one of my chief teachings is to disregard pleasure." Only the notion that it would somehow benefit his pursuits of power and glory permitted him to continue to entertain the thought: "I hope it will consist with my glory—duty, nosology & pathology. I will perhaps endeavor to understand."[37]

But only with difficulty could Hughes control his passions and urges.

---

35. *Ibid.,* July 31, 1848.

36. *Ibid.,* September 17, 1848. One wonders whether Hughes's lifelong bachelorhood resulted from such "contempt" for "wedded beatitude."

37. *Ibid.,* October 7, 1849.

On September 29, 1850, he noted that "I have added to my daily prayers—sunday's excepted—one to 'restrain to health, my appetites & pleasures.'" Hughes's resort to prayer reflected his sense of a loss of self-control. Just less than a month later, on October 27, 1850, Hughes recorded his most explicit meditation on his battle with his "appetites." "My appetites," he wrote, "are—all—strong,—impetuous. I would without cogitant self-control be libertine, glutton and drunkard." He then shifted from the first person to the third person plural, suggesting that it was easier for him to examine his own feelings by locating and analyzing them in others. "There is in some an antipathy to the Sensual. It disgusts them. They fear it. Yet they are to the luxury of it, acutely sensible. While enjoyment is thus rolled under the tongue it is with self-rebuke made intensely bitter; this sometimes is also an after-taste. Sensual pleasures are to them of this aloe-dust never rid. It if they are not stupefying; ~~this all~~ [Hughes's correction] disgusts from more than fitful indulgence. Great men may be drunkards; they never are gluttons or excessive libertines. Their effulgence scatters before they can reach a large size, these sin-fat clouds." He then returned to the first person and directly confronted his fears regarding these appetites and his ability to control them: "I have of animal gratifications, this dread and disgust, yet with these, almost ungovernable appetites. Prayer is my chief means of controlling them; for in resolve I place there no trust." [38]

Hughes's continuing struggle between his "ungovernable appetites" and his desire for greatness and power illustrates two central facets of his personality. His insecurity, his inability to "trust" himself, permeated not only his relation with his senses but also decisions he made regarding almost every aspect of his life. Yet he saw himself as "chosen" for greatness. Hughes resembled the popular image of the romantic hero or genius, and he himself acknowledged the resemblance. Drew Gilpin Faust, in her study of five antebellum southern intellectuals, has commented on the concept of "genius" that her subjects shared: "The doctrine of genius thus incorporated both religious and scientific justifications for their plight, for it explained their gifts as at once an indisputable physiological reality and a kind of divine grace. The genius was both selected by nature and elected by God." [39]

38. *Ibid.,* September 29, October 27, 1850.

39. Drew Gilpin Faust, *A Sacred Circle: The Dilemma of the Intellectual in the Old South, 1840–1860* (Baltimore, 1977), 24.

For Hughes, his recognition of his genius meant that conventional life was an impossibility, yet it was often conventional life that he longed for. "Wedded beatitude" appealed to him, but he had to have contempt for it in order to fulfill his destiny, a destiny he, like Faust's geniuses, only partly chose. He came to view his genius as a curse that prevented him from enjoying the simple comforts of life: "I wished I labored with my hands. I wish a little cottage, with honeysuckles around it was mine."[40] But such dreams, like his feelings for love and companionship, fell victim to his overriding quest for power and glory. Hughes's ambivalence toward sex, the tensions that racked his experiences with women and with pleasure of any sort, resulted from and in turn strengthened his view of himself as a chosen genius plagued by worldly temptation. Hughes viewed the world around him through the perspective of his destiny. His day-to-day life certainly did not continually revolve around his preoccupation with glory and the fears that threatened his acquisition of it. Yet that he chose to devote so much of his weekly reflections to what he perceived to be an intense and critical struggle allows us to see both his excessive and melodramatic view of his role in human history and the ways that view led him to make professional and intellectual choices he might not have otherwise made.

Just as Hughes's personal life exhibited a conflict between convention and greatness, so too did his professional life. Throughout the course of his diary he pursued law, first as a student and after April, 1850, as a lawyer. His work in his chosen profession further illustrates the conflict he experienced between the reality of his daily life and his dreams of glory and power. Hughes could view law only as it affected the pursuit of his destiny. As he spent year after year learning and then practicing law, he became more and more disillusioned by its inability to hasten his acquisition of fame. His legal career, like his personal life, posed the central problem of his early adulthood: the sacrifices that had to made to realize power. The elusiveness of power would lead him to question not only his profession but also his conviction that he was indeed destined to be "the greatest mortal man that can be."[41]

40. Hughes Diary, October 20, 1850.
41. Hughes frequently referred to himself in these terms. For examples see *ibid.*, February 13, 1848, February 3, 1850, and May 25, 1851.

On December 24, 1848, soon after completing his first year as a law student in New Orleans, Hughes asked himself, "Why am I averse to being a practical lawyer?" He answered, in part, in the rest of the entry: "It is said that if all would labor in production, four hours in every day; the remaining portion of the day could be spent as desire prompted." The demands of law thus interfered with his "desire," and such interference led him to consider other professional options that would better allow for his chosen pursuits: "I have a longing to cultivate with my own hands a 'few paternal acres', for this little part of the day, and then be free."[42] The ideal of the country squire who met his needs with just a few hours of work and then turned his attention to the cultivation of more important tasks contrasted sharply with the long hours of a young law student. But there was more to the law than time, and Hughes found himself alternately attracted to and repulsed by these features.

Hughes's attitude toward legal practice reached a high point in late 1850, soon after he was admitted to the bar. In one of his most enthusiastic entries, from September 29, he noted a change in perspective: "I have hitherto nursed for, my profession a regard of which its utility was the cold sire. But a new, warm and ruby-cheeked affection leaps, like a father's prattler to my arms. It is the child of my soul's own bosom." Hughes proceeded to detail how he would nurture this "child," but he remained, as ever, cryptic about exactly what the "child" was. In a subsequent paragraph of the same entry, however, he did elaborate somewhat on his new attitude toward his profession and the reasons for it: "I have been in my mind, developing of logic, Evidence, Civil & Criminal Practice & General Law, the leading doctrines, the physiology, the causes. I still, to my aim of intention design of wooing Criminal Practice adhere. Its bar is more a rostrum. I will wed, to it, my young eloquence. Apollo shall marry Hecate. The fullfledged eaglet, & aged phoenix' unburnt grizzliness shall mate."[43] Hughes, the young Apollo, would transform the bar into a vehicle for personal advancement. The law would serve his needs, further his ambitions. This burst of excitement for the law may, in part, be attributed to Hughes's work in developing "the leading

42. *Ibid.,* December 24, 1848.

43. *Ibid.,* September 29, 1850. Note Hughes's use of the words *woo, wed, marry,* and *mate.* Even when speaking of his profession he employed language more appropriate to romantic, even conjugal, relations.

doctrines, the physiology, the causes" of "Civil & Criminal Practice & General Law." Hughes appeared to have found a way for his profession to aid his vocation.

Hughes maintained this enthusiasm in the months ahead. In November, 1850, he returned to New Orleans after spending the summer in Port Gibson. As he had for the previous two years, he reported to the law office of Thomas J. Durant. But this fall, he returned as an accredited lawyer. More than that, he returned full of the hope for his profession that marked the September 29 entry. He expressed this hope on November 3, while still in Port Gibson: "I expect to, on Tuesday next, depart for New Orleans. I will be Caesar; it shall be my Pharsalia." He then added, with as much insecurity as confidence: "In God, my faith that I shall be the greatest mortal man that can be, & the best mortal man: is supreme & indestructible. Such is, if there is a God, my destiny; if there is not; I care not what it is." Although unsure about God's existence, Hughes remained hopeful. Upon arriving in New Orleans he wrote: "Here, earnest life begins."[44]

For the first few weeks after his arrival Hughes wrote positively about his career. Though not as ecstatic as before, he nonetheless appeared interested in his cases and his performances in them. But disillusionment came quickly. Not surprisingly, this disillusionment coincided with a renewed sense of his destiny. On January 1, 1851, after reconsecrating himself to glory, he laid out his goal. But he could not eliminate the insecurity and doubt that rivaled his conviction about his role in the world: "I am by God set apart;—O, I know that I am—for my fellow-being's happiness. I am to be the Greatest Mortal Man that can be; & the best Mortal Man. God loves me. I am not raving! I am not mad, I pray." As if to put his doubt behind him, in the next paragraph Hughes once again confidently set forth his dream: "I am God's implement to reveal the philosophy of the Human Mind; & to illustrate it; to reform legislation; to reveal perfect politics;—these, of thoughts and words—; of deeds; to be the leader, and beloved of the World."[45]

As he struggled to reassure himself of his destined greatness, Hughes vacillated between despair and confidence. But to whichever pole he tended, his attitude toward his career suffered. If he felt confident, then

44. *Ibid.,* November 3, 10, 1850.
45. *Ibid.,* January 1, 1851.

law became an obstacle, a weight that held him to a menial position. If he despaired, then law was a source of his misery, a path that was taking him nowhere. His dissatisfaction became apparent by mid-January, 1851. On January 12, after mentioning his difficulties in cross-examining witnesses, he lashed out at the intellectual limits of law: "The most Successful lawyers have, I observe, but brief opportunities of extraprofessional reflection. I would rather be a basketmaker and think; than the most opulent counsellor, and attorney at law." Hughes did not totally reject the law, only his position within it. Indeed, the law remained his destined profession: "I think God has not condemned me to the perishable and indifferent acts of the law-practitioners; I am to be a jurisprudent; a maker, not a fitter."[46] As a "jurisprudent" Hughes would be better able "to be the leader, and beloved of the World."

Just twenty-one years old, Hughes was nonetheless impatient with the delay of greatness and the tediousness of legal practice. At times his despair over his progress led him to contemplate the simplicity of conventional life, much as did his relations with women. In these moments Hughes revealed his conflicts about his place in the world and his power to influence that position. On January 19, 1851, he confronted his ambivalence. For a rare moment he seemed balanced between the opposing tensions of unlimited hope of greatness and frustrated bitterness of despair. He even wrote of his law practice in an unusually tempered way: "Law-business not, I think, decreased. I have in addressing the Court, preferred in style the Serene. I study my cases. I build on each one, a hope of glory. I for that pray, and in each suit, I am a man. It now neither grieves or glads me." But such claims to indifference could not block feelings of resignation. "Yet,—alas, why yet? I yet wish that I were a mere chaser of butterflies; a gatherer of wild roses in the valley; and shells on the shore." In such a mood, Hughes considered not how to become "the leader, and beloved of the World," but whether his happiness could be achieved only in the afterworld: "Are there on continents of Eternity, butterflies, wild roses, white and dimpled shells, forests and rivers swimming to the sea."[47]

Such moments of resignation did not, however, last very long. Hughes continued to view the practice of law negatively, especially as his ambi-

46. *Ibid.*, January 12, 1851.
47. *Ibid.*, January 19, 1851.

tions remained unrealized. At times, he sought to channel his frustration, to use it to reinvigorate his hopes. On May 4, 1851, he wrote: "Law-business punctually regarded. It yields some trifle, pecuniarily. But exorts no action of soul. Shall I be content. If discontent is a devil; let it find in my breast a hell. Leap to me, you subtle power, stir me to something of courage, wisdom or goodness."[48] Hughes's dissatisfaction with his career soon led him to consider other professions that might better serve his goal.

Journalism appealed to Hughes. In May, 1851, he asked his brother William and his brother-in-law William Thomas Magruder "to procure for me the editorial chair of a Newspaper in Port Gibson." He then recorded his motives in seeking such a position: "My investigations, into physical and metaphysical had been so satisfactory, fruitful indeed, & promissory of success; the prospect of a law-practice here [New Orleans], so despising; mechanical labor, so repulsive; that I could not but yearn for some attitude which would secure subsistence, & action in exchange, political opportunities & leisure for philosophy."[49] Being an editor would have allowed Hughes to make a living and pursue his intellectual work, something the law had been unable to do. But no editorship was available.

Hughes's reaction to the news revealed not only his disappointment but also his vision of what he could have accomplished as an editor. All the dreams of his destiny, all his plans for himself and the world, informed that vision: "How would I have loved the Ultimun Organum. How speeded the Universal Republic, How consummated the action, expression, & reasonings of the orator, How pondered the question of Slavery, How lived, loved, How worshipped God. But I submit."[50] Hughes found himself in one profession that prevented him from real-

48. *Ibid.,* May 4, 1851.

49. *Ibid.,* May 11, 1851. This was not the first time Hughes had expressed interest in becoming an editor. On December 8, 1850, while living in New Orleans, he wrote that he had "directed a friend to inquire whether any editorial chair of two of the leading City Newspapers, were vacant." He made no further mention of this inquiry. See *ibid.,* December 8, 1850.

50. *Ibid.,* May 11, 1851. Hughes remained interested in journalism and convinced that it was a career of great influence and power. His most forceful discussion of the importance of editors can be found in an unpublished April 26, 1856, lecture, "The New Governing Class," in Folder 3, Box 1, Hughes Papers. He reiterated this point in *Speech of Henry Hughes, On Our Administration of Justice; or, The New Bar and New Court . . .* (Port Gibson, Miss., 1860), 12.

izing his goals and unable to enter another that might allow their attainment. He would spend several more years searching for a way to express and implement his ideas.

What were these ideas? Where did they come from? The diary abounds with comments on the books, pamphlets, and periodicals Hughes read and shows that he, like many southern thinkers, actively and thoughtfully took part in the major intellectual, literary, and scientific debates of his time. His discussions of those debates and the relevant literature provide us with insight into the ways in which Hughes's personality and his social context influenced both what and how he read.

Hughes perceived himself an intellectual, and his diary testifies to his attempts to master almost every field of intellectual inquiry. The scope of his interests led his contemporary biographer, Reverend William D. Moore, to state in his eulogy that "an unusual combination of gifts met in him and so equally that it was difficult to say what was his special endowment." On October 21, 1849, Hughes noted his unlimited appetite in a succinct and serious statement: "I propose to make the whole circuit of human knowledge." The sincerity of this proposal runs throughout the diary; no subject escaped his consideration. Although he would focus more narrowly on social questions in later years, Hughes maintained an interest in a wide variety of fields throughout his adult life.[51]

Hughes often provided a breakdown of his typical daily activities. On November 18, 1849, for example, he composed before breakfast and thereafter studied "a little in Vegetable Physiology." "Then," he continued, "to the office. There I study law. This from 9 o'clock A.M. to 2 P.M." Upon returning home, "I glance into a French book; then until dinner, which in about a quarter of an hour occurs, read Shakespeare." The time after dinner was spent reading "Young's Night Thoughts, and Carpenters [sic] Human Physiology." After reviewing by candlelight he

51. Moore, *Life and Works of Col. Henry Hughes,* 11; Hughes Diary, October 21, 1849. For evidence of Hughes's continued interest in scientific or nonpolitical matters, see Hughes, "Theory of Capillarity, January 1, 1855," and Hughes, "Hebe or Hygienic Worship," both in Folder 4, Box 1, Hughes Papers; and Hughes, "The New Science: Aristology; or, That Branch of Philology whose end is the Perfection of the English Language—Aristologic Formulas," read before the New Orleans Academy of Science, March 8, 1858, clipping in Hughes Scrapbook, Hughes Papers. This last essay is also in Lyman, ed., *Selected Writings of Henry Hughes,* 197–205.

"memorized a classification in Law & Political Economy; from Logic, & my Law Note Book, learn something; memorize a passage from the poets and exercise in gesticulation." The day's other activities also presented opportunities for improvement: "While walking, I anal[y]ze, classify, combine, & study the principles of conversation, discover a rhetorical resemblance & synonyms. At a disengaged interval, exercise in facial expression.— — —Thoughts of writing a tragedy 'The Aspirant.' Thoughts of improving the process of setting (or composing?) type." Hughes did not exaggerate his activities. A casual examination of the books he recorded reading supports his contention that all knowledge was his domain.[52]

His reading served both narrow, practical ends and his broader ambitions. He was thus able to consider nearly any reading valuable in some way. As he put it on June 7, 1852, "How every book makes me wiser." Although he read much law in preparation for his professional life, he also read it with an eye toward what he hoped would be his far more important historical role. His interest in oratory, especially Cicero's and James Rush's works, similarly aided his immediate and more long-term interests. And his interest in novels, poetry, and plays provided him with insight and understanding of human behavior, including his own, which, as we have seen regarding his "experiments" in "sensual gratification," would enable him to better "control . . . the emotions of the multitude."[53]

Hughes's reading also suggests that he had more than a casual interest in scientific and mechanical knowledge. And, as with his other reading, he sought to put into practice the knowledge he had acquired in these fields. In addition to his idea of modifying "the process of setting (or composing) type," he also "Invented a cotton-press: a combination of the lever & screw, with a cone instead of a cylinder." He contemplated inventions for steamboats and wagons.[54] Fascinated with the senses, Hughes

52. Hughes Diary, November 18, 1849. For similar accounts of his daily activities, see *ibid.*, April 21, June 16, 1850. Hughes recorded the books he read week by week, entry by entry. See the Appendix to this book for a complete list of his readings.

53. *Ibid.*, June 7, 1852. For references to Cicero see *ibid.*, January 23, 30, 1848, and February 4, 1849. For those to Rush see *ibid.*, February 4, 1849, April 21, 28, 1850, and June 15, 1851. After finishing Rush's *Philosophy of the Human Voice* on June 15, 1851, Hughes noted, "That work I, in gratitude, kissed."

54. For the cotton press see *ibid.*, October 3, December 28, 1851, and March 14, 1852; for the steamboat see December 14, 1851; for the wagon see December 28, 1851.

speculated: "Are not the four of the Senses, Modifications of the Sense of Touch? Are not the eye, ear, nostril, tongue, nerves of Touch adapted to Light, Atmosphere, Odorous particles and Sapid particles." For months thereafter, Hughes read and analyzed the physiology of the senses, seeking to confirm his speculations. Gravitation, motion, the nature and character of atoms, capillary action, and hydraulics were just some of Hughes's other scientific interests.[55] As his continued interest in some of these topics would demonstrate, his desire to understand nature, much like his wish to "feel every variety of Woe and enjoyment," was directly related to his interest in using that knowledge to control nature, just as his knowledge of emotions would enable him to "govern" "human passions." The natural world, like the human one, would have to be studied before it could be controlled.

Although law and the sciences interested Hughes deeply, the liberal arts attracted him even more. Literature, philosophy, history, and the classics occupied the greater part of his reading and speculations. The men and women of these fields aroused his interest, challenged his ideas, and influenced the development of his thought. Hughes's absorption of and responses to these writings laid the groundwork for his maturation as a "sociologist" committed to the realization of a "Slavery Perfect Society."[56]

Ascertaining the influence of specific thinkers on Hughes proves difficult in part because of his strong reluctance to acknowledge such influence. To admit that someone else had developed a theory or idea threatened his sense of his own originality and creativity. Thus in one of his earliest references to another intellectual, John Locke, Hughes expressed disillusionment over the similarities in their thought: "Mr. John Locke & myself agreed most flatteringly in our views of the origin of the idea of God. I confess my disappointment; I indulged the hope that I was exploring an untrodden field. Lock[e] anticipated me, & I consent. May the results of my next investigations be such as will not dread to confront the past." A year later Hughes had a similar reaction to Immanuel Kant.

---

55. *Ibid.,* January 21, 1849. For further references to the senses see *ibid.,* March 18, June 10, October 14, 29, 1849. For expressions of Hughes's scientific interests, see *ibid.,* August 5, 12, 26, November 25, 1849, March 24, April 17, May 16, 1850, September 12, December 5, 19, 1852, and February 13, 1853.

56. The reference to "Slavery Perfect Society" is from *ibid.,* October 24, 1852.

He indicated not only his disappointment in being "anticipated" but also his fear that his own fame would be compromised by such "anticipation." After reading a life of Kant in the *Edinburgh Encyclopedia,* he wrote: "I was filled with pride and wretchedness. I was proud that the philosophy of that divine mind was so like that System the result of my own young reflections which I vainly flattered myself to have been alone in developing. I was bitterly wretched to think that my Glory would be in part deprived of the praise, of novelty."[57]

Such feelings of "wretchedness" betrayed an intense sense of competition. And when Hughes did not "dread" confronting past thinkers, he often dreamed of surpassing them. This was especially true of his views toward Francis Bacon, whom he frequently mentioned in the diary.

For Hughes, Bacon was both model and rival, someone he wished to emulate and best. Part of Hughes's interest in Bacon surely resulted from Bacon's encyclopedic knowledge and scope of inquiry, two characteristics Hughes desired for himself. But his admiration may also have resulted from what Bacon had done to the scientific world. Although historians continue to debate the rival influences of Baconian induction and Cartesian deduction in the seventeenth through nineteenth centuries, Bacon's impact on the intellectual world of antebellum America, especially in the Old School Presbyterianism in which Hughes was educated, has been persuasively demonstrated by Theodore Dwight Bozeman and others.[58] Hughes saw Bacon like many others had, as someone who had revolutionized the scientific system and supplanted outdated "idols" with his *Novum Organum.* This, Bacon's masterwork, called for a total reformation of all of science—methods, education, application, and institutions. It boldly set forth a new system of knowledge, one closely tied to practical use. For Bacon, science had to serve humanity's needs. The inductive method he systematized sought to allow men the means by which they could acquire knowledge and then use that knowledge "for the benefit and use of life."[59] Bacon combined his scientific thought with a life in

57. *Ibid.,* July 31, 1848, July 29, 1849.

58. See especially Bozeman, *Protestants in an Age of Science, passim;* Herbert Hovenkamp, *Science and Religion in America, 1800–1860* (Philadelphia, 1978), esp. 23–36.

59. Francis Bacon, *Novum Organum* (1620), in *The Philosophical Works of Francis Bacon,* ed. John M. Robertson (Freeport, N.Y., 1970), 256–387. The quote is from Bacon, *The Great Instauration* (1620), *ibid.,* 247.

public service, and he advocated his method as one that could provide pragmatic social benefits.

This combination of revolutionary thinker and social reformer no doubt appealed to and attracted Hughes, who saw himself as nothing less. In fact, while still in his teens he desired to see himself as something more. Early in the diary Hughes pleaded: "My Father, let [me] surpass Bacon." He eventually, however, moderated such ambitions. In 1852, after having read more of Bacon's works, Hughes appeared more respectful toward him: "Read Lord Bacon. There I met a man. He is a peer; with him I feel an intellectual equality." Such peerage did not come easily; Hughes excluded Alexander the Great (too young), Cromwell (not "high taught"), and Napoleon ("not freeminded when young"). Even Aristotle and Shakespeare did not make the grade, although they came close. Along with Bacon, Hughes included only the general, historian, and statesman Julius Caesar.[60]

Although Hughes mentioned Bacon far more often than Caesar, he also frequently paired them. Both epitomized aspects of Hughes's character, particularly his desire to combine thought and action, to be both mind and body. Hughes expressed this wish, and the concomitant fear of never realizing it, on May 28, 1848: "O My Father let not my divine desires satisfy themselves with words; Let them not evaporate in vain declarations to my friends & prayers to Thee. Let me be the perfect orator, reasoner, statesman, philosopher, warrior, philanthropist." The fear of remaining a mere thinker, of never achieving anything concrete, plagued Hughes throughout the diary years. After reading an article on "Influence of Authority in matters of Opinion," Hughes voiced a familiar refrain: "That [article] will be of use in my political & social plans—works I mean. For if all my life, I am but to plan and dream, had I not now better die?"[61] Hughes feared that his wisdom would be the kind Bacon had ridiculed. Writing of the wisdom of the Greeks but including by implication all abstracted thought, Bacon declared that "it can talk, but it

60. Hughes Diary, June 27, 1848, July 18, 1852.
61. *Ibid.,* May 28, 1848, June 13, 1852. Hughes read James Chesnut, Jr.'s, harsh review of George Cornwall Lewis' *Influence of Authority in Matters of Opinion* (London, 1849). Chesnut's review appeared in the *Southern Quarterly Review,* n.s., V (April, 1852), 341–72. I am grateful to Professor Michael O'Brien for providing me with this citation.

cannot generate; for it is fruitful of controversies but barren of works."[62] Nothing worried Hughes more than the idea that his life would be "barren of works." Bacon thus provided him not only with a model to emulate but also standards by which to judge his own thoughts and actions.

Hughes's concern with works, with action, did not prevent him from devoting much of his time to study. As a good Baconian, he recognized the need to gather data before drawing conclusions. Hughes expressed this process in a June 29, 1851, entry: "Have the wish to classify all science art & literature, & arrange them in note-books. I wish then to collect or create all notions useful to the orator, philosopher & statesman."[63] Notwithstanding his continued frustrations with mere thought, Hughes recognized that only a thorough knowledge of all aspects of inquiry would prepare him for his destiny. He accordingly read broadly but rigorously. Although he simply noted most of the titles of works he read, two writers besides Bacon received extended treatment. Their influence would prove significant for the course of Hughes's subsequent career.

While steaming down the Mississippi River from Port Gibson to New Orleans on October 24, 1852, Hughes pondered: "Why, why does Carlyle thrust himself into my thoughts." In the next paragraph, although not directly answering his own query, he penned a passage that revealed Thomas Carlyle's influence: "A Universal Republic, Ultiman Organum, Longitude, Slavery Perfect Society; Myself, the God-beloved, the human supreme of Earth's Politics, Society, Philosophy, Economics, Religion & Aesthetics; Of these I am the devotee." This passage exemplifies Hughes's heroic vision of himself, a vision he partly derived from Carlyle's writings on heroes and hero worship. Although Carlyle himself was hardly responsible for the notion of the heroic during the first three-quarters of the nineteenth century, he helped promote hero worship, which he termed "the basis of all possible good, religious or social, for mankind." Hughes acknowledged Carlyle's role in his sense of his own heroism in a January 5, 1851, entry: "In the purpose of my existence, my earnestness becomes greater; my self-ambition, less. I feel more—more, my heroism; thus Carlyle terms it. I feel as if I could dignify Jove's throne; hold the

62. Bacon, *Great Instauration,* in *Philosophical Works of Bacon,* ed. Robertson, 243.
63. Hughes Diary, June 29, 1851.

chain which holds the world; hurl thunderbolt, and shake the poles."[64]

Hughes dutifully mentioned his lack of "self-ambition," which Carlyle attributed to the "sham hero" as opposed to the genuine hero. Hughes's reference to "earnestness" also reflects Carlyle's insistence that the hero be "sincere." But it was less these attributes of Carlyle's hero that Hughes responded to than the overall conception of the hero as political savior. Carlyle viewed the modern world as dominated by anarchy and political decay, most clearly evidenced by the mediocrity of political leadership. The hero, although not exclusively a political figure, would lead human-kind, which in turn would be grateful for such leadership. Guided by his intellect and his sincerity, and in part an agent of divine will, the hero would restore order and provide the guidance necessary for proper social development. When Hughes read the following passage in Carlyle's *Latter-Day Pamphlets*, he surely understood and sympathized with Car-lyle's message: "Intellect exists in all countries; and the function appointed it by Heaven,—Governments had better not attempt to contradict that, for they cannot! Intellect *has* to govern in this world."[65]

Carlyle's writings on heroes and the heroic confirmed Hughes's sense of his destiny and legitimated his vision of himself as one worthy of respect and reverence. Carlyle's influence on Hughes cannot be delineated in every respect, but he surely helped shape and strengthen Hughes's notions regarding power, intellect, and the relations between them. The idea of the hero squared nicely with Hughes's conception of himself and his place in the world, while Carlyle's corresponding idea of the need for stability and order in an anarchistic and unguided world informed Hughes's broader vision of social organization and leadership. Although Hughes generally refrained from citing those figures who influenced him, his few brief references to Carlyle and the presence of Carlyle's ideas in his diary and subsequent writings testify to Carlyle's impact. As a con-servative who combined romantic notions of an ordered and harmonious society with a impassioned critique of capitalistic social relations, Carlyle

64. *Ibid.,* October 24, 1852, January 5, 1851; Thomas Carlyle, *On Heroes, Hero-Worship and the Heroic in History* (Lincoln, Neb., 1966). See Gerald Milton Straka, "The Influence of Thomas Carlyle in the Old South, 1848–1865" (M.A. thesis, University of Virginia, 1953).

65. Thomas Carlyle, *The Works of Thomas Carlyle* (New York, 1903), XX (*Latter-Day Pamphlets*), 130.

proved to be a model for Hughes's own career as social critic and theorist.

Carlyle was just one of the countless writers who addressed the historic changes in Western society in the first half of the nineteenth century. Hughes read many of them, including Jeremy Bentham, John Stuart Mill, Henri Saint-Simon, and Charles Fourier.[66] Of these four, Fourier had the greatest initial impact on Hughes. In Fourier, Hughes found a different kind of thinker than he had in Carlyle, although both forced him to confront what he called the "Social problem." From late February until early June, 1852, Hughes read with sustained interest Fourier's *Passions of the Human Soul,* a work that presented some of Fourier's most significant thoughts on social organization and development.[67] Although Hughes characteristically avoided identifying the specific ideas of Fourier that appealed to him, we nonetheless can locate tendencies in Fourier's thought the young Hughes may have found appealing and later incorporated into his own social writings.

Although Fourier held his share of romantic notions, most notably in his thoughts on cosmology, and roundly condemned the philosophes, he nonetheless shared the Enlightenment's belief in human perfectibility. Writing in the first three decades of the nineteenth century, Fourier drew from and developed Enlightenment ideas regarding society's operation

66. For references to Bentham see Hughes Diary, September 12, 19, 1852; for Mill see September 22, 1850, May 25, June 6, 1851; for Saint-Simon see August 19, 1849; for Fourier see August 19, 1849, and those references in note 67 below. Although many scholars have noted Hughes's indebtedness to Auguste Comte, which I will discuss more fully in Chapter 3, in the diary Comte is a minor figure. Hughes refers to him briefly, and those references do not suggest a deep familiarity with Comte's works. His first reference, on July 13, 1851, states, "Began 'Philosophy of Mathematics,' translated from the French of Compte [*sic*]." Several weeks later, on August 17, he notes that he had "Finished 'Compte's [*sic*] Philosophy of Mathematics,' by 'Gillespie,' " but makes no further mention of the book or its author. William M. Gillespie's translation was published by Harpers in New York in 1851, but it represented but a small portion of Comte's *Cours de philosophie positive.* Hughes, may, however, have read Comte after he stopped keeping his diary; he certainly displayed a greater familiarity with his style and substance after 1853.

67. Fourier's thoughts on the passions can be found throughout much of his work. For a convenient sampling see Jonathan Beecher and Richard Bienvenu, eds., *The Utopian Vision of Charles Fourier: Selected Texts on Work, Love, and Passionate Attraction* (Boston, 1971). For Hughes's references to Fourier and his writings, see Hughes Diary, February 29, March 14, 21, April 4, 11, May 2, 9, 16, 23, 30, June 7, 1852.

according to natural laws that could be discovered through reason and investigation. Once humankind knew these laws, society could be reformed so as to function in accordance with them and could thereby eliminate the suffering and misery caused by the improperly organized societies of the present. Fourier believed that human perfectibility could be achieved only through a societal reorganization that eliminated the atomistic and exploitative individualism that dominated contemporary bourgeois civilization. Labeled by many, beginning with Friedrich Engels, as a "utopian" socialist, Fourier advocated the creation of "phalanxes" that emphasized the interdependence and unity of human beings. Phalanxes, organized scientifically according to social and psychological laws, would permit the full realization of individual happiness through communal living. The market relations that dominated current society would be replaced by relations based on the free and natural exercise of human passion and attraction.[68]

Like Fourier, Hughes believed strongly in using one's knowledge of the human condition to reform and even restructure society. On March 14, 1852, Hughes wondered whether he should apply his knowledge and devise a solution to "the Social problem." Revealingly, this thought comes after a reference to Fourier: "Continued Fourier on 'the Passions of the Human Soul.' The Social problem: Shall I solve it?" Fourier served to draw Hughes's attention and interest to the "Social problem," and by doing so may well have stimulated Hughes to devote most of his adult life to questions about social organization and social relations. On May 2, 1852, Hughes acknowledged Fourier's impact: "Finished the first volume of Fourier's 'Passions of the Human Soul.' That book's influence on me! May God guide and govern it."[69]

As this entry suggests, Hughes was not altogether comfortable with the degree of influence Fourier seemed to have on him. Why this might have been the case cannot be determined, but it would not be unreasonable to attribute this discomfort in part to Hughes's excitement and his

68. In addition to Fourier's own writings see Nicholas Riasanovsky, *The Teaching of Charles Fourier* (Berkeley, 1969); Frank Manuel, *The Prophets of Paris* (Cambridge, Mass., 1962), Chap. 5; Jonathan Beecher, *Charles Fourier: The Visionary and His World* (Baltimore, 1986); and Carl J. Guarreri, *The Utopian Alternative; Fourierism in Nineteenth-Century America* (Ithaca, 1991).

69. Hughes Diary, March 14, May 2, 1852.

corresponding fear that such excitement might prevent him from developing his own thought. We have seen how much emphasis Hughes placed on being original in his ideas, of relying as little as possible on other thinkers. Thus even with someone who clearly influenced him, such as Fourier, Hughes remained wary of attributing too much influence to another. On May 23, 1852, as he read the second volume of *Passions,* Hughes again qualified the impact Fourier had on him: "Continued Fourier on the Passions. I do not think that this book will mislead, nor make me visionary. It will generate conceptions; it will supply elements. These I can combine; can accept or reject."[70] As usual, Hughes would control his own thought, although others would "supply elements."

With both Carlyle and Fourier, Hughes exposed himself to two of the most bitter critics of contemporary Western society. Both attacked the social atomization, materialism, and exploitation of the emerging capitalist order, and, although they differed on specifics, both longed for the establishment of a society that would restore order, interdependence, and harmony. The influence of Fourier and Carlyle on Hughes, like all intellectual influences, was affected by a myriad of personal factors that limit our ability to establish accurately the nature of the influences. Hughes read and responded to these men in ways that strongly suggest that he found what they had to say of more merit than almost all the other writers he read. Knowing what he read and combining that with what we know of him, we can conclude that the attraction to Carlyle and Fourier served both personal and political functions. Carlyle's theory of the hero and Fourier's ideas of social reorganization, along with their different but common critique of bourgeois individualism and the nature of contemporary society and desire for a unified and harmonious social order, all contributed to the formation of Hughes's sense of self and of the world. And although Hughes's later writings would only hint at the influence of both Carlyle and Fourier, these men and their ideas strengthened and added to Hughes's belief that he could develop and implement ideas that would change a world that desperately needed changing.

But how should the world be changed? How did Hughes define the "Social problem"? For a man who would emerge in 1854 as one of the South's staunchest defenders of slavery, Henry Hughes did not appear

70. *Ibid.,* May 23, 1852.

as such in his diary. Hughes discussed slavery and the South only briefly, and those brief comments do not suggest coherent or highly developed views on the subjects. Throughout the diary Hughes focused on his life, his thoughts. He rarely provided glimpses of the world outside of himself, and then only when that world impinged upon or related to his personal concerns. What we have seen throughout this chapter holds true regarding Hughes's comments and ideas on social issues: his sense of his destiny, his craving for power, and his desire to satisfy these personal needs affected his actions at every turn. Only gradually and subtly did Hughes merge his personal ambitions with a social vision that encompassed and addressed the world in which he lived.

The extent to which Hughes viewed political and social events in reference to his own interests can be seen in his responses to the revolutions of 1848. On April 16, 1848, Hughes first mentioned the events in Europe: "The World is preparing for me.—France is a Republic. Universal dominion is my aim.—a consolidation of all the powers and principalities of earth into one happy, sublime Republic."[71] This entry reveals far more about Hughes's sense of himself than his sense or understanding of the world and the events shaping it. The notion that the "World is preparing for me" clearly reflects the youthful Hughes's belief in his destiny but hardly expresses much knowledge of the nature of what was happening in Europe. Any disruption in the world, regardless of its character, sparked hope in Hughes that his destiny would somehow reach fulfillment. The content of world events mattered little; what mattered was the significance Hughes attributed to them, a significance that related directly to his desire for power.

The degree to which Hughes subordinated specific knowledge of world events to this desire for power closely resembles his subordination of his sexual and professional lives to the same desire. But whereas personal relations or professional obligations might interfere with his quest for power, political and social issues could directly serve his aspirations. Hughes recognized that knowledge and understanding of these issues, rather than simple awareness of them, could further his ambitions. Thus, although in 1848 and 1849 he exhibited a shallow view of world and national political and social questions, he increasingly broadened and

71. *Ibid.*, April 16, 1848.

deepened his knowledge of these matters as he matured in the early years of the 1850s. It is in these last years of the diary that we begin to see the emergence of someone for whom these questions would form the basis of his adult intellectual life.

Hughes testified to the development of his political outlook in a November 13, 1849, entry. "In politics," he noted, "my principles have gradually assumed shape. But are still not as definite as they should be. Of *Socialism,* I have obtained a knowledge, by no means perfect." In contradistinction to the grandiose claims to "World dominion" Hughes now clearly recognized the limitations of his own position. But even as he became more knowledgeable he did not completely abandon his notion of world leadership. Personal ambition continued to play a central role in his thought even as specific issues gained his attention. On March 9, 1851, Hughes referred to several contemporary political topics, but his references still contained his unique and inflated view of his destiny: "Thought of the bearing of Liberia & the American Colonization Society on the abolition of slavery. Through the Report of the Committee of Congress on the establishment of Steamers to Liberia, skated. This week am to investigate the annexation of Cuba. How shall I accomplish it. . . . The world shall be a Republic, and I its President. Now my God, I feel the impulse; I begin my Active Career. Here commences the political life of Henry Hughes."[72] God still was present, guiding Hughes to his appointed destiny, but perhaps more important than the continued emphasis on this divinely ordained mission is Hughes's more practical mention of the beginning of his "Active Career." What before had been some divine plan to be realized through the exercise of God's will now became a self-conscious, "Active Career," one that Hughes termed a new "life." He was developing a new way of thinking about himself and the world.

This new way of thinking did not, however, entail a wholesale rejection of the divine in favor of a purely secular worldview. Hughes's relation with God had, throughout the diary, vacillated between intense devotion and defiant questioning of God's existence. His desire to believe in a providential plan that included a prominent role for himself often conflicted with his similarly strong conviction that he, through his own mind and will, would make his own destiny. On November 19, 1848,

---

72. *Ibid.,* November 13, 1849, March 9, 1851.

Hughes wrote: "If there is a God, I trust in him, and feel that he dwells within my soul, and incites me to my destiny.—If there is not a God, my proud mind trusts to its own power here and hereafter." He often tried to reconcile these competing notions, attributing his faith in himself to a divine source. "There must be a God," he wrote in May, 1848, "else whence this holy confidence, this contempt of wealth, this consent to live?" Yet such evidence could neither allay his doubts nor permit him to envisage himself proceeding without faith. "Can I not receive a sign, a proof. . . . I must believe, or I will die. My faith is interwoven with my ambition. . . . I will be the greatest mortal man that ever was." Only a final, resolute affirmation, one that reappears throughout the diary, permitted Hughes to lay to rest, at least temporarily, his existential fears. "I am the darling of my heavenly Father. I still shall stand upon the pinnacle of Fame and look down on Washington & Napoleon. O God clasp me to Thy breast, press Thy lips to mine."[73]

As these passages make clear, Hughes's view of God was directly, even inexorably, bound to his vision of his earthly destiny. On several occasions he wrote: "This is my prayer: 'My Father in Heaven? let me be the greatest mortal man that can be.'"[74] Faith for Hughes meant faith in a God who would make him "the greatest mortal man that ever was." His use of sensual, even sexual, language to express his relation with God forcefully demonstrates that only by conceiving of that relationship as an intimate, unique, practically monogamous one could Hughes assure himself that he was set apart from all other human beings. His religion, in this sense, was excessively personal; he related to God as did no other. "My Father press to my lips, love me Thy Pet, Thy Darling." He used such language throughout the diary.[75] And even when he refrained from using lover-like language, he continued to see his relation with Him as *sui generis*. In the entry for March 9, 1851, in which he concludes by asserting, "Here commences the political life of Henry Hughes," both Hughes's doubts and his need to believe himself set apart remain pro-

---

73. *Ibid.,* November 19, May 21, 1848.

74. *Ibid.,* April 21, 1850. For other references to this prayer, see *ibid.,* January 7, 1849, and May 19, 1850.

75. *Ibid.,* July 2, 1848. For examples of Hughes's use of sensual language in his writings about God, see, in addition to those cited in notes 73 and 74, *ibid.,* July 2, 1848, October 7, 1849, July 28, September 29, 1850, December 21, 1851, March 14, July 4, 1852.

nounced. "Is God present. Is He ever by my side. Does He rule specially the affairs of men. Of All? Or yet of some? Of, One? and through him, the Chosen One, All mankind. Am I not he? Am I not his chosen One, his viceroy, his Pope. My Father, address me; Tell me how I may know."[76]

Hughes's messianic view of himself remained prominent throughout the diary. On January 25, 1852, he declared "Kossuth is my fore-runner. He is St. John: I am the——." On April 10, 1853, he conversely wondered whether he would be the Saint John to the second coming. "Who shall be Christ's forerunner? Lord is it I?" The final entry of the diary, on May 1, 1853, ominously asks, "Do we want a new-Jesus." Thus, even as he devoted himself to a more serious and mature study of social questions, his need to believe in a God who would bestow unparalleled power upon him persisted. Although in his post-diary writings Hughes invoked religious ideas and elements sparingly, if at all, the diary portrays him as someone who moved from intense religiosity to secular study and then back again. His struggle to reconcile his earthly desires with his faith was often painful, and it too remained unresolved. "Would I exchange my soul for the 'World?'" he pondered in November, 1848. "If I become a Christian, will I not have to abandon the earthly destiny which I have appointed myself?"[77] Hughes's solution to this dilemma, in the diary at least, was to remain convinced that his and God's will coincided, that both his efforts and God's would lead him to power. Although he could write in January, 1851, that "I am God's implement to reveal the philosophy of the Human Mind," he would not be a passive implement.[78] His turn to an "Active Career" in politics meant not a rejection of his divine destiny but rather a conscious decision to act in accordance with it. Hughes's political vision thus rested upon both his long-standing belief that he was chosen by God and the knowledge of the world he gained through his reading and political activity. Although the religious element

76. *Ibid.,* March 9, 1851.

77. *Ibid.,* January 25, 1852, April 10, May 1, 1853, November 5, 1848. Hughes had expressed similar doubts just months earlier. After once again questioning the existence of God, as well as a yearning "for omniscience & omnipotence" that would allow him "to be separated from my fellows," he prayed, "O God, let me be perfect. If thou art, I shall worship thee. Yet I feel that I would give my soul for the unprofitable World" (*ibid.,* August 27, 1848).

78. *Ibid.,* January 1, 1851.

would become nearly totally muted after 1853, the notion derived from his religious beliefs that Hughes had a historic role to play must have persisted. The intensity of his diary's dialogue with God, though certainly in part the result of youthful indulgence, was also, no doubt, the sincere expression of one who burned with an ambition that, in his mind at least, could only have come from God.

Yet while Hughes in the final two years of the diary continued to appeal to and affirm his faith in God, he focused more and more attention on politics. Just over a month after he announced the beginning of his "Active Career," he again expressed this new outlook: "Earnestly attracted towards the politics of the South." He followed with one of his few overt yet ambiguous references to slavery. "The relation of land-lord & tenant is as sinful as that [of] master & slave. Both relations shall be abolished; but not to the hurt of the South." We shall see in the next chapter that Hughes could believe that slavery was sinful but still defend unfree labor, social inequality, and hierarchy. This mention of the South, one of the earliest in the diary, was followed by others in the weeks and months ahead. In April, 1851, Hughes read some articles on "Southern manufactures." On June 22 he read "some Congressional Speeches on the Compromise [probably of 1850] Measures." On July 6, he discussed his membership in the "states-rights party in Claiborne County." Two weeks later he related that "political discussion is here [Claiborne] animated" and again mentioned his attachment to the states'-rights party. Less than a week later he attended a "political Barbecue" in Claiborne County and discussed with his brother-in-law William Thomas Magruder the possibility of giving a speech at a barbecue the following week. Hughes even began considering "the notion of procuring [a State convention candidate's] withdrawal from the present of candidacy, & my nomination." Politics was on Henry's mind in the spring and summer of 1851.[79]

Hughes never again wrote so regularly about party politics, but his interest continued throughout the final year and a half of the diary. Although he did not articulate a clear and well-defined political agenda, he revealed the increasing orientation of his thought toward social and political questions. The content of this thought in the diary remains oblique

79. *Ibid.*, April 13, 27, June 22, July 6, 20, 27, 1851.

and inconsistent. Hughes was not yet the ideologue he would become, and his passages on specific topics are far too brief to make any firm conclusions. But that he was heading toward a life centered around social and political issues is clear.

This turn toward social and political questions can be illustrated by examining some of his reading during the last six months of 1852. His reactions to that reading were only spottily recorded, but a pattern emerged from his choice of books.

As he had done throughout the years of the diary, Hughes continued to read broadly and to keep abreast of the latest publications. In addition to Fourier, whose *Passions of the Human Soul* was published in English in 1851, Hughes read contemporaries such as Thomas Macaulay (Essay on Bacon), Nathaniel Hawthorne (*Blithedale Romance*), Ralph Waldo Emerson (essays), Elizabeth Barrett Browning (poems), and Alfred Lord Tennyson (poems), whom he especially liked.[80] But what is most striking and significant is the high percentage of works that either directly or indirectly relate to social topics. In July and August, 1852, Hughes almost exclusively read materials concerning slavery and the sectional struggle. He began with John Fletcher's *Studies on Slavery,* published in 1852. He proceeded to John C. Calhoun's *Disquisition on Government,* "looked through" Harriet Beecher Stowe's *Uncle Tom's Cabin* (Hughes commented, "That book is womanish & I am afraid absurdly unprincipled; written by a woman clearly"), and then read Daniel Webster's reply to Robert Y. Hayne "on the South Carolina Tariff Matter." In September he examined Jeremy Bentham's work on legislation, after which he commented: "I wish I had all of Bentham's works." In yet another instance of Carlyle's influence, Hughes added, "Was he [Bentham] heroic?" In October Hughes "looked into" a southern reply to *Uncle Tom's Cabin* entitled *Aunt Phyllis' Cabin*. Finally, in November he read J. Thorton Randolph's "tale about slavery."[81] The precise effect of all these works

---

80. *Ibid.,* July 27, 1851.

81. For Macaulay see *ibid.,* June 27, 1852; for Hawthorne see November 21, 1852; for Emerson see November 28, 1852; for Browning see November 28, 1852; for Tennyson see July 25, 1852; for Fletcher see July 25, August 1, 8, 15, 1852; for Calhoun see August 15, 1852, in which Hughes labeled the *Disquisition on Government* an "able work"; for Stowe see August 15, 1852; for the Webster/Calhoun tariff matter see August 22, 1852. Although Hughes's entry states that he "Read Webster's Reply to Calhoun on the South

cannot be determined. But Hughes surely was interested in topics that in previous years he was not. The future sociologist was well into the making.

Hughes's personal, intellectual, and political development continued throughout the diary. His visions of world dominion, of heroic leadership, of being the chosen representative of God on earth, did not cease as Hughes turned some of his attention to political and social matters. Rather, Hughes tried to meld these diverse and often conflicting interests into a stable sense of self, one that satisfied his psychological need to believe himself set apart but at the same time based in the real world of antebellum America. The forging of this personality may never have been completed; Hughes might never have reconciled his humble accomplishments with his boundless dreams. The diary reveals, however, the clear direction this process took in the years before he assumed his position as a public defender of slavery. A different Hughes would emerge in the years that followed, but the difference would be accompanied by many of the personal and political characteristics that found expression, often unwittingly, in Henry Hughes's diary.

Carolina Tariff Matter," I have assumed that he meant Webster's reply to Hayne. Further revealing Carlyle's influence, he noted: "The heroic element is larger in Calhoun." For Bentham see September 12, 1852. Mary H. Eastman wrote *Aunt Phillis's Cabin; or, Southern Life As It Is* (1852; rpr. Upper Saddle River, N.J., 1968). For Hughes's reference to the novel, see October 10, 1852. J. Thorton Randolph was the pseudonym for Charles Jacobs Peterson. The "tale about slavery" was probably Peterson's *The Cabin and Parlor; or, Slaves and Masters*. See November 14, 1852.

3

THE *TREATISE ON SOCIOLOGY:*
SLAVERY, WARRANTEEISM, AND THE STATE

O n April 24, 1853, in his penultimate diary entry, Hughes noted casually: "I leave home in a few days to make the tour of Europe." Whether his decision was as sudden as the entry suggests remains unclear. Unhappy with his legal work and having just turned twenty-four one week earlier, Hughes may have been seeking a change that would benefit his ambitions. Indeed, later in the April 24 entry he stated, "This tour is to complete my education."[1] In a sense, the tour was the culmination of a period in Hughes's life, one marked by the introspection and self-doubt so clearly evidenced in his diary. Although these feelings most likely persisted until his death in 1862, we know little about his personal life or thoughts during his last eight years. Very few personal papers from this period have survived, and those that have provide few glimpses into Hughes's interior life. He became a public figure during this period—an author, speaker, and political activist. His writings and speeches from these years are some of the most interesting and intriguing contributions of proslavery thought to appear in the antebellum United States. In no other work are these contributions more apparent than in his first and most significant publication, *Treatise on Sociology,*

---

1. Hughes Diary, April 24, 1853. Years earlier, on August 20, 1848, Hughes wrote, "I entertain the idea of visiting Europe," but he never discussed the idea again until the April 24, 1853, entry.

Theoretical and Practical, published in 1854, when Hughes was twenty-five.

Any connection between Hughes's trip to Europe and the subsequent appearance of the *Treatise* remains open to speculation. Although his passport has survived, no letters or other correspondence shed light on his activities during his stay. The passport charts his journey from his arrival in Le Havre on June 30, 1853, through to August 6, 1853, when he received permission to travel in France, Belgium, and Prussia. After stopping in Marseilles on July 7, Hughes proceeded to Italy and arrived in Naples on July 16. He spent the rest of July making a quick tour of several major Italian cities, including Rome, Florence, and Genoa. But Hughes stayed in Italy only briefly and arrived in Geneva on August 3.[2] Although we know little of what he did in Italy or what impression it had on him, he did make reference to his time there in a newspaper article located in the scrapbook in which he kept articles by or about him. Titled "Barbee's Coquette" and signed "Hughes," the article reviews sculptor Randolph Barbee's statue *Coquette*. In it Hughes wrote: "You know that I have studied both sculpture and painting in the Louvre in Paris, the Pitti Palace at Florence, and the Vatican in Rome."[3] We do not know what he did in Paris, but his claim that he "studied both sculpture and painting" in Florence and Rome strains credulity because he spent less than one week in each city. Yet this passage, even with its hyperbole, suggests that Hughes conceived and perceived his trip as one of study, in the words of his diary, "to complete my education." However brief, the time he spent in Italy furthered his sense of himself as a broad-minded intellectual, qualified to comment on everything from art to politics.[4]

Whatever impression Italy may have made on Hughes, scholars have focused almost entirely on his time in France. Ironically, they have done so without one piece of hard evidence that places him there, except for his passport's recording of his stops in Le Havre and Marseilles. Although

2. Henry Hughes Passport, Folder 7, Box 11, Daniell IV Collection.

3. [Henry] Hughes, "Barbee's Coquette," clipping, Hughes Scrapbook, Hughes Papers.

4. For an interesting examination of other antebellum southern travelers' experiences in Europe, see O'Brien, "Italy and the Southern Romantics," in his *Rethinking the South,* 87–111.

he undoubtedly did spend time in France, the absence of evidence even about the places he visited makes any analysis of the effects of his visit problematic. We can accept his claim in "Barbee's Coquette" that he "studied" at the Louvre (taking account of what qualified as studied), but beyond that we can only speculate as to his activities in France and how they affected him.

Perhaps the most important—and difficult—question about Hughes's time in France concerns his reaction to its intellectual milieu. Those who have written about his trip have made some suggestions, but none have corroborated their claims with satisfying evidence. Reverend William D. Moore, Hughes's friend and eulogist, first placed him in Paris. In *The Life and Works of Col. Henry Hughes; A Funeral Sermon,* published in 1863, Moore claimed that while in Paris Hughes "became acquainted with the leading writers of his time, on social questions, made himself more familiar with the language and literature of France, [and] revised and completed" what Moore believed to be the *Treatise on Sociology.*[5] Moore probably based his comments on personal contact with Hughes, which strengthens their credibility, but their vagueness prevents us from fully grasping Hughes's thoughts of and actions in the Parisian intellectual environment.

In 1936, the sociologist L. L. Bernard argued that Hughes not only visited Paris but that there he "met the leading sociological thinkers of the time, including Comte."[6] Bernard, who helped resurrect Hughes as a subject of study, posited the link between him and Comte that later writers have accepted even in the absence of any documentation.[7] But whether Hughes actually met or knew or studied with Comte matters little. Hughes had read Comte before leaving Mississippi, although with-

5. Moore, *Life and Works of Col. Henry Hughes,* 13.

6. L. L. Bernard, "Henry Hughes, First American Sociologist," *Social Forces,* XV (December, 1936), 155.

7. See, for example, Joseph Dorfman, *The Economic Mind in American Civilization, 1606–1865* (5 vols.; New York, 1946–59), II, 936; Louis Hartz, *The Liberal Tradition in America: An Interpretation of American Political Thought Since the Revolution* (New York, 1955), 180; Wyatt-Brown, "Modernizing Southern Slavery," 36; Drew Gilpin Faust, ed., *The Ideology of Slavery: Proslavery Thought in the Antebellum South, 1830–1860* (Baton Rouge, 1981), 239; John Shelton Reed, *One South: An Ethnic Approach to a Regional Culture* (Baton Rouge, 1982), 46; and Takaki, *Pro-Slavery Crusade,* 86–102.

out any apparent excitement or intense interest.[8] And as the modern sociologist Stanford Lyman has convincingly pointed out, he surely had absorbed more knowledge about Comte and his ideas from other works he read, including John Stuart Mill's *System of Logic* and Victor Cousin's *Course of the History of Modern Philosophy*.[9] Finally, given Hughes's predisposition to "study" and "complete [his] education," he most likely encountered and pondered Comte's ideas while in Paris.

It is, nonetheless, a bit misleading to focus exclusively on Hughes's exposure to Comte, for Paris in 1853 offered far more to the eager intellectual than Comtean positivism. Although we cannot identify specific ideas that he acquired while in Paris, we can safely conclude on the basis of the scope of interests recorded in his diary and his boasts in "Barbee's Coquette" that he availed himself of whatever knowledge he could locate. His visits to the Louvre constituted but one of what must have been a series of edifying endeavors. Gustave Flaubert's *Sentimental Education* richly evokes the artistic, political, and intellectual excitement that nineteenth-century Paris generated in the mind of a young, eager provincial like Hughes. Indeed, it is not difficult to envision him, in Flaubert's words, "savoring that delicious Paris air, which seems fraught with the redolence of love and the exhalations of the intellect."[10]

That Hughes initiated his tour of the Continent suggests that he had developed a need to break out of the confines of a small-town legal practice in which he had been suffering. And the tour itself may well have strengthened his desire not to return to the unsatisfying routine he complained of so bitterly in the diary. Perhaps Paris and Europe generally did expose him to ideas on social organization that provided him with a framework or an intellectual perspective from which he could "solve the social problem" and begin to realize his dream of a "Universal Repub-

8. See Hughes Diary, July 13, August 17, 1851.

9. John Stuart Mill, *A System of Logic* . . . (London, 1941); Victor Cousin, *Course of the History of Modern Philosophy* (New York, 1852). For references to Mill's *Logic,* see Hughes Diary, June 6, 22, 1851. For those to Cousin's *Course,* which Hughes's elder sister Mary Ann gave to him, see *ibid.,* April 18, May 30, July 18, October 31, November 7, 14, 28, December 12, 1852. See also Stanford Lyman's interesting discussion in his "Henry Hughes and American Sociology," in Lyman, ed., *Selected Writings of Henry Hughes,* 14–17.

10. Gustave Flaubert, *Sentimental Education* (London, 1966), 99.

lic."[11] Whatever he did or learned in Paris, his trip, above all else, helped to focus his hitherto wandering ambition. In 1854, just months after his return, Lippincott, Grambo & Co. published his *Treatise on Sociology: Theoretical and Practical*.[12]

The appearance of the *Treatise* so quickly after Hughes's return from Europe suggests that he had composed it before the trip. Hughes's first biographer, the Reverend Moore, asserted, "Before leaving College [Hughes] had methodized his thoughts and in some measure prepared himself for their public vindication in a treatise entitled 'Sociology.' Its publication was postponed until after his visit to Paris." Once again, Moore's close relationship with Hughes gives his account much weight, but that Hughes never explicitly mentioned this work in all the years of his diary makes one question Moore's accuracy. In October, 1850, Hughes stated, "I commenced on the 19th of October 1850 ... the Ultimum Organum," and though he afterward occasionally referred to the "Ultimum Organum," one does not get the sense that it was either a revision of a college-era work or a systematic treatise on social organization and politics. Whatever its origins, the *Treatise* initiated Hughes's public attempt to articulate and promote his vision of a unique social order that, although emerging out of southern slavery, would represent that to which all societies would and must "progress." The *Treatise* is, as the Reverend Moore pointed out, "the key to [Hughes's] life."[13]

Superficially, the *Treatise* testifies to the various influences on Hughes's intellectual development. Organizationally, it resembles antebellum moral philosophy texts, following the same division between a short opening "Theoretical" section and a longer "Practical" section as Francis Wayland's *Elements of Moral Science,* which Hughes studied

---

11. The reference to the "social problem" is from Hughes's Diary, March 14, 1852, and the reference to the "Universal Republic" is from the entry of October 17, 1852.

12. Lippincott, Grambo & Co. published many proslavery tracts. Located in Philadelphia, they published, among other works, Josiah C. Nott and George Gliddon's *Types of Mankind; or, Ethnological Researches* ... (1854), Nott and Gliddon's *Indigenous Races of the Earth; or, New Chapters of Ethnological Inquiry* (1857), and George S. Sawyer's *Southern Institutes; or, An Inquiry into the Origin and Early Prevalence of Slavery and the Slave Trade* ... (1859).

13. Moore, *Life and Works of Col. Henry Hughes,* 13; Hughes Diary, October 20, 1850, October 10, 24, 1852.

while at Oakland College.[14] Other aspects of its organization suggest
Comte's influence, especially the division of society into seven "systems"
and the use of jargon, which makes Hughes almost as difficult to read
as Comte.[15] Finally, the *Treatise* displays Hughes's legal training throughout, most prominently in Book V, "Law of Warranteeism." Of interest
as well is the unmistakably secular tone and message of the *Treatise,*
which contrasts sharply with the religiosity of Hughes's diary. Although
the *Treatise* occasionally refers to God, these references are mere gloss;
Hughes presents his arguments in the secular language of science and
reason. Although Hughes may have continued to grapple with his complex relation with God, his writings after the diary, beginning with the
Treatise, display little if any concern with religion. Yet these formal features of the *Treatise* tell us little about its content and purpose. We must
turn to the text and the arguments contained within it to understand
how the *Treatise* constituted an original contribution to southern proslavery thought.

Hughes began the *Treatise* with a short definition of sociology: "Sociology is the science of societary organization. It is, 1, Theoretical, and
2, Practical." The ensuing twenty-eight-page section titled "Theoretical
Sociology" lays out what he considered some of the essential tenets of
social organization. Paramount among these was order. "The essence of
power is orderliness." Without order, society could not function: "Anarchy is impotence. Men, therefore, must be orderly; the whole power of
society, must be orderly."[16] Order, as Hughes conceived it, resulted from
the application of "societary wisdom" to "societary power" to ensure the
proper "association, adaptation, and regulation" of society's members.
Only through the application of these three constituent elements of order
could society fulfill its primary task, the "existence of all," and its secondary task, the "progress of all." Hughes left no doubt as to the correct
ranking of these two goals; progress was desirable and necessary, but it

14. Francis Wayland, *The Elements of Moral Science,* ed. Joseph L. Blau (Cambridge,
1963). The *Oakland College Catalog and Commencement Proceedings for 1845* mentions
Wayland's book as the standard text for the senior year class in moral philosophy. See
the catalog in Box 4, Oakland College Papers.

15. For a discussion of the structure of the *Treatise* and its Comtean flavor, see Bernard, "Henry Hughes," 156–57.

16. Hughes, *Treatise,* 47, 51.

could only follow subsistence, which could never be neglected or qualified.

From his emphasis on order Hughes moved quickly to the necessity of duty. "Duty," he wrote, "is its [order's] essence and modulus." His concern with duty led directly to his critique of freedom and individual will. The essence of order was duty, but "the essence of freedom is not duty; it is choice.... Conscience is the faculty of duty; will, of choice." Hughes argued that order forbade free choice; one had to do what duty demanded. This point proves fundamental to an understanding of the *Treatise*'s central contention regarding the social roles of individuals and the corresponding limits to personal freedom. Social order regulated, indeed dictated, the actions of society's members; conscience, understood as recognizing and fulfilling one's social obligations, subordinated will. As he reiterated much later in the *Treatise,* the duty of contributing to "the subsistence and progress of all" imposed "an obligation to which consent issues not from the will, but from the conscience, and the general reason. It is an obligation coupled to the reciprocal duties of man and society." [17]

The subordination of individual freedom to social duty formed just one of the pillars upon which Hughes constructed his theoretical edifice. Equally important was his emphatic endorsement of inequality and hierarchy as central features of proper social organization. He posited that order required the inequality of social relations: "In every society there must ... be both orderers and orderees. Some must order; some, be ordered. These are subordinates; those, superordinates." This inequality flowed from what Hughes termed the "sovereign power," the "supreme orderer of the society." [18] The need for a "supreme orderer" grew out of the need for order, which he argued could be assured only through the exercise of a public, or sovereign, power. Thus only that order which the sovereign power realized was itself sovereign; order that resulted from nonsovereign, or private, means he termed "free order."

The distinction between these two forms of order provided the basis for one of Hughes's most important points: the nature and the necessary exercise of legitimate state power. Only sovereign order, that which the sovereign exercised, was "warranted." For Hughes, "warranted" meant

17. *Ibid.,* 52, 209.
18. *Ibid.,* 53.

more than guaranteed. Central to his conception of "warranted order" was the role of the state in creating and enforcing it. He rejected totally the increasingly popular idea, drawn from bourgeois political economy, that order resulted naturally from the operation of free market forces. For Hughes, not freedom but state control and guidance assured order. "Sovereign order is therefore warranted. It is not natural or accidental; it is necessary or certain. It is not from choice, but from duty. It is ordained and established. It is authoritative. It is magisterial. It is not private; it is publicly organized; it is municipal."[19]

Hughes praised warranted order over free order, and by so doing he embraced state-exercised power, in large part because he believed that freedom could not guarantee the order necessary for proper social maintenance and development. People, members of society, had to be associated, adapted, and regulated for society to meet its principal goals of universal subsistence and progress. Freedom, he argued, made association, adaptation, and regulation, and thus subsistence and progress, uncertain by permitting choice rather than ensuring duty. But how could society guarantee that its members did their duty? Hughes's answer to this question, like his rejection of order through freedom, revealed the vast differences between his views and those of contemporary bourgeois political economists.

Hughes, following Bentham, whom he had read in 1852, maintained that there existed two basic and related human motivations: desire and fear. Although related, desire and fear were not equal motives of action. "Some desires and fears are certain springs of action. They warrant action. Some do not." Among the desires that did not warrant action was the "desire of a better condition." Individual preference, or choice, resulted in some people acting to better themselves and others remaining content with certain living standards. Hughes clearly did not share the increasingly popular view of many contemporary political economists that individual desire for increased pleasure would improve the economic and social well-being of society. He argued instead that fear, especially "fear of adequate punishment," guaranteed action. "Desire of a better condition" varied and thus "is neither universal, apt, or regular." "Fear of adequate punishment," by contrast, "is a certain spring. . . . It is universal,

19. *Ibid.,* 54.

adaptable, and regular."[20] Only fear could ensure consistent action and order. Fear of punishment therefore provided the basis of social organization—the means by which society could order its members.

For Hughes, the exercise of the "sovereign will," particularly its ability to use punitive means, constituted the most efficient and reliable way of ensuring universal subsistence and progress.[21] The use of state power to fulfill the fundamental goals of any social organization was more than practical; it was moral as well. What Hughes established in the "theoretical" section of the *Treatise* was no less than the logical and thus moral basis of state intervention and control of social relations. Only an authority that could punish any and all of society's members, that could elicit fear from all of them, could "warrant action." Hughes's authoritarianism thus grew directly out of his understanding of human motivation and his belief that the state must both act in accordance with that theory of human motivation and possess the power to act, if necessary, upon all of society. As he pointed out when speaking of sovereign order, "It is realized. The supreme power in the state legislates and executes it. The degree of its realization is the degree of its sovereignty." Only a state that "executes" and "realizes" order was sovereign. And only a state that employed fear of punishment could provide order. A state that did not intervene to provide order would be neither sovereign nor moral. Hughes insisted that just as duty bound the individual, so it bound the state. And ultimately, he argued, it was the duty of the state to "enforce" the duties of the individual. Although he had stated that "conscience" as the "faculty of duty" would make one do his or her duty, he ultimately did not trust individual conscience to ensure the fulfillment of duty. The state had to "warrant" the fulfillment of individual duty to fulfill its own duty to provide for the "existence and progress of all." The sovereign will, Hughes stated, "has the power of gratification and privation. If that fails, this follows. It compels. It civilly enforces the civil obligations of all. . . . It realizes by all necessary means, its order. This is its power and its duty. For in a society, such warranted association, adaptation, and regulation,

---

20. *Ibid.,* 55.

21. In "Theoretical Sociology" Hughes uses "sovereign will," "sovereign power," and "supreme orderer" when referring to the exercise of public authority. In "Practical Sociology" he simply uses the term *State*.

as are sufficient to realize the existence and progress of all, are morally necessary."[22]

By employing the words "all necessary means" and "sufficient" Hughes well knew that he was extending the potential power of his "theoretical" state far beyond what most Americans would have considered appropriate. His vision of the state in "Theoretical Sociology" demonstrates the ways in which he borrowed from American political discourse only to construct a state that represented a radical departure from the American model.

"Theoretical Sociology" contains Hughes's discussion of the seven "systems"—the economic, political, hygienic, philosophic (educational), aesthetic, ethical, and religious—that constitute a "heptarchy," or society. Every society must decide how best to divide power among these systems, although Hughes believed that at least five of them, the economic, political, hygienic, philosophic, and aesthetic, "ought to be warranted. They ought to be municipalities or public bodies." To permit these systems to be "free" or "private," he argued, would jeopardize society's ability "to actualize the existence and progress of all." Each of these public "municipalities" could have its own legislature, or "there may be for all the systems, one common legislature, one common executive, and one common judiciary," or, he continued, there could be fewer than five but more than one. The intricate complexity of this scheme is less significant than the ways in which it highlights Hughes's notion of what constituted the legitimate scope of state activity. The "body economic," for instance, would have power to "order or regulate commerce, agriculture, and manufactures," "to adjudicate wages, interest, rent, prices, and other parts of economic distribution," and "to order migration," while the "body hygienic" would be able to "regulate the structure of all habitations and houses; of all tenements" and "provide for the inspection, and prohibit the adulteration, of food, and of drugs and medicines."[23] This state's

22. *Ibid.,* 54, 56.

23. *Ibid.,* 62, 60, 65, 66. The "body philosophic" would have power to "order public schools," "regulate the powers, rights, duties, responsibilities, and qualifications of scholars, teachers, and other philosophic orderers," and "have jurisdiction of institutions for the increase, or diffusion, of knowledge." See *ibid.,* 67. The "body esthetic" would have power to "regulate common entertainments: as theatres, operas, concerts, circuses, fireworks, and other exhibitions," "to order public museums and galleries," "to order

theoretical authority far exceeded that of any state or the federal government, yet Hughes delineated the powers it and its constituent "municipalities" would have in language and forms taken directly from Article
I, Section 8, of the United States Constitution. Rather than "The Congress
shall have power," Hughes simply wrote, "It [the body economic, hygienic, philosophic, aesthetic, or politic] shall have power." Just as Article
I, Section 8, lists the enumerated powers of the Congress in the infinitive
form, so too did Hughes list the powers of his "municipalities." Most
revealingly, however, Hughes made sure to give an elastic clause to each
of his "municipalities," to provide far more "implied power" than the
elastic clause of the Constitution. Hughes used the words *necessary and
proper* only in his discussion of the body economic; he claimed that the
others would "have all powers incidental to the foregoing." "Among
incidental powers," he continued, "that of taxation is eminent and essential." Each municipality "may have the power of limited or unlimited
taxation." Hughes's interest in taxation and its relation to social and political questions was apparent in his diary.[24] And we shall see in subsequent chapters that as Hughes moved from "Theoretical Sociology" to
practical politics, the state's ability to tax continued to intrigue him as he
sought to expand the state's role in social and economic life.

Hughes's use of the language of the Constitution to further statist
ends reveals both his grounding in American political and legal traditions
and his desire to go far beyond them. His "Theoretical Sociology," like
the *Treatise* as a whole, thus appears both familiar and foreign. But the
familiar forms only thinly veil the radically different substance within
them. Hughes recognized that enumerating powers did not necessarily
limit a state's authority, especially if that state possessed "all powers incidental to the foregoing." Antebellum southerners had long been known
as strict constitutionalists, suspicious of state authority. But Hughes was

---

pageants, public honors, public feasts, and games and sports," and "to order public parks,
gardens, and squares; public arbors, seats, recesses, groves, grounds, and promenades;
public fountains, statues, columns, monuments, and decorations" (*ibid.,* 68). In his discussion of these systems, Hughes somewhat resembles John Quincy Adams, who, as
president, urged a vast expansion of government-supported art and educational projects.
Hughes mentioned Adams, positively, in his diary, April 30, 1848.

24. Hughes, *Treatise,* 65, 66, 67, 68, 69; see, for instance, Hughes Diary, December
15, 1850, May 25, 1851, and October 10, 1852.

contemplating something other than antebellum politics in the *Treatise*. What if southerners, free from northern domination, controlled the state? What if an expanding, activist state represented not the encroachment of hostile northern power but the expression of the South's "collective wisdom and goodness"?[25] In "Theoretical Sociology" Hughes raised the possibility that although southerners had been forced by practical political necessity to resist state power generally and centralized state power in particular, statism *per se* might yet be of value, might yet, in fact, be the best means for the South's future development. He elaborated upon this possibility more fully in the section titled "Practical Sociology," which makes up the bulk of the *Treatise*.

"Practical Sociology" includes more of Hughes's views of the nature of and hopes for antebellum southern society than "Theoretical Sociology." But he did not dispense entirely with abstract meditations on the nature of humanity, society, and the state. Indeed, Hughes's tendency to move from abstract, theoretical discussions to concrete, material ones and then back again constitutes one of the most perplexing aspects of the *Treatise*. At times the *Treatise* seems to describe an artificial model of a proposed society; other times it appears to describe the contemporary South. This tendency reveals Hughes's dual purpose: to defend the basic principles of the southern social order while simultaneously advocating major reforms that would place it on a firmer, more theoretically sound foundation. Hughes sought to elaborate a defense of slavery that not only would have silenced critics from without but also would have stimulated reformers from within. Yet in urging substantial changes in southern society, Hughes moved well beyond most of his fellow defenders of slavery and articulated a vision of social order that in many ways differed significantly from slavery as southerners knew it.

The *Treatise* does not follow a single organizational pattern. It moves from topic to topic without an explicit unifying argument, more like a series of essays, some of which overlap and repeat one another, than a coherent statement. Yet taken together, Hughes's ideas in the *Treatise* do form a body of thought, which, although never entirely free of contradiction and faulty logic, offers a strong, clear vision of a proper social order.

25. Hughes, *Treatise,* 209.

The core of this vision lies in Hughes's ideas about the nature of humanity and society, which rest on two *a priori* suppositions: "Man is gregarious" and "Of society, the substance is order." But although nature demanded that humans live together in an orderly manner, humans had to determine the way they lived. "The substance of society is by nature; the form, by art. . . . The substance of society is immutable and ingressive; the form, mutable and progressive." Thus nature brought humans together, but they had to devise the practical means of realizing social order. In this sense, nature limited humans' ability to act, even as it required them to do so. Sounding very much like a positivist, Hughes argued that once humanity discovered a natural law, humans had to live by it. Human gregariousness and the overriding need for order not only had to be accepted but had to form the basis of all future human action. Since "man is rational" as well as gregarious, "rational gregation" as opposed to "instinctive" "subhuman gregation" "is the means of existence; reason discovers and realizes it; and reason prescribes or promulgates the law of Nature." Humans, through their use of reason, uncovered the laws by which they had to structure their lives.[26]

Hughes's use of the "law of Nature" underscored one of the main points he had put forth in "Theoretical Sociology": the subordination of choice to duty. Gregation and order were "laws," and individuals could not avoid either. To have done so would have been not only inexpedient but contrary to nature and thus immoral. Hughes employed this reasoning to subvert the compact theory of social organization. "Of a compact or agreement," he wrote, "the essence is free will, or choice." But society was not and could not be based on choice. "The origin of rational association is morally, not in a compact or agreement of the associates. Because the association is not free but commanded." Duty to natural law, not free will, formed the basis of human association and morality. "It [association] is a duty or law of God. And the will is not free to do or not to do, a duty. There is no choice. Duty is without alternative." Since "every individual is under an obligation to associate, for the existence and progress of himself and others," to violate such an obligation would have placed one outside the natural order. "Disassociation is immoral and unnatural."[27]

26. *Ibid.*, 175, 176.
27. *Ibid.*, 176.

Society arose naturally according to laws that demanded human obedience. But once society was formed as a result of these laws, what dictated its function? Hughes, as we have seen, placed central emphasis on subsistence as any society's first priority. Although he did not locate this fundamental duty of society in natural law, he assumed throughout the *Treatise* that societal performance could be evaluated only according to how well each society met "its first object; and the chief reason for its formation." A society's obligation to assure subsistence to all "is primary, capital, necessary, overriding and supreme. All other ends are secondary, subordinate, and collateral. Subsistence ought to be warranted to all. Everything ought to be stopped, till that is done." [28] Humans had to associate, Hughes argued, and once associated they had to do everything necessary to guarantee the subsistence of everyone in that society. Neither individual nor social actions could rightfully exceed or neglect these parameters.

By establishing the priority of subsistence and hence the economic system, Hughes posited that freedom had to be limited to that which did not impede or interfere with the economy's ability to guarantee subsistence. It is hardly surprising, then, that his insistence on the restricted freedom of individuals attained its purest expression in his discussion of their economic responsibilities. In these passages he exhibited the degree to which he had rejected the premises of individualism that even as he wrote were becoming firmly established as the basis of bourgeois society.

"Man is by nature related to society," Hughes wrote, and that relation qualified his personal liberties. Hughes did not deny that individuals had rights, but he consistently maintained that those rights followed from and were subordinate to the rights of society. He thus rejected "natural rights," as did many other proslavery theorists. The absolute right of all to subsistence superseded all individual rights. "Existence and Progress," he asserted, "are ultimate rights. They are the final and supreme objects of social organization. They are its end and aim. All other rights are incidental. They are means." These other "rights" were thus "actualized" or not depending on their relation to the "ultimate rights" of existence and progress. Rights, in Hughes's view, did not reside within individuals but were social creations, which society could, accordingly, qualify; if they

28. *Ibid.,* 81.

furthered existence and progress, they could be exercised; if they hampered or interfered, they could be restricted or prohibited. Until society's paramount obligation had been fulfilled, individual freedom must be controlled. All individuals had to contribute to the realization of universal subsistence and could exercise their freedom only within the order needed to realize this goal. Hughes never permitted doubt about the respective rights of society and the individual: "They [humans] are born free and equal. But this is freedom to do not what they would, but what they ought; and equality not of power but of justice."[29] Justice consisted of receiving from society the subsistence that everyone deserved and to which everyone had to contribute.

Hughes conceived of individuals as mere components of society, bound by and subject to its needs. No aspect of an individual's personal freedom could be permitted to compromise society's goals. "A man has not a right to use his mind and body as he will. . . . Man must do what he ought." Focusing on the fundamentally economic character of the individual's and society's actions, Hughes continued: "He cannot as he wills, work or be idle; pursue, one, another, or no, calling; be dissociate, unadapted or irregular." He then expanded the discussion to include political freedoms and maintained the essential primacy of duty over choice: "In economics as in politics; he must adjust his economic pleasure to his economic duty. The freeborn power of every man over his labor, is morally qualified." Hughes concluded this important passage with a cogent summary of his ideas of the nature, rights, and duties of both man and society: "Man is a social being; order is Heaven's first law. None have the right of the selfish; they have the right of the social use only, of their bodily and mental powers. . . . The freedom of every man is therefore, qualified by a duty. That duty is to use it, as a social being ought. But a social being ought to use his labor socially, or for the existence and progress of all."[30]

Hughes's thoughts in these passages echo those found in "Theoretical Sociology." And as in that section, the emphasis on duty and the subordination of individual freedom to societal needs led him to embrace inequality and hierarchy as unavoidable and proper aspects of social organization. He reiterated the point made in "Theoretical Sociology" that

29. *Ibid.*, 182, 232, 186.
30. *Ibid.*, 186.

universal subsistence could be assured only through order, which required "orderers and orderees, or inequality." He then concluded, "Inequality is therefore, natural and necessary. For the substance of society, is order."[31] Inequality of power did not, however, mean inequality of justice. For society could provide equality of justice by providing universal subsistence, which could be assured only by social inequality. Some had to order, others had to be ordered, so that all could eat.

The defense of southern society, which constituted Hughes's primary objective in the *Treatise,* logically followed from his discussion of subsistence, order, and inequality. He considered these principles objective, indisputable laws of social organization, and he based his analyses of contemporary societies on them and the larger "sociology" that he constructed around them. Only by appreciating the centrality of these principles to Hughes's social thought can one understand his unique defense of and proposals for southern society.

Hughes devoted much of "Practical Sociology" to an elaboration of his conception of southern society and his original vision of the course of southern social development. His discussion is important not for its accurate dissection of actual conditions in the South, but for his interpretation of how southern slavery should best evolve. In this sense Hughes meant the *Treatise* to be both descriptive and prescriptive. His prescriptive interpretation challenged many of the contemporary and historical views of what constituted the essential character of antebellum southern society and thought.

Hughes argued early on in "Practical Sociology," and maintained throughout the rest of the text, that the social organization of the South was not slavery but what he termed "warranteeism." For him it was a set of social and economic relations and, by extension, the governing principle of political relations. "Warranteeism is a fundamental obligation enforced from a fundamental duty. That is the duty of the subsistence and progress of all. It is an obligation to which consent issues not from the will, but from the conscience, and the general reason. It is an obligation coupled to the reciprocal duties of man and society."[32] Often dismissed by historians as euphemistic, Hughes's distinction between slavery and warranteeism actually represented an attempt to highlight and ex-

31. *Ibid.,* 174.
32. *Ibid.,* 209.

tend the major developments of the evolution of southern society from colonial times into the future.[33] Employing the term *warranteeism* to describe both the current and future South allowed him to avoid becoming entangled in citing and commenting on examples of specific conditions. His writing remained abstract, detached, even though he clearly described and defended much of existing southern society. Warranteeism acted as Hughes's idealized society, but its numerous and substantial links with the actual antebellum South prevented it from being purely utopian. Thus his seemingly abstract discussions of warranteeism can more properly be understood as prospects and proposals for the future development of southern slave society.

If warranteeism was not slavery, how did the two differ? Hughes defined slavery in a way similar to Locke and Montesquieu as a total institution in which the slave has no rights and the master has nearly complete control over the slave. Most southern defenders of slavery, particularly ministers, denied that their system of slavery resembled this model.[34] But Hughes went to great lengths to repudiate the notion that warranteeism contained even semblances of slavery. "What is slavery?" Hughes asked. "It is want, oppression, hatred, outrage, cruelty, and injustice. . . . It is a moral evil. It is abhorred by God and man." In contrast, he asserted, "The warranted economic system of the United States South, is not slavery. Its placard errs. The simple-laborer in that system is not a slave; he is a warrantee. He has essentially all his rights. There are no slaves in the United States South."[35] Hughes continually reiterated his claim that "warrantees," unlike slaves, had "all their rights." Those "rights" and their qualified character will be discussed below. For our purposes here, Hughes's insistence on warrantees' "rights" was one way he attempted to distinguish warranteeism from slavery.

33. Studies that minimize the differences between Hughes's warranteeism and southern slavery include Hartz, *Liberal Tradition*, 149, and Eric L. McKitrick, ed., *Slavery Defended: The Views of the Old South* (Englewood Cliffs, N.J., 1963), 51.

34. For one minister's rejection of the notion that southern slavery deprived slaves of all their rights, see James Henley Thornwell, *The Rights and Duties of Masters* (Charleston, 1850). Also see Bertram Wyatt-Brown, *Yankee Saints and Southern Sinners* (Baton Rouge, 1985), 155–82; Willie Lee Rose, "The Domestication of Domestic Slavery," in her *Slavery and Freedom*, ed. William W. Freehling (New York, 1982), 18–36.

35. Hughes, *Treatise*, 82–83. For other examples of Hughes's claim that warrantees had "all their rights," see *ibid.*, 209, 227, and 243.

Much of this effort to demonstrate the differences between slavery and warranteeism revolved around and was based on Hughes's notion of the "State" and its role in warranteeism. In "Theoretical Sociology" Hughes argued that only "sovereign power" could ensure the order required for universal subsistence, and therefore its exercise was not only legitimate but morally necessary. In "Practical Sociology" he reaffirmed these positions and broadened his discussions of both the scope of state action and its relation to "warrantors," or masters, and "warrantees," or slaves.[36]

The most fundamental difference between slavery and warranteeism was that slavery was a private relation between a master who owned a slave, whereas warranteeism constituted a system in which the state sanctioned and regulated the public relation between a warrantor and a warrantee. Warranteeism therefore lacked one of the essential characteristics of slavery: property in human beings. Hughes emphatically and repeatedly rejected the concept that one person could own another. Warranteeism, in direct contrast, consisted of "parties" to an "obligation," each of whom derived benefits from the obligation. "The parties to the warrantee-obligation, have no property in each other. Property in man is absurd. Men cannot be owned."[37] Instead of owning the person, the warrantor owned the person's "labor-obligation."

Concerned with the duties each individual owed society and society owed its members, Hughes used the term *obligation* throughout the *Treatise*. All people were obligated to labor for the subsistence and progress of all; labor was the primary social obligation of each individual. "Everybody," he wrote, "ought to work. Labor whether of mind or body is a duty." Since "we are morally obliged to contribute to the subsistence and progress of society," this labor obligation was not private, but public, owed to society, not another person.[38] No one's labor could be devoted solely

36. Since Hughes argued that warrantees were not slaves, my equating them in this sentence is merely for identification purposes. I will use the term *warrantee* throughout this book in the same way that Hughes employed it.

37. *Ibid.*, 167. Thornwell also repudiated the notion that humans could own one another or that persons could be reduced to chattel. Like Hughes, Thornwell insisted that southern slavery was "a relation of man to man—a form of civil society, of which persons are the only elements, and not a relation of man to things" (*Rights and Duties of Masters*, 19).

38. Hughes, *Treatise*, 95.

to the benefit of an individual but had to redound to society's benefit by helping society meet its primary obligations.

Because the state existed to ensure the subsistence of all, it had to guarantee that each individual's labor contributed to that all-important social goal. With labor, as with all other social duties, the state could require all members of society to perform their economic duty. "Production is a societary obligation," hence the "obligation of every consumer to produce, may, as any other moral obligation, be if necessary, civilly enforced." In the case of southern warranteeism, Hughes asserted, the state "civilly enforces" the labor obligation of the "simple-laborer" class by "warranting" each "simple-laborer" to a "capitalist," who then became, respectively, a warrantee and a warrantor. Hughes claimed that this uniting or "association" of capital and labor was "a right of society; and its perfection, a duty."[39] Society's ultimate right of universal subsistence permitted, indeed required, it to "perfect production," which, in turn, gave it the "right" to "warrant" laborers to capitalists.

The process of "warranting" "simple-laborers" to "capitalists," thereby transforming them into "warrantees" and "warrantors" respectively, reveals Hughes's rather simple and uncritical division of society into three classes. "The three economic classes," he noted, "are simple-laborers, skilled-laborers, and capitalists." Hughes asserted that all societies contain these three "economic classes," but one society was differentiated from another by the ways these economic classes related to one another socially and politically. Thus the "civil enforcement" of the simple laborer class's labor obligation produced the classes of warrantees and warrantors. I will examine the social and political character of the class of "skilled-laborers," who were neither warrantees nor warrantors, below. Yet the question of why only the simple laborer's labor obligation required civil enforcement remains. Although Hughes claimed that all classes were "obliged" to work, he maintained that "while all [classes] are morally; all are not civilly, obliged to labor." He firmly and repeatedly emphasized, however, the state's absolute right to enforce civilly the labor obligations of all classes. "These three classes may, in a system, be civilly enforced to work, or do their economic duty." Such enforcement depended upon social needs: "The need qualifies the enforcement. What

39. *Ibid.*

classes, how many, shall be civilly enforced, what and how many, morally, only; this is a matter of mere expediency."[40] What mattered to Hughes was not whether one, two, or all three classes were so enforced but that the state retained the right to exercise such power. Whatever the state deemed "expedient," classes and individuals had to accept.

Although Hughes posited the abstract right of the state to enforce everyone's labor obligation, he argued that in the South the civil enforcement of simple laborers' obligation assured the other classes' obligations, thereby making civil enforcement of them unnecessary, at least for now. He based his reasoning on a rather vague and unsophisticated theory of value that highlights a tension in his work between state direction of economic and social activity and individual fulfillment of social duty through self-interest. Each class, he suggested, added to the value of a product through its different form of labor. In the productive process each class depended on the others to perform their labor adequately so as to realize the goal of a "perfect product," one that each class developed and refined. Since simple labor began this process, its labor had to be guaranteed so that the other classes could then contribute their labor. But whereas civil enforcement compelled the simple laborers to work, a combination of moral obligation and pecuniary interest motivated skilled laborers and capitalists to continue the process. If skilled laborers and capitalists did not perform their labor satisfactorily, not only would society fail to achieve subsistence, but also these classes stood to lose financially because their livelihoods depended on "perfecting" the products produced by simple laborers. According to Hughes, economic and moral motivation among skilled laborers and capitalists sufficiently ensured their labor, thereby permitting them to remain free of civil enforcement as long as these other motives proved expedient. Simple laborers, however, lacked such motivation and thus civil enforcement was required so they carried out their obligation to labor.[41] Hughes implicitly recognized the need to ensure that the least attractive, most offensive tasks be executed regularly. Only compulsion, he asserted, could guarantee such execution.

40. *Ibid.,* 95–96. Hughes reiterates this point throughout the *Treatise.* For examples see *ibid.,* 112, 165, and 194–95.

41. For more on Hughes's ideas about production, "perfect products," and the economic motivation of capitalists, see *ibid.,* 96–97, 105, 165, 224, 271–74, and 281–82.

Hughes's reasoning as to why only the simple laborer class's labor obligation needed to be civilly enforced should not prevent us from recognizing the importance of his basic point: state creation and regulation of warrantee-warrantor relations and of all aspects of economic life. Although Hughes did not discuss the historical development of warranteeism, he did maintain that the state exercised its role at the very origin of the warrantee-warrantor relation. A simple laborer became warranted to a capitalist by the latter's purchase of the former's labor obligation. To make this possible, Hughes wrote, "Their [simple laborers'] labor obligation is capitalized." This labor obligation as an item to be purchased represented a public creation; the state permitted the natural duty of an individual to labor for society to become "capital." It could extend this permission, revoke it, or do whatever else it considered necessary to provide subsistence to all because the obligation itself always remained due to society, which could not alienate it, only entrust it to warrantors. For the state, Hughes pointed out, "specially retains, and publicly substantiates, the labor-obligations of the class of simple-laborers. It makes them civil obligations." Thus, even after the obligation was purchased, the state "retained" it and thereby continued its supervising interest in the relation between the purchasing warrantor and the warrantee whose labor obligation that warrantor now held.[42]

By making the labor obligation of a simple laborer capital, the state in warranteeism made possible the social classes of warrantor and warrantee. Whatever authority an individual warrantor held over a warrantee derived from the state, which created and continued to sanction the relation. Thus a labor obligation, even when capitalized, did not become private property in the sense of a slave. Nor did the capitalized labor obligation constitute the same thing as the labor power of an individual in a free labor market. Labor power is the property of an individual that that individual exchanges in the market for a wage. As Karl Marx pointed out, each person "must constantly look upon his labor-power as his own property, his own commodity" of which he is the "untrammeled owner." To maintain one's ownership of his labor power, Marx continued, he can only place "it at the disposal of the buyer temporarily, for a definite period

42. *Ibid.,* 163, 106.

of time."[43] Labor power thus can never be divorced from the individual to whom it represents property and from whom it can never be totally alienated. It is exchanged in a market wherein its possessor acts as an owner of a commodity that he chooses to sell at a price determined by the market.

Capitalized labor obligations superficially resembled labor power. They too resided in individuals, and buyers purchased them in a market.[44] Notwithstanding these similarities, capitalized labor obligations differed from labor power in significant ways. First, whereas an individual owns his labor power and chooses to exchange it for a wage, an individual did not own his labor obligation and did not choose the terms or affect the process by which another acquired it. Here it is important to reiterate that a labor obligation, as the term implies, constituted a duty to society, not a personal possession. In warranteeism, the social obligation of all to labor constituted a state concern. The state thus made the labor obligations of simple laborers purchasable, but it, not simple laborers or warrantors, retained control of them. The labor obligation was the property of neither the simple laborer nor the warrantor. It always remained a social duty subject to state regulation.

Second, labor power as a commodity is bought and sold according to market forces, even when law regulates aspects of this buying and selling, as for instance the length of a contract. If the market for labor power is depressed, some labor power may not be purchased. This would not necessarily be an issue of public policy in a free labor society, although it could become so. But the labor obligation of a simple laborer in warranteeism could never not be held by a warrantor.[45] Because of the fundamental relation of the labor obligation to subsistence, the state in warranteeism had to guarantee that the labor obligations of all simple laborers were always warranted to warrantors. Thus unlike the relation of an owner of labor power to a buyer of it, which occurs in a market in which both are legally free to sell and buy, however unequal the terms of the

43. Karl Marx, *Capital: A Critique of Political Economy* (3 vols.; New York, 1967), I, 168.

44. The market for labor obligations is more fully discussed in Chapter 4. For relevant passages see Hughes, *Treatise,* 106–107, 163, 168, 194–95, and 220.

45. For more on the impossibility of an unheld labor obligation, see the discussion of manumission later in this chapter.

contract, the relation of a simple laborer's labor obligation to the warrantor who held it constituted not a free exchange but a state arrangement in which neither party was free. Warrantors had to provide not what the market determined to be a wage but what the state dictated to be a "comfortable sufficiency of necessaries for health and strength."[46] Simple laborers did not choose to have their labor obligations "purchased," nor did they influence any of the terms of their service. Whereas labor power acts according to market forces, labor obligations acted according to state directives.

The distinctions between labor power and labor obligation reveal the centrality of state supervision in Hughes's vision of warranteeism. Labor power in a free labor society is a commodity; a capitalized labor obligation in warranteeism was a person. To allow labor to be subject to anything but state control, Hughes argued, would have jeopardized the essence of social organization. Free labor society allows wages—the source of laborers' subsistence—to be determined privately, in the market. "In the free-labor system," Hughes wrote, "the relation of . . . capitalist and laborer, is private. This relation is the key or modulus of the system. Progress is by a change in it; and can be by no other change." For Hughes, such a system did not and could not ensure universal subsistence because the market could not ensure that everyone's labor power would be purchased. "Men must not be free-laborers. For if they are; some must starve." The solution, then, was to transform the private relation of capitalist to laborer into the "public" relation of warrantor to warrantee. Only state-enforced labor relations could guarantee subsistence. "Because subsistence is the right of all; the relation of capital and labor, ought to be public. It ought to be that of magistrate to people."[47] And since the relation of capital to labor in warranteeism was public, the state not only regulated the buying and selling of warrantees' labor obligations but also supervised the warrantor's power over and treatment of the warrantee.

"The power of the master," Judge Thomas Ruffin wrote in 1829, "must be absolute, to render the submission of the slave perfect."[48] Al-

46. Hughes uses this phrase and slight variations of it throughout the *Treatise*. For examples see 113, 124, 141–42, 152, 154, 156–57, 168–69, 187, 200, 202, 230, and 284. For more on wages in free labor and warranteeism see Chapter 4.

47. *Ibid.,* 196–97.

48. *State of North Carolina* v. *Mann,* 1829, in Willie Lee Rose, ed., *A Documentary History of Slavery in North America* (New York, 1976), 222.

though many historians, following antebellum southerners, have distanced actual southern practice from Ruffin's brutal logic, his words nonetheless reflect one of the essential aspects of slavery: the power of one human over another.[49] The degree to which southern defenders of slavery articulated how law, Christianity, and social convention mitigated that power illustrates both their desire to portray their slavery and themselves as humane and their often contradictory reasoning on social versus personal responsibilities.

The contradiction in southern law between "questions of humanity and interest," so skillfully analyzed by legal historian Mark Tushnet, plagued Hughes.[50] He did better than most other southern jurists and ideologues in attempting to ground authority in society and thereby eliminate the tension between the freedom of the master and the claims of society. But his attempt dramatically reduced the master's personal power over his laborers and elevated the state's authority to affect that power to such a degree that the relation of master to slave or, more accurately, warrantor to warrantee lost much of its alleged paternalistic character. What Hughes constructed in the *Treatise* resembled nothing so much as an unfree labor system in which the state controlled both warrantor and warrantee in the interests of society.

Hughes devoted considerable attention to the warrantor and especially to his relations to warrantees and the state. What emerges from the *Treatise* is a contradictory picture of the warrantor as both dutiful public officer and benevolent paternalist. The paternalistic aspects of warran-

---

49. For more on antebellum southern law, see Helen T. Catterall, ed., *Judicial Cases Concerning American Slavery and the Negro* (5 vols.; Washington, D.C., 1926–36); Thomas R. R. Cobb, *An Inquiry into the Law of Negro Slavery in the United States of America* (1858; rpr., New York, 1968); James Codman Hurd, *The Law of Freedom and Bondage in the United States* (2 vols.; Boston, 1858); Charles S. Sydnor, "The Southerner and the Laws," *Journal of Southern History,* VI (1940), 3–24; A. E. Keir Nash, "Reason of Slavery: Understanding the Judicial Role in the Peculiar Institution," *Vanderbilt Law Review,* XXXII (1979), 8–218; Mark V. Tushnet, *The American Law of Slavery, 1810–1860: Considerations of Humanity and Interest* (Princeton, 1981); Genovese and Fox-Genovese, "Slavery, Economic Development, and the Law"; Paul Finkelman, "Exploring Southern Legal History," *North Carolina Law Review,* LXIV (1985), 77–116; and Andrew Fede, *People Without Rights: An Interpretation of the Fundamentals of the Law of Slavery in the U.S. South* (New York, 1992).

50. See Tushnet, *American Law of Slavery, passim.*

teeism served Hughes well in his critique of free labor society. But though expedient in that effort, the paternalism he attributed to warranteeism conflicted with his more persistent effort to portray warranteeism as a system that performed properly, that is, ensured subsistence to all, not because of personal relations between labor and capital but because of state planning and control. In such a system, the warrantor assumed importance because of his execution of the state's policy, not his personal good intentions.

Hughes's concept of "obligation" provided the basis of his analysis of class-state relations, just as it did that of the larger question of social organization. The capitalization of the labor obligations of simple laborers and the purchase of those obligations by capitalists transformed simple laborers and capitalists into warrantees and warrantors, respectively. But just as this process resulted from state action, the subsequent relations between these classes remained within the province of state regulation. "Both warrantor and warrantee, are economic lieges of the State." As "lieges," both classes owed allegiance to the state that determined the obligations of them both. "The warrantee is obliged by the State in favor of the warrantor; but the warrantor is reciprocally obliged by the State, in favor of the warrantee. The warrantor is an obligee to the warrantee; the warrantee, to the warrantor. They are both bound to each other."[51] Throughout the *Treatise,* Hughes expanded on the nature of these recip-rocal obligations and on the role of the state in creating and maintaining them. It should come as no surprise that Hughes devoted far more time and space to warrantors' obligations than to those of warrantees. As much as warranteeism might have differed from slavery, the warrantee, like the slave, primarily owed labor and obedience. Hughes's warranteeism was unique not in its description of the duties of the warrantee but in its depiction of the warrantor's obligation to the warrantee and the state. In detailing the warrantor's obligations, duties, and public character Hughes most clearly established warranteeism as a social system in which an activist state regulated the relations between all classes.

What was the warrantor's "obligation"? Although Hughes used the terms *warrantor* and *master* interchangeably at times, we have seen that the inherent power of the two positions constituted one of the primary

51. Hughes, *Treatise,* 167–68.

differences between slavery and warranteeism. Warranteeism eliminated the unlimited authority of the master over the slave. The warrantor was a mere "agent of the state," bound by law and dependent on the state for whatever authority he possessed over warrantees. The simple laborer's obligation to labor, Hughes again emphasized, was owed to society, and society only delegated the management of that obligation to the warrantor. The state, which created warrantors and warrantees, remained the party to whom all were obliged. "The warrantor capitalist or master, is not the obligor of the warrantee labor-obligation. He is an agent of the State; nothing more. He is the State per proxy. The State is supreme and principal warrantor. The capitalist is deputy warrantor. That is a public office. The master is a magistrate."[52] By insisting that no master was above the law or had unlimited power over a slave, Hughes remained consistent with prevailing southern opinion and law. It was less this insistence than his concomitant conception of the state as the sole source of all earthly authority that set him apart from other southern defenders of slavery.

Throughout his discussion of warranteeism Hughes argued that such things as "classes," "property," and "rights" constituted mere social constructs that emanated from society through the actions of the state. The specific relation of warrantor to warrantee represented one form of the general social obligation of all to labor, a form that humans created and modified to meet natural laws, especially the fundamental law of universal subsistence. Thus there was nothing "natural" about warranteeism; it was based on utility and judged by its ability to maintain subsistence and order. In this sense, Hughes differed from other southerners who displayed a conservative appreciation for tradition and precedent. For Hughes, the past mattered little when determining social policy, although it would have to be considered when implementing that policy.[53] Hughes's tendency to reason from "ultimate rights" or "natural laws" rather than from tradition may have developed out of his legal training, particularly his reading of works on the civil law. As his diary richly documents, he read such classics of the civilian tradition as Jean Domat's *Civil Law in Its Natural Order,* Robert Pothier's *Treatise on Obligations,* and Emmerich de Vattel's *Law of Nations,* as well as the Civil Code of

52. *Ibid.,* 166.
53. See, for example, *ibid.,* 291.

Louisiana.[54] Domat's claim that "there is nothing more necessary in sciences, than to possess the first principles of them, and that every science begins with establishing its own principles ... that they may serve for a foundation to all the particulars which are to depend upon them" strikingly resembles Hughes's ideas regarding the "science of societary organization." For Hughes, as we have repeatedly seen, "subsistence and progress" were society's "ultimate rights. . . . the final and supreme objects of social organization," much like Domat's "first principles." And, as with Domat's "first principles," subsistence and progress served as a "foundation to all the particulars," or, in Hughes's words, "All other rights are incidental. They are means." The civilian tradition, particularly Domat, provided Hughes with a logic that enabled him to argue that subsistence constituted a "natural" or "immutable law" that was "so essential to the engagements which form the order of society, that it is impossible to alter them without destroying the foundations of the said order."[55] Only those "engagements," or social relations, that fulfilled the "natural, immutable law" were acceptable; only those practices that flowed from and conformed to first principles were legitimate.

Basing and judging a social system on its performance forced Hughes to subordinate all individuals and classes to the interests of society, particularly its need to provide universal subsistence. What allowed a warrantor to compel a warrantee to work was the state's decision that this was expedient, not the right of an owner of property to use that property as he wished. The obligation of the warrantee to labor was an obligation to society, and society determined how it would best be performed. "The obliger," Hughes noted, "is the State. . . . All the powers, rights, duties, and responsibilities of the obligation issue from it. It is the economic sovereign, or lord-paramount. All are its lieges." And since only utility and performance qualified the state's actions, a state emerged from Hughes's *Treatise* that theoretically had no bounds, no fundamental limits, particularly as it related to individuals. The state, Hughes argued, "has in the premises, supreme executive legislative and judicial powers. Justice is its only limit; and it is the judge of that." In such a system, all

54. For Domat see Hughes Diary, February 17, 1850; for Pothier see *ibid.*, March 25, 1849; for Vattel see *ibid.*, March 11, 1849; and for the Civil Code of Louisiana, see *ibid.*, September 23, 1849.

55. Jean Domat, *The Civil Law in Its Natural Order* (2 vols.; Boston, 1850), I, 2, 50.

individuals and classes derived their status and power, or lack thereof, from the state: "Parties to the labor-obligation, have no rights, duties, or powers, which the State does not authorize; over which the State has not jurisdiction; and which the State may not according to justice, amend, remedy, enlarge or restrain."[56]

Hughes avoided linking warrantors' control of labor and other resources, such as land, to "property rights." In fact, he never mentioned land or the relations of different classes to it in the *Treatise*. Rather, he implied that the control of any resource, although reserved to certain classes, resulted only from the action of the state. His failure to explain or explore the relation between property, especially in land, and class position reveals the recurring difficulty he encountered in trying both to defend existing social relations and to promote a fundamentally different social system. For whereas slavery arose and to a large extent was defined by property relations, in warranteeism such property relations were replaced by relations created by the state on the basis of efficiency and justice, not "property rights."

In articulating the character of this leviathan-like state Hughes expressed a number of significant points concerning his ideas of southern slave society. Obviously, no such state existed in the South in 1854, and Hughes did not claim that it did. He did not even make clear whether his "State" represented a centralized government or a state government, nor did he touch upon the question of federalism. His "State" clearly represented part of a vision of an idealized southern society, one based on warranteeism, not slavery. And warranteeism differed from slavery especially in the diminished power of the warrantor. Yet Hughes's vision never totally transcended the actual conditions of the antebellum South; he remained bound by time and place even as he abstracted from them. But he sought in the *Treatise* to expound on the relations between the theory of warranteeism and the practice of slavery, to construct a model of social organization that incorporated elements of slavery while it departed from slavery's basis in human property. By advocating the illegitimacy of human property, the "public" character of the warrantor, and the unlimited scope of state control over labor relations, Hughes proposed

56. Hughes, *Treatise*, 166.

drastic changes in the existing structure of southern society. Nowhere are these changes more evident than in his depiction of the warrantor.

In his discussion of the warrantor's circumscribed authority, Hughes may well have been responding to the portrayal of masters as despots, such as the one of Simon Legree he found in Harriet Beecher Stowe's *Uncle Tom's Cabin,* which he had read in 1852. That any master could have behaved like Legree because of the nature of southern slavery led many southerners, including Hughes, to develop arguments that not only defended the South against outside attacks but also asserted the need for internal reform. For Hughes, as we have seen, the *Treatise* served both these purposes.

Hughes hardly introduced the idea of limiting the master's authority over the slave. Many historians, including Drew Faust in her discussion of slavery reform in the Confederacy, have noted that "the state had long intervened in the relation of master and slave." The most noted examples of this intervention, the outlawing of slave murder and the prohibition of certain forms of punishment such as castration and branding, placed the state, albeit marginally, between master and slave. In the 1840s and 1850s some southerners, particularly clergymen such as James Henley Thornwell, called for more wide-ranging reforms, such as legalization of slave marriage, permission of slave literacy, and prevention of the separation of slave children from their mothers.[57]

57. Drew Gilpin Faust, *The Creation of Confederate Nationalism: Ideology and Identity in the Civil War South* (Baton Rouge, 1988), 79. For other secondary studies, see Eugene Genovese, *Roll, Jordan, Roll: The World the Slaves Made* (New York, 1974), 25–49; Rose, "Domestication of Domestic Slavery," in *Slavery and Freedom,* ed. Freehling; and Tushnet, *American Law of Slavery,* 188–91. For the laws themselves see Hurd, *Law of Freedom and Bondage,* II, 1–218; and Cobb, *Inquiry into the Law of Negro Slavery.* For more on southern calls for reform, see Faust, *Creation of Confederate Nationalism,* Chap. 4; Fede, *People Without Rights;* and Rosser Taylor, "Humanizing the Slave Code of North Carolina," *North Carolina Historical Review,* II (1925), 323–31. On appeals from the churches and clergy, see, for example, Thornwell, *Rights and Duties of Masters.* Useful secondary studies include Anne C. Loveland, *Southern Evangelicals and the Social Order, 1800–1860* (Baton Rouge, 1980), 206–18; Mitchell Snay, *Gospel of Disunion: Religion and Separatism in the Antebellum South* (New York, 1993), 88–99; Jack Maddex, Jr., "A Paradox of Christian Amelioration: Proslavery Ideology and Church Ministries to Slaves," in *The Southern Enigma: Essays on Race, Class, and Folk Culture,* ed. Walter J. Fraser and Winfred B. Moore, Jr. (Westport, Conn., 1983), 105–17; Donald G. Mathews, "Charles Colcock Jones and the Southern Evangelical Crusade to Form a Biracial Community," *Journal of*

Yet even these reforms amounted to far less than Hughes's warranteeism. And the difference was not one of degree. These reforms would have increased the role of the state in master-slave relations, just as the outlawing of slave murder had. But whereas these reforms in a piecemeal manner limited the master's authority over his property, warranteeism rejected the notion of human property and instead of limiting a pre-existing property right located the source of the warrantor's authority in the state. "All warrantors are special government-officers. Their official powers issue from the State, are subject to the State, and under review and visitation of the State; The State is supreme and supervising. It is the fountain of power."[58] By denying that the warrantor had any power over warrantees other than that provided by the state, Hughes envisioned a fundamentally different set of social relations than did reformers of slavery. Although state intervention and the limits it imposed on the master resembled warranteeism, they nonetheless stopped well short of it.[59] Hughes did not seek modifications in slavery; he sought to reconstruct southern society on an alternate set of social principles.

Although Hughes's vision of warranteeism did not and was not intended to correspond precisely to actual southern practice, his depiction of warranteeism closely resembled what Mark Tushnet has suggested southern law and politics were moving toward in the 1850s. Sketching out what a "rationalized law of slavery," free of the contradictions that bourgeois law and legal reasoning imposed on it, might have looked like, Tushnet suggests that the "primary alteration" of such a law "would have been a transformation in the notion of property." The transformation he sketches appears strikingly similar to Hughes's ideas of the nature of warrantor-warrantee relations and his differentiation of those relations with slavery. Property, Tushnet suggests, "would no longer be defined as the expression of individual will, subject to regulation only for

---

Southern History, XLI (1975), 299–320; Farmer, *Metaphysical Confederacy;* and William W. Freehling, *The Reintegration of American History: Slavery and the Civil War* (New York, 1994), 59–81.

58. Hughes, *Treatise,* 227.

59. The most forceful argument demonstrating the limited scope and application of these laws can be found in Fede, *People Without Rights,* esp. Chaps. 4, 7, and 11. For the limited effectiveness of the clergy's calls for reform, see, in particular, Freehling, *Reintegration of American History,* 59–81.

the most pressing social goals." Instead, he posits that property first in slaves but eventually in everything "would be defined as the delegation by society as a whole of certain limited authority to 'owners,' who would be charged with exercising that authority only in socially prescribed ways." Tushnet goes on to point out that such a transformation would do exactly what Hughes did when he made the warrantor's power over the warrantee derive from state delegation, not property rights. By replacing property rights with social duties, Tushnet argues, "social control [would be] embodied in all relationships rather than . . . superimposed on them." [60]

State intervention under slavery required encroaching upon property rights that most slaveholders considered nearly absolute. Thus is was only with great difficulty that southern states passed laws designed to curtail the will of the master.[61] Warranteeism eliminated this difficulty by denying the warrantor any claim to absolute or even partial property rights in the warrantee. State intervention therefore did not encroach upon warrantors' "rights" but rather constituted the legitimate and moral, in Hughes's terms, right of the state to maintain the proper functioning of society. Embodied in the relation of warrantor to warrantee, in fact the creator of it, the state did not have to justify regulating what in essence was its primary concern: social relations.

Hughes's warrantee state, therefore, would have related to warrantors in a fundamentally different way than southern states did to masters. Even as southern courts and legislatures restricted an individual master's actions, the master's property right in his slave and the legal and ideological implications of that right restrained the scope of restriction. As Tushnet and other historians have pointed out, southern society throughout the antebellum period failed to resolve the contradiction that spawned conflicts between the state's right to limit a socially irresponsible master and the master's right to control his property. Warranteeism would have resolved the contradiction by removing any individual property right. The warrantor would have had no legal rights derived from property in the warrantee, and thus the state would not have faced the obstacles to action that southern states did. The inconsistencies of southern law, in which a judge could side with an individual master against state restric-

60. Tushnet, *American Law of Slavery*, 231.
61. See Fede, *People Without Rights, passim.*

tions and another judge on the same court could side with the state against the master and both judges could cite precedents, were just what warranteeism would have eliminated.[62] In opposing, in essence, the foundation of the common law, Hughes advocated a near total break with the legal and ideological framework that had provided individuals with the means of limiting state action.

Warranteeism thus did preserve those elements of slavery that Hughes revered: order, hierarchy, and interdependence. But it replaced the essence of slavery, one person's ownership of another, with a new relation based on state mandate. Of course, slavery, like all other forms of property, requires legal sanction and protection. In that sense, slavery is a state creation. And as David Brion Davis, Orlando Patterson, and others have reminded us, slavery is a most difficult term to define.[63] Nevertheless, the distinctions between southern slavery and warranteeism involve more than mere semantics. Hughes envisioned something quite different from slavery, even though he staunchly defended elements of it. He argued in effect that if unfree labor, broadly understood as one class's ability to coerce and control the labor of a legally and politically subordinate class, was to survive, then slavery had to change dramatically. Hughes responded to the increasingly hostile antislavery climate of world and national opinion, strongly influenced by a bourgeois worldview based on individual liberty, by proposing that the South develop an authoritarian, activist state. Such a state would eliminate the abuses of slavery by eliminating their ultimate source: the personal power of the master.

Writing of warrantors, Hughes stated unequivocally: "All their rights, duties, powers, and responsibilities issue from the law, pursue the law, are limited by the law. and are created, continued, modified or terminated by the law." Only by envisaging a fundamentally different social and political order than that of the antebellum South could one claim that

62. Tushnet, *American Law of Slavery, passim;* also see Genovese, *Roll, Jordan, Roll,* 25–49; Wyatt-Brown, *Yankee Saints and Southern Sinners,* 158–68; Fede, *People Without Rights.* For an example of conflicting opinions, see Tushnet's discussion of *Bailey* v. *Poindexter,* 55 Va. (1858), in *American Law of Slavery,* 209–11.

63. For the problem of defining slavery, see David Brion Davis, *Slavery and Human Progress* (New York, 1984), esp. 8–22; Orlando Patterson, *Slavery and Social Death: A Comparative Study* (Cambridge, 1982); on the changing character of American slavery see Rose, "Domestication of Domestic Slavery," in *Slavery and Freedom,* ed. Freehling, and Wyatt-Brown, *Yankee Saints and Southern Sinners.*

"rights" could be created and terminated by "law," without regard to either the Constitution or the common law. Hughes devoted considerable space to detailing the ways in which the state, through the law, regulated warrantor-warrantee relations. "The powers, rights, duties, and responsibilities of laborers and capitalists, must be adapted and regulated by law; their private relations superseded; public relations, ordained and established."[64]

The need for such adaptation and regulation resulted from the nature of warranteeism itself. Because universal subsistence guided every social policy, the state had to control economic life in order to guarantee subsistence. "The function of subsistence, is the economic system; but because existence is the right of all, and because the function of right or justice is the State or civil organization; the economic system is an implement of the State." The state had to ensure not only that everyone received a sufficient amount of sustenance but also that everyone worked to produce that sustenance. Both production and distribution required state direction. The state therefore determined wages and work hours. "In the public method [of distribution], the state adjudicates the wages. This is the laborer's share of the produce. It is what justly belongs to him. But to adjudicate wages, is also to adjudicate labor. For labor comes before wages." The need for ensuring both work and wages required state control of both: "When the State decrees the wages, it must decree the work; the quantity of one that justifies the quantity of the other; how much work is entitled to how much wages. An ordinance of wages is therefore an ordinance of work. If the state adjudicates distribution, it must of necessity, adjudicate production."[65]

Given the "necessity" of state adjudication of wages and work, the warrantor's treatment of his warrantees became circumscribed by law. In this regard, Hughes built upon actual southern practice. State statutes prohibited work on Sundays, established minimum standards for food and clothing, and some, such as those of Mississippi, set maximum hour limits.[66] But Hughes wanted to do more than set limits on a master's

---

64. Hughes, *Treatise,* 212, 204.

65. *Ibid.,* 178, 126. Also see *ibid.,* 151–53.

66. For state laws relating to slavery, see Hurd, *Law of Freedom and Bondage,* II, 1–218. Also see Fede, *People Without Rights,* 132–34, on laws relating to feeding and clothing slaves.

prerogative. By constantly emphasizing the source of the warrantor's authority and the public character of his relation to the warrantee, he placed the state at the center of the warrantor-warrantee relation and made it the most powerful party to that relation. And although Hughes cited the familiar case of the fining of a warrantor/master who failed to provide adequate "wages" to his warrantee/slave as an example of state protection of the warrantee/slave, his conception of the state's role went well beyond such limited action.[67]

The state in warranteeism, Hughes posited, could have conceivably interceded between warrantor and warrantee whenever it felt justified. In "Theoretical Sociology," for instance, Hughes argued that the "body hygienic" organ of government should have power to "order sanitary inspections, or surveys ... to establish sanitary police, watchmen, and surveyors.... To regulate the structure of all habitations and houses.... To provide for the inspection, and prohibit the adulteration, of food, and of drugs and medicines."[68] Such regulation far exceeded any existing southern law, and it represented the breadth of what Hughes considered legitimate state action.

The *Treatise* fluctuates between adamant claims of state power, limited warrantor authority, and the "rights" of warrantees, and familiar southern arguments about the ways in which the warrantor/master's interest in his warrantee/slave provided the latter with all the protection and care that the law failed to. While claiming that warrantees had various judicial, political, and economic rights, Hughes wrote little of actual state enforcement of these rights; at best he suggested that such enforcement was a matter for future consideration.[69] More frequently he stated that just as warrantors were motivated to work by their self-interest, so they were motivated to do right by their warrantees.

The personal interest of the warrantor in the warrantee meant that any damage to the warrantee also damaged the warrantor, who depended on the warrantee's labor for his livelihood. In these discussions Hughes no longer spoke of "civil" enforcement but tellingly used the term *economic* enforcement: "The warrantor is economically enforced therefore to warrant health, strength, and justice to the warrantee. Sickness, want

67. Hughes, *Treatise,* 214.
68. *Ibid.,* 66.
69. See *ibid.,* 227–46.

or injustice to the warrantee, mulct the warrantor. The wrongs by their consequences right themselves. They fine the wronger, and are self-executing."[70] Such reasoning, which defenders of slavery frequently employed, revealed the contradictory nature of Hughes's argument. Although positing a system in which the state ensured universal subsistence through active regulation and supervision of social relations, he made the system rely to a great extent on the economic motivations of warrantors. Such contradictions indicate the difficulty Hughes encountered in attempting simultaneously to bolster the image of the benevolent paternalistic master through appeals to economic rationality and shift the basis of the defense of southern society from the friendly master to the efficient and authoritarian state. Once again, Hughes found himself caught between a defense of the South and advocacy of a new order.

The fundamental contradiction of relying on the master to follow "logically" his economic self-interest while claiming that he was a mere "agent of the State" who "executes the State's commands" illustrates the ultimate incompatibility of southern slavery and warranteeism.[71] Although he clearly did not intend to, Hughes demonstrated that the paternal master and the public magistrate were at fundamental odds with each other. The inconsistency in Hughes's argument in the *Treatise* does not negate the significance of his central point: the proper subordination of the will of the master to the will of the state. The inconsistency arose from his desire and attempt to link current practice with the goals of warranteeism. Thus if the master cared for the health of his slaves, the goal of healthy laborers was achieved without state intervention. But as we have seen, Hughes maintained the theoretical right of the state to monitor the health of warrantees and intervene directly if necessary. It is this theoretical right that, although unrealized in actual southern practice, remained at the center of Hughes's vision of a properly ordered society. One final example, that of manumission, illustrates both the conflict between the freedom of the master and the will of the state and Hughes's belief that only by ordering society on the latter could the contradictions of southern slavery be resolved.

Hughes brought together many strands of his thought concerning masters' rights, state prerogatives, and the future development of south-

70. *Ibid.,* 224.
71. *Ibid.,* 166, 110.

ern society in his discussion of manumission. He attacked manumission and argued that it was incompatible with true warranteeism. He based this position on two major theoretical pillars of warranteeism: the warrantor's limited authority over the warrantee and the primacy of universal subsistence.

These two points are interrelated. The state's need to ensure subsistence to everyone necessitated the subordination of all individuals to the state's will. Warranteeism, Hughes held, guaranteed subsistence by binding laborers to capital under a system of state supervision. In warranteeism, he wrote, "Every simple-laborer is ascribed to capital. . . . Warrantee laborers are not adscripts of the soil; that is not sufficient. They are more than this. They are adscripts of capital: so that while life lasts; they are warranted the means of livelihood." The uniting of labor and capital assured production: "Association in this system is essentially perfect. Production therefore, is so far perfect."[72] Production, and thus subsistence, depended on the labor of warrantees. That labor, Hughes argued, was "systematic" only if warrantees remained "associated" to warrantors.

The obligation of the warrantee to labor was matched by the obligation of the warrantor to provide sustenance and care to the warrantee. Both parties' obligations derived not from contract but from state directive aimed at ensuring subsistence. It therefore followed that an individual warrantor who "freed" a warrantee not only violated his "civic" and legal duty but also jeopardized the ability of the society to meet its essential goal of universal subsistence. Manumission severed what theoretically had to be a permanent bond; a simple laborer without a warrantor would have been outside the scope of public control and thus vulnerable to the twin evils of all societies: idleness and want. Hughes envisioned no want in warranteeism because he envisioned no idleness. "In [warranteeism]," he stated, "idlers are industrialized. There are no beggars, or vagabonds. . . . All work; none are idle." All simple laborers were bound to warrantors, and neither party could alter the relation. Warrantors could only "transfer" or sell the labor obligations of their warrantees to other warrantors. A warrantee, by definition, always had to have a warrantor. "Warrantors have no power to terminate or qualify their warranties. Warrantees must always be warranted. A warrantor has no power to

---

72. *Ibid.*, 91.

withdraw or resign his warranty otherwise than by the subrogation of another good and sufficient warrantor. This is the essence of the system. Whatever is in derogation of it, is void."[73]

Hughes's unqualified opposition to manumission was logically consistent with his theory of warranteeism. Although he could entrust warrantors with certain responsibilities that they performed out of self-interest and that therefore did not require direct state control, he could not allow them to "terminate" their "obligation" to a warrantee; the obligation could only be transferred to another warrantor. The warrantor's freedom to act toward his warrantee within the relation differed fundamentally from freedom to end the relation itself. Hughes generally believed that the warrantor would act properly within the relation. And if the warrantor did not, the state maintained the right to intervene. But the state could never permit a "mere agent" of it to undermine the basis of warranteeism. Hughes recognized the incompatibility of freedom and warranteeism; either all simple laborers were bound to warrantors and thereby guaranteed labor and subsistence, or some were free and not guaranteed either. To allow the possibility of such freedom was to admit that society had failed to meet its first end. "Idleness is a crime, and the dam of crimes. No subsistee ought to be an idler. Everybody ought to work.... This should not be the State's intention only; it should be the State's obtention.... There ought to be no mendicants, no vagrants, no idlers. This is the fundamental rule of warranteeism."[74] Manumission would have created a free laborer, a potential "idler." Warranteeism could not tolerate such a potentiality.

Hughes's position on manumission clarifies some of the inconsistencies in his earlier discussion of warrantors' duties and responsibilities. His reliance on the self-interest of the warrantor conflicted with his insistence on state regulation of social relations, but this reliance did not negate warranteeism as a system. Hughes could rely on warrantors and still maintain the theoretical right of the state to increase its role in warrantor-warrantee relations. If a warrantor acted contrary to state wishes, that problem could be remedied within the system because the warrantor was a public official subject to law. The freedom the warrantor exercised was freedom that the state granted and could modify at its will. By denying

73. *Ibid.,* 282, 220.
74. *Ibid.,* 281.

the warrantor any freedom to manumit his warrantees Hughes demonstrated not only how the state could limit the actions of the warrantor but also the logic by which the state could establish such limits. Warranteeism, with its emphasis on state guarantee of subsistence, effectively made all freedom contingent on state prerogative.

Hughes's dismissal of manumission within warranteeism reflected actual southern developments.[75] But his discussion of manumission in particular and of warranteeism in general suggests a more dramatic and far more sweeping reform of existing southern society. Southern laws that restricted manumission were, in general, based on the notion that former slaves constituted, in the language of the common law, a "public nuisance." These laws, as historian Andrew Fede has demonstrated, did "manifest the exercise of community control over the slave owner's property rights."[76] But they were based on a different principle from Hughes's in opposing manumission. According to his reasoning, the "freedom" of the manumitted warrantee did not create a "public nuisance," as the concept was understood in the common law, but rather presented the possibility of want and therefore undermined warranteeism's central purpose. Here again Hughes argued not from common law principles but from the logic his insistence on the primacy of universal subsistence imposed on him. It was not the practical dangers or inconveniences of manumission that led him to denounce it but the inconsistency of "free" laborers in warranteeism. Warranteeism necessitated that every laborer be warranted at all times. As a social system, warranteeism thus implied that there be but two classes—warrantees and warrantors—for only by binding every laborer to a warrantor could subsistence be assured. Just as a nonwarranted warrantee contradicted warranteeism, so would the existence of any "free" laborer. All laborers would have to be warrantees if warranteeism was to achieve its ultimate goal of universal subsistence.

The logic of warranteeism thus implied that all southern laborers be made warrantees. Yet this implication remains unarticulated and is even contradicted by Hughes's racism, which severely qualified his attempt to develop a nonracial basis for the defense of southern unfree labor. Indeed,

75. For discussions of legal developments limiting manumission in the antebellum South, see Tushnet, *American Law of Slavery,* 191–228, and Fede, *People Without Rights,* 135–53.

76. Fede, *People Without Rights,* 131.

Hughes's treatment of race demonstrates the extreme difficulties southern intellectuals encountered in their efforts to construct an abstract defense of slavery. Hughes carefully kept race out of his theory of warranteeism; it was applicable to any and all societies, irrespective of their racial makeup. But when he did discuss race, he drastically if not irreparably weakened the applicability of his theoretical argument to the antebellum South.

"In the United States South," Hughes wrote, "there are two races. These are related." The presence of different races meant that southern warranteeism had a specific character, although its essential nature was not, he argued, thereby altered. "The organization of these [southern] States, is therefore not unqualified warranteeism; because its population is not homogeneous. The societary organization of the United States South, is warranteeism with the ethnical qualification." But even as Hughes acknowledged the racial character of southern warranteeism, he firmly repudiated the ideas that race was the basis of warranteeism and that warranteeism was suitable only to societies composed of different races: "This qualification is not essential to theoretical or abstract warranteeism. It is accidental. Warranteeism without the ethnical qualification, is that to which every society of one race, must progress."[77]

Hughes thus understood warranteeism as essentially a system of class, not race, relations. The *Treatise,* accordingly, contains few extended discussions of race. But when Hughes turned from theoretical discussions and wrote specifically of the South, he often mentioned race. And he focused extensively on race in relation to one topic: miscegenation. It is in his analysis of miscegenation that the profound influence of racism reveals itself most clearly and problematically.

Although Hughes claimed that the races were "related," he did not say that they were equal. He noted that the two races "must be either peers ethnically, or not peers." He then surprisingly commented that if "not peers ethnically, the black race must be either superior or inferior." Hughes of course never meant to suggest that blacks were superior to whites. His point was to argue that different races, of different capacities, could not engage in miscegenation without negatively affecting the "superior race." Thus he hypothetically and disingenuously suggested that

---

77. Hughes, *Treatise,* 207.

if blacks were "superior [to whites], their ethnical progress forbids amalgamation with an inferior race." And, logically, "If the white race is superior; their ethnical progress forbids intermixture with an inferior race."[78]

"Ethnical progress" thus prohibited miscegenation. "Hygienic duties" were no less important than economic or political duties, and to violate them was to violate a "law of nature." Hughes reached unprecedented levels of emotion in his denunciations of such violations: "Degeneration is evil. . . . Hybridism is heinous. Impurity of the races is against the law of nature. Mulattoes are monsters."[79] Hughes's outrage was even more pronounced than typical antebellum southern sentiment and inexplicably uncharacteristic of his *Treatise*. But his solution to the potential horrors of miscegenation forced him away from the logical conclusion of his thought regarding manumission and warranteeism generally. In his efforts to ensure the "preservation and progress of a race" Hughes avoided confronting the dilemma of the "progress" of "free" "nonwarrantor" whites in southern warranteeism.

Rigid racial caste, Hughes argued, provided the only effective means to preserve the progress of the races. "It is the duty of caste," he wrote, "to prevent amalgamation: it is, caste for the purity of the races." Whites and blacks had to be segregated "for sexual intercourse follows social intercourse. In a society of two races, therefore, ethnical segregation was essential." In the context of the antebellum South, however, this meant that caste lines had to coincide with class lines: "One race must be superordinate and warrantors; the other subordinate and warrantees." Blacks, and only blacks, could have been warrantees, for to have permitted whites to be warrantees would have invited the evil of miscegenation and the violation of natural law.[80]

Whether Hughes descended into racial demagoguery to win support from race-conscious southerners or whether his thoughts on miscegenation reflect some deep-seated personal fears cannot be ascertained. What is clear, however, is that his endorsement of a caste system of white dominance over blacks compromised his advocacy of warranteeism as a color-blind social system. By forbidding the existence of two races within

78. *Ibid.*, 239.
79. *Ibid.*, 239–40.
80. *Ibid.*, 240, 242, 243.

the same class Hughes portrayed all whites as warrantors ("one race must be ... warrantors"). Yet he knew that not all whites were warrantors, and he even referred to this class of "nonwarrantors" in the *Treatise*. This class, which roughly corresponded to nonslaveholding southern whites, received little specific attention from Hughes. It is not difficult to understand why.

The position of nonslaveholding whites posed a peculiar problem for Hughes in his attempt both to defend slavery and to establish a firmer foundation for southern social relations and development. Warranteeism essentially recognized but two classes: warrantors and warrantees. In "abstract or theoretical warranteeism" each laborer was bound to another and obliged, through law, to perform specific duties for society's benefit in general and universal subsistence in particular. Only the "enforcement" of everyone's obligation to labor could guarantee subsistence. But whereas black "simple-laborers" were "civilly enforced" to perform their duty to labor, "nonwarrantor" "skilled-laborers," Hughes maintained, were "economically enforced" to execute their obligation. Hughes thus expected "nonwarrantors," like warrantors, to be motivated to labor out of self-interest. We have seen how this aspect of Hughes's reasoning reveals an assumption that different groups responded better to different motivations; simple laborers needed to be civilly compelled to work but skilled laborers and capitalists worked because of self-interest and "moral obligation." But we have also seen that Hughes consistently claimed that the lack of civil enforcement of skilled laborer and capitalist labor obligations was mere expedience, subject to revision whenever the state deemed it necessary. Nonetheless, such assertions do not altogether eliminate the difficulties nonwarrantors posed to the theory of warranteeism.

The existence of a third class between warrantees and warrantors raises the question of how their labor would have been "civilly enforced" if the state decided that was necessary. Warranteeism, by capitalizing the labor obligations of simple laborers, provided for capitalist "magistrates" to supervise the labor and ensure the subsistence of simple laborer warrantees. How exactly the subsistence of nonwarrantors would have been ensured is never made clear in the *Treatise*. By referring to nonwarrantors as "skilled-laborers," Hughes suggested that it was their "skills" rather than their access to or control of land that distinguished them as a class. Had he focused on their ability, through access to land, to provide their own subsistence he could have incorporated them into warranteeism with little difficulty. But by ignoring land and nonwarrantors' relation to it, he implied that their means of subsistence depended upon their ability to labor, just like simple laborers.

Although political expediency, not to mention personal survival, prevented Hughes from explicitly calling for the capitalization of nonwarrantors' labor obligations, such a development would have followed logically from the nature of warranteeism and Hughes's depiction of nonwarrantors. A "free class," such as nonwarrantors, without any apparent means of subsistence other than their labor, constituted an anomaly in warranteeism. Its existence in actual southern society, like that of manumitted slaves, represented an inconsistency that had to be eliminated if warranteeism was to achieve universal subsistence. It is thus not difficult, and only logical, to extend Hughes's rejection of manumission to freedom generally. Freedom, understood as being outside the scope of state action—outside the warrantor-warrantee relation—presented an obstacle to the full realization of warranteeism, which held that no one ought to have to starve.

The political realities of the South in 1854 prevented Hughes from calling for the incorporation of nonwarrantors into warrantor-warrantee relations. But his own racism also prevented him from extending warranteeism's progress to such an incorporation. Hughes clearly stated that caste was necessary to preserve racial purity. Therefore, no white could have been a warrantee, for that would have violated such caste distinctions. He thus was forced into claiming that "one race must be . . . warrantors," even though he acknowledged the existence of nonwarrantors and his theory contained no place for them. Only a two-class system of warranteeism could have ensured subsistence; only a two-caste system of warranteeism could have ensured racial purity. Hughes's discussion of manumission, as well as the entire logic of warranteeism, suggests that the free class of nonwarrantors would have been gradually and inexorably eliminated. Perhaps he envisioned an eventual consolidation of landholding and the separation of nonwarrantors from the soil. Nonwarrantors would then be made either warrantors or warrantees. But his racial policy did not allow for such a culmination of warranteeism's progress; no white could ever be a warrantee as long as black warrantees existed, and yet not all nonwarrantors could become warrantors. This fundamental con-

tradition reveals the difficulties Hughes encountered as a racist southerner attempting simultaneously to defend an existing social and racial
order and to construct an abstract defense of unfree labor. Nonwarrantors, who in reality constituted the majority of white southerners, presented Hughes with theoretical and political obstacles that he could not
or would not confront. His racism and the realities in which he lived
prevented him from explicitly stating the logical outcome of his theory.
Notwithstanding these inconsistencies, Hughes insisted that warranteeism was the social organization "to which every duteous society must
progress." [81]

For Hughes, "progress" consisted of society's movement toward guaranteed universal subsistence, which necessitated a powerful regulatory
state. In noting the centrality of the state in warranteeism, it is important
to understand not only the powers of this state but also its character.
Hughes presented the state as a transcendent force, acting in the interests
of all society, regardless of class. Warrantors and warrantees faced the
state in the same way and were equally bound to carry out its wishes,
which were determined by justice. The state acted not in the interest of
any particular class but in the broad, social interest. "The State regulates
the standard of public distribution. It adjudicates the wages. Capitalists
and laborers in this, are not antagonistic; they are anagonistic. They do
not act against each other; they are inactive." When writing of the unequal relations of capitalists and laborers in free labor societies, Hughes
referred to the state as "a disinterested or just third party." Notwithstanding these attempts to portray the state as beyond class control or influence,
it is ultimately clear that the state's primary functions served to strengthen
the collective power of warrantors over warrantees even as they limited
the wills of individual warrantors. [82]

Hughes wanted the state to be seen as an objective, neutral institution
that decided how to act solely on the basis of social necessity. In this
respect he followed other nineteenth-century social thinkers, especially
Saint-Simon and Comte, both of whom he had mentioned in his diary,
who saw the state as the rightful preserve of experts who approached and
solved social problems scientifically. Sociology, which Hughes termed
"the science of societary organization," enabled sociologists to rise above

81. *Ibid.*, 207.
82. *Ibid.*, 158, 135.

narrow, particularistic interests and administer the state according to laws of human and social development. In a passage that Hughes surely would have concurred with if he had read it, Comte pointed out that in such a "scientific polity" the necessity of recognizing and acting according to natural law removed much of politics from human will. In a scientific polity, Comte wrote, "the human race is regarded as subject to a natural law of development that can be ascertained by observation and that prescribes for each epoch, in the most unequivocal manner, the political course it is possible to pursue." This view of politics envisioned the state not as a battlefield of competing parties or interests but as an institution above such divisive and subjective forces: "Government by measures replaces government by men. . . . In politics all is settled by a truly supreme law, recognized as superior to human forces."[83]

The modern sociologist Gertrud Lenzer has argued that "the very purpose and result of extending the positive scientific method to human and social phenomena are to secure in the public at large the acceptance of the existing order and its predominant forces." She has further pointed out that "in the hands of the governing classes it is indeed a most powerful instrument, guaranteeing the continuation of that very order."[84] In this understanding of the character of the positivist state, we see if not Hughes's debt to Comte at least the affinity of his ideas to those of Comte. "Every social system," Comte wrote, "whether constructed for a handful of men or for several millions, aims definitively at directing all special forces towards a general result, for the exercise of a general and combined activity is the essence of society."[85] For Hughes this "general result" was universal subsistence. By declaring subsistence the "primary" and "overriding" goal of society, a goal that Hughes likened to an inflexible law, he established the basis for his defense of "the existing order and its predominant forces."[86]

We have seen how Hughes's emphasis on subsistence allowed him to

---

83. Auguste Comte, "Plan of the Scientific Operations for Reorganizing Society" (1822), in Gertrud Lenzer, ed., *Auguste Comte and Positivism: The Essential Writings* (Chicago, 1975), 49.

84. Gertrud Lenzer, "Auguste Comte and Modern Positivism," *ibid.,* xli.

85. Comte, "Plan of the Scientific Operations," *ibid.,* 20.

86. For examples of Hughes's elevation of subsistence to the level of inflexible law see Hughes, *Treatise,* 81, 174–75, 178–79, 201.

praise the interdependence, inequality, and hierarchy that characterized southern social relations. But to assure subsistence required as well the elimination of property and property rights in human beings and the substitution of state control of class relations. Hughes recognized that to preserve the fundamental features of southern society changes had to be made to place that society on a firmer basis. The transfer of authority over labor from individual masters to the state meant challenging the foundation of the master class's power. But Hughes proved himself a true conservative in calling for such a transfer. As Lenzer says of Comte, Hughes too believed that those "who cling to a disintegrated past and who are unwilling to accept any changes whatever will be overruled by events and the very changes they reject."[87] For Hughes, as for many southerners, those events and changes centered around the increasingly hostile relation of northern to southern society in particular and of free labor to slavery in general. Hughes sought not to strip the master class of power but to institutionalize it on a new basis so that it could better defend itself against the impending domination of northerners. In essence, he advocated, as did George Fitzhugh, "centralization within" to prevent the "evils of centralization from without."[88]

Although this new basis would mean the creation of an authoritarian state with the power to subordinate warrantors, Hughes did not envisage an adversarial relation between the state and the warrantors as a class. Although he never discussed the specific form the state would take, who would serve in it, or how they would be chosen or appointed, his writings suggest that he remained committed to some form of representative republicanism even while he embraced an activist state. In an 1860 address at his alma mater, Oakland College, Hughes spoke of citizenship and its obligations. Asserting that "our duties to the State are as sacred as our duties to the family," Hughes urged his audience to conceive of citizenship as "an office," with "powers, rights, duties, and responsibilities which cannot be ignored." Citizens, he argued, should not passively "let the State take its course," for then they would not be citizens but "subjects" who "listlessly let others rule." Since "politics is our progress," and "by

87. Lenzer, "Auguste Comte and Modern Positivism," in Lenzer, ed., *Auguste Comte and Positivism,* xxxiii.

88. George Fitzhugh, *Cannibals All! or, Slaves Without Masters,* ed. C. Vann Woodward (1857; rpr., Cambridge, Mass., 1960), 3.

politics comes Paradise," each "citizen of wisdom, skill, wealth or learning" should be evaluated according to "what public good he has done. If he has done little, let his corpse be spit upon, but if has done much, let his corpse be wept upon." This conception of citizenship, particularly its emphasis on participation, reveals Hughes's commitment to republican ideals. Yet the concept does not preclude an activist state that, even while it sought citizen participation—especially of those citizens of "wisdom, skill, wealth or learning"—could also forcefully guide society toward "Paradise." Hughes was not here calling for broad, participatory democracy; he was calling the elite to their sacred public duty. "For whether of skill, or will, or wit, or wealth," he declared, "power is of God and for God. The powerful, therefore, must be godly, and the people's good, the public good is godliness." The powerful owed society their services. And that service to the state, Hughes maintained, represented the pinnacle of earthly achievement. The state remained central; the "public good" continued to command obedience and fulfillment of duty. Although citizens did participate, that participation did not necessarily lessen the state's role in society. Hughes could not advocate or perhaps even foresee a state run without citizen involvement. But neither could he abandon the notion that individuals owed society, that "our duties to the State are as sacred as our duties to the family." And while the powerful had to serve the state, they simultaneously were the state. Although the state would restrict and control their individual actions, it would also maintain, albeit on different legal grounds, their dominant position in society. Change, in this case, would both ensure the hierarchical nature of southern society and, equally important, better protect that society from northern assault.[89]

"There are in practice," Hughes wrote in the beginning of "Practical Sociology," "two forms of society.... These forms essentially differ. The difference is in their economic system, whose order qualifies all the other systems."[90] His critique of free labor will be examined in depth in the following chapter. For our purposes here, however, it is important to recognize the clear and critical importance he placed on understanding warranteeism in the context of free labor. From the opening of the major section of the *Treatise* with the above-quoted lines through the extended critique of free labor society found in the rest of the text, Hughes re-

89. Hughes, *Speech ... on Our Administration of Justice,* 6–8.
90. Hughes, *Treatise,* 79.

mained engaged in a determined effort to establish the superiority of warranteeism over free labor. And it is in this dominant theme and purpose of the *Treatise* that we understand why Hughes insisted on the need for warranteeism and not slavery.

Warranteeism not only prevented the outrages of slavery such as those found in *Uncle Tom's Cabin,* but it also provided for a rational, efficient, and orderly system of social relations based on and guided by a responsible state. Warranteeism challenged the efficiency and orderliness of the market with an authoritative, regulatory state. Such a state eliminated both the "want, oppression, hatred, outrage, cruelty and injustice" that Hughes claimed slavery produced and the "Want, idleness, vagrancy, mendicancy, and other economic irregularities" of free labor.[91] By elevating slavery to warranteeism, therefore, the South could have defended itself more ably and criticized those systems of social relations that failed the essential test of all societies.

Warranteeism was thus more than simply a defense of unfree labor. Hughes presented it as a superior form of social organization, based on neither the subjective will of the master nor the unpredictable fluctuations of the market. No other aspect of warranteeism mattered as much as order. Like Comte, Hughes saw order as even more essential than progress. Order to Hughes meant guaranteed subsistence, and only a social system controlled by a state capable of controlling everything related to subsistence could have provided order. Warranteeism therefore provided Hughes with a model that allowed him to defend the South not on its own terms but as a society that more than any other approximated the objective standard that measured the performance of all societies. Free labor, like slavery, had to be eliminated to ensure universal subsistence. Warranteeism constituted not merely one proper social system but the only one. Social progress equaled warranteeism.

By equating social progress with a society's ability to provide subsistence to all its members, Hughes conveniently avoided confronting any other notion of what constituted progress. He never wavered from his commitment to the primacy of subsistence, and for good reason. Insisting that all societies absolutely guarantee subsistence permitted him to condemn free labor without ever having to address the questions of eco-

91. *Ibid.,* 82.

nomic, political, and social progress that a thorough comparison would entail. The only test the free labor society had to face was subsistence, and Hughes found it failing. The "Free-labor organization," he wrote, "does not actualize the subsistence of all. Its imperfections are organic and essential. . . . Its economic system must progress. . . . This reformation must pursue the laws of progress." Progress became, in Hughes's analysis, the transformation of free labor into warranteeism. He stated this conclusion with the assurance of one not troubled by doubts; he had established a universal law of social organization and then pronounced what had to be done to assure compliance: "Wherefore; the system of Free-labor must progress. All must be obliged to labor; because this is the duty of all; this obligation must be civilly enforced, because it is necessary to the subsistence of all."[92]

Hughes's solution to the problem of a free labor society demonstrates the ways in which warranteeism represented the only legitimate basis of social relations. Only in a society in which labor and capital were bound together permanently by state regulation could the unalterable law of universal subsistence be satisfactorily obeyed. Hughes thus shifted the ground of the debate between slavery and free labor. By denying the legitimacy of human property and the rights conferred upon owners of such property, Hughes sought to deny antislavery forces the main target of their attacks. At the same time, he located the free labor society's dependence on the market in labor power as the basis of its inefficiency and disorder. In both instances, he elevated the state to center stage. The state in warranteeism controlled masters who no longer could claim property rights in their laborers and whose authority derived completely from state command, and it eliminated the market in labor power by requiring all laborers to be "associated" to a warrantor at all times. Hughes was not proposing an unqualified defense of slavery. He was advocating a new, universal basis of social relations. Like many of the thinkers he read, Hughes wanted a permanent solution to the "social problem." He found it in the modern authoritarian state under whose watchful eye all social, economic, and political activity took place.

92. *Ibid.,* 182, 195. On the complex relation of southern intellectuals to the concept of "progress," see Genovese, *Slaveholders' Dilemma.*

4

WARRANTEEISM AND FREE LABOR:
HOUSEHOLDS, FAMILIES, AND MARKETS

I n the *Treatise on Sociology* Hughes sought not only to develop his claim that southern society more closely resembled warranteeism than slavery but also to highlight the essential differences between warranteeism and free labor society. He provided the basis for this latter purpose in his theoretical discussion of the nature and function of societies, especially his emphasis on universal subsistence as the first end of any society. But he also focused on specific aspects of life to illustrate societal performance as it related to subsistence, order, and stability. Hughes placed the difference between the plantation household of the South and the free labor household of the North at the center of his defense of the superior character of southern society. Through his examination of the different ways in which households distributed income, related to external market forces, and affected the development of families, Hughes predated present-day historians, anthropologists, and sociologists who have only recently turned to households as vital subjects of historical inquiry and analysis.[1] The *Treatise* testifies strongly to the no-

1. See, for example, Peter Laslett, ed., with Richard Wall, *Household and Family in Past Time: Comparative Studies in the Size and Structure of the Domestic Group over the Last Three Centuries in England, France, Serbia, Japan, and Colonial North America, with Further Materials from Western Europe* (Cambridge, Eng., 1972), esp. Laslett's introduction; Christopher Clark, "The Household Economy, Market Exchange and the Rise of Capitalism in the Connecticut Valley, 1800–1860," *Journal of Social History,* XIII (1979), 169–90; Michael Merrill, "Cash Is Good to Eat: Self-Sufficiency and Exchange in the Rural Econ-

tion that the plantation, understood as a household, and the social relations that developed within it fundamentally contributed to the growth of a distinct southern society. Hughes's examination of the plantation household and its relation to warranteeism also unintentionally but unavoidably illustrates the contradictions that racked both that society and the arguments of those, like Hughes, who sought to defend and promote it.

Most scholars today acknowledge the ubiquity of households throughout history, but problems of definition and application remain. Today's debates over the meaning of the term *household* center around a number of theoretical and practical questions: How should one, if one should, differentiate between family and household? What has been the nature of household production over time and place? How has that production, or lack thereof, related to the dominant mode of production in the broader society? Central to all these questions is the historical context, for households can properly be understood only as units within social systems. The degree to which households incorporate the dominant values and relations of the social systems in which they are embedded varies over time and place. But this variation depends on the nature of the social system, the stage of its historical development, and its relations to other contemporary systems.[2]

---

omy of the United States," *Radical History Review,* IV (1977), 42–71; Harriet Friedmann, "Household Production and the National Economy: Concepts for the Analysis of Agrarian Formation," *Journal of Peasant Studies,* VII (1980), 158-84; Olivia Harris, "Households and Their Boundaries," *History Workshop Journal,* XIII (1982), 143–52; Elizabeth Fox-Genovese, "Antebellum Southern Households: A New Perspective on a Familiar Question," *Review,* VII (1983), 215–53; Fox-Genovese, *Within the Plantation Household;* Gavin Wright, *The Political Economy of the Cotton South: Households, Markets, and Wealth in the Nineteenth Century* (New York, 1978); Allan Kulikoff, *Tobacco and Slaves: The Development of Southern Cultures in the Chesapeake, 1680–1800* (Chapel Hill, 1986); Stephanie McCurry, "Defense of Their World: Gender, Class, and the Yeomanry of the South Carolina Low Country, 1820–1860" (Ph.D. dissertation, State University of New York at Binghamton, 1989); McCurry, "The Politics of Yeoman Households in South Carolina," in *Divided Houses: Gender and the Civil War,* ed. Catherine Clinton and Nina Silber (New York, 1992); and Steven Hahn, "The 'Unmaking' of the Southern Yeomanry: The Transformation of the Georgia Upcountry, 1860–1890," in *The Countryside in the Age of Capitalist Transformation: Essays in the Social History of Rural America,* ed. Steven Hahn and Jonathan Prude (Chapel Hill, 1985), 179–203.

2. Fox-Genovese's *Within the Plantation Household* contains a discussion of recent

The slave South constituted a unique social system. It had been created by the expansion of merchant capital, yet its dominant social relations limited the intrusion of capitalist values and relations even as they assumed prominence in the North. In this unique setting, southern households took form as part of that system, one in which slavery permeated every aspect of life. Hughes recognized the centrality of slavery in southern society in general and in the southern household in particular. Although he did not discuss nonslaveholding southern households, his focus on slaveholding households correctly recognized their dominance in setting the tone and often the conditions of southern life for all southerners, slaveholding and nonslaveholding, black and white, male and female.

Hughes developed his own working definition of households in the *Treatise* but did not make it explicit. Rather, it emerges from his discussions of households in both warranteeism and free labor society. And though he pointed to direct aspects of household life in both societies, he used his concept of the household primarily to illuminate fundamental differences between the two social orders and the labor systems on which they were based.

Proceeding from his notion that warranteeism "associates every laborer to a capitalist," Hughes articulated what was for him an essentially familial relation between the warrantee and the warrantor, both of whom resided in a common household: "The capitalists and laborers are economically affamiliated. The State consists of Families; Families, of (1) Warrantors and (2) Warrantees. . . . The laborer and capitalist belong to the same family. They have a home-association. The household is instituted."[3] This passage contains important points regarding Hughes's conceptions of southern society in general and the nature of the southern household in particular. First, Hughes highlighted the essential but not exclusive economic basis of the "family" in warranteeism. Since the plantation existed, in an economic sense, to produce commodities for the world market and consequently provide subsistence to society's members, the initial "associating" of warrantor and warrantee derived primarily from economic concerns. But once brought together, the "association"

---

treatments of these questions. Most of the works cited in note 1 above touch upon one or more of these questions.

3. Hughes, *Treatise,* 113.

developed into a relation which Hughes believed resembled that of family members residing in a common household. Hughes used the terms *family* and *household* as synonyms, thereby indicating the nonbiological nature of these terms as they applied to southern society. Coresidence, based on economic association, determined the boundary of the household. Hughes did not explicitly state that the southern household he discussed was a plantation, nor did it have to be for his general argument. What matters for this discussion is his assertion that the cohabitation of slaves and slaveholders on the same residential and productive unit and their sharing of a common income pool constitute distinctive elements of southern households.

Hughes, arguing that warrantee and warrantor were members of the same "family," considered the relation between them to resemble most closely that of child to father. The analogy of plantation as family rested on the notion of the warrantor as provider and "father figure." "The head of the family is the capitalist. He warrants subsistence to all." Hughes forcefully emphasized the role of the warrantor as the vital center of the household. The warrantor acted as the political and legal representative to his "constituency," which was composed of all the members of his community. As the "legislative representatives of warrantees," warrantors were obliged "to represent in the government, the interests of the warrantees. The warrantor is the political servant of the warranty [the household or plantation]." But unlike a conventional political representative's relation to his constituents, Hughes likened the warrantor's relation to that of a father to his dependent family members: "It is therefore his duty to act for the political good of the association, as an honest father of family acts for the good of his household." Hughes's use of the father/family analogy not only illustrates the warrantor's paternal relation to his warrantees but also the warrantor's dominant relation to his wife and children. In warranteeism, women, children, and warrantees all related to the polity in the same way: through the warrantor. The household's connection to the polity consisted of the warrantor, who acted for all members of the household.[4]

Just as the warrantor acted for the household in political matters, so too did he in legal ones. Hughes's use of an archaic English legal concept,

<hr />

4. *Ibid.,* 113, 216–17.

the "frankpledge," reveals the ways in which he understood southern households to be both "familial" and composed of nonrelated members. What made those members parts of a "family" was their common relation to the corporate unit headed by the warrantor.

Hughes drew upon the executive method of King Alfred, who reigned from 871 to 899, for a historical model that for him illuminated certain corporate aspects of southern households and southern society generally. In this model, the nation was divided into counties, counties into hundreds, and hundreds into tithings. A tithing consisted of ten families and a hundred consisted of ten tithings. A "tithing man" presided over the other tithing inhabitants, and a "high constable" governed the hundred. According to the law of frankpledge, all of the inhabitants of a tithing were collectively responsible for the good behavior of each adult member of the tithing and were to compel any wrongdoer to come forward and answer for any infraction of the law. *Black's Law Dictionary* succinctly defines a frankpledge as "the pledge, or corporate responsibility, of all . . . to the sovereign for the collective good conduct of a group."[5] In the event that someone committed an offense, the members of the tithing had to pay a fine. This system, Hughes reasoned, used self-interest and corporate responsibility to prevent crime: "Their [tithing members'] economic interest for the execution of laws, was the fear of loss. They were responsible in damages for wrongs within their jurisdictions. In case of laches [neglect to do what is lawful] on the part of the association, this loss for damages was divided, and [a] rate levied on each. The implement for the prevention of wrong, was the fear of this special loss."[6]

Hughes's discussion of tithings and frankpledge and his likening of them to southern warranteeism reflects his understanding of the South as a society that consisted of masters and slaves interdependently bound together in corporate units. He also saw the problem that slavery, or warranteeism, presented in the realm of civil law. Warrantees, as dependents under the control of others, could not be held responsible for their actions as were free persons. Hughes consequently bifurcated warrantees' actions and responsibilities, arguing that warrantees were responsible for their criminal actions but could not be directly responsible for civil ones. Concerning private suits for damages, Hughes argued that

5. Henry Campbell Black, *Black's Law Dictionary* (5th ed.; St. Paul, 1979), 593–94.
6. Hughes, *Treatise,* 267.

"if damages are recovered, they are not paid by the warrantee." Since "warrantees are simple-laborers," and "simple-laborers' means of paying are their wages only," any "reduction of wages" would produce "want." "Damages therefore for wrong by [the] warrantee are not paid by him. They are paid by the warrantee association." In this way, the "association is responsible for the warrantee's wrongs. It answers in its property; and is by this property-responsibility, a general security against wrongs."[7] The warrantee association, or household, as a corporate unit like a tithing, was thus responsible for damages resulting from the actions of an individual warrantee.

The "association is a tithing or hundred," Hughes asserted, and "warrantors are tithing-men or high-constables." Warrantors, as such, functioned as "securities that the warrantees ... keep the peace and be of good behavior," and "warrantees are hundredors and frankpledges: they are a general security for each other."[8] In this model, both warrantors and warrantees, as unequal but interdependent parts of the same household, had vested interests in the behavior of its members. The warrantor, of course, would have to pay whatever fines warrantees were obliged to pay. And warrantees, although incapable of paying monetary fines directly, lost as well because those fines were paid out of the common income pool of the household. Hughes here recognized the corporate reality of the southern household, particularly the way all slaves could be punished if the household suffered economic setbacks such as civil damages or criminal fines. Not only could food rations be cut or work intensified, but slaves could be sold to meet the household's expenses. By asserting that "warrantees are ... a general security for each other," Hughes laid bare an all-too-real aspect of the corporate nature of southern households. For better and especially for worse, the individual slave's, or warrantee's, actions often had collective repercussions.

Hughes's use of the frankpledge model, though flawed in several ways,[9] reinforced his basic point regarding the "familial" character of

7. *Ibid.*, 272.

8. *Ibid.*, 273.

9. Part of the problem of Hughes's likening of the household of warranteeism to the English tithing resided in their fundamentally different component parts. A tithing consisted of freemen, and they were directly responsible for their fellows. These freemen, unlike warrantees, controlled at least some personal wealth, whereas warrantees directly

southern households and particularly the relation of warrantees to warrantors. When the warrantor either brought suit on behalf of one of his warrantees or had suit brought against him because of the actions of one of his warrantees, he acted as any white male in the antebellum South did for dependent members of his family. In these respects, the warrantor household differed primarily from nonwarrantor households in that it contained warrantees as well as dependent kin. Hughes referred explicitly to these similarities when writing of other aspects of the law, further asserting the familial relation of warrantees to warrantors: "By the essence of warranteeism, the interests of warrantors and warrantees, are affamiliated; they are syntagonistic; they are family interests. Grievance to warrantees, is grievance to warrantors; as grievance to wife is grievance to husband." [10] Yet as central as the warrantor was to these legal aspects of the household, his position as the head of that household assumed greatest importance in the realm of economic relations. It was there that the warrantor household most clearly emerged as qualitatively different from nonwarrantor households in general and free labor households in particular.

As we saw in the previous chapter, Hughes argued that free labor society and warranteeism differed essentially in their economic systems. What he termed the "economic order," the way the "laborer" related to the "capitalist," qualified all other aspects of social and private life. For Hughes, the household's fundamental character derived from its relation to the wider economy. In warranteeism, the household related to the economy as it did to political and legal matters: through the warrantor. He linked the household to the outside world while remaining the dominant force within the household as well. As head of the household, Hughes posited, the warrantor acted as the economic agent of the association, participating in the market relations necessary to maintain its viability. Regarding warrantors, Hughes wrote: "The duty for Exchange,

---

controlled none. Thus, although Hughes claimed that "warrantees are hundredors and frankpledges," he had to acknowledge that "in practice now, the loss [from civil damages] falls altogether on the warrantor," rather than directly on each member of the community. Although Hughes's analogy did highlight the corporate, collective similarities between the warrantee household and the tithing, it could not ignore their very significant differences. See *ibid.,* 273.

10. *Ibid.,* 253.

is to act to the best of their ability as the public exchanger and agent of the warranty. They must therefore buy and sell whatever, according to the ability of the association, is best for its welfare." The warrantor acquired the income necessary for the functioning of the household through the market. Although the warrantees produced the goods that yielded this income, the warrantor retained exclusive control of both those goods and that income. Hughes insisted that warrantors monopolize the process of exchange in the market and exclude the warrantees. "They [warrantors] must forbid and prevent buying and selling by orderees [warrantees] to the detriment of industry, health, or police; exchange must be by the exchanger of the association; and production by the producers; the division of labor must be enforced." [11]

Hughes's notion of division of labor entailed that warrantees produced within the household, into which the market did not directly intrude, and that warrantors engaged in market exchange, which ensured the maintenance of the productive household. Warranteeism, Hughes argued, preserved the warrantee's right of exchange, but it was exercised in the form of an "association right." In this sense the warrantee, as part of the household, had his exchange "right" performed by the warrantor: "In warranteeism, the exchanges of the associates are transacted by the head of the association. In the division of labor, that is his function. He aliens, purchases, and administers for all." [12] The division of labor maintained the separation of warrantees from the market and necessitated the participation of warrantors in it.

Hughes's warranteeism household thus related to the market in a peculiar way. As a unit of production, the household responded to the demands of the world market. Yet the relations of production within the household remained fundamentally different than those in capitalist societies in which laborers exchange their labor power for a wage. [13] In short,

11. *Ibid.,* 214. Drew Faust, in *James Henry Hammond and the Old South: A Design for Mastery* (Baton Rouge, 1982), 75, notes that Hammond attempted to prevent his slaves from participating in exchange as a way of reinforcing their recognition of his "omnipotent rule" over his plantation.

12. Hughes, *Treatise,* 231.

13. I emphasize the commodification of labor power as a fundamental element of capitalism to distinguish it historically from other societies, including that of the Old South, that participated in exchange and sought profit but cannot be labeled capitalist without draining the concept of historical precision. I argue that the separation of labor

capitalism did not penetrate the household. For Hughes, this fact directly shaped the status of the laborer in warranteeism, for it affected society's primary obligation to him: subsistence. Hughes's fundamental concern with subsistence for all members of society led him to focus on what he considered the elemental differences in the status of warrantees and free laborers. As members of qualitatively different households, warrantees and free laborers related to the market in different ways. Warrantees, as members of households outside the market, were guaranteed subsistence, whereas free laborers, whom Hughes argued lived in households directly affected by market forces, enjoyed no such guarantee.

Hughes clearly saw the warrantee household as an institution that not only produced a surplus but also pooled income and allocated it to individual members. In all these aspects, control resided with the warrantor. The warrantor, as we have seen, both sold the surplus and purchased the supplies necessary for the household's maintenance. But his obligations also included distributing to all household members their share of the income pool. Warrantees, according to Hughes, received a "wage" for their labor, which constituted their share of the income produced by the household. But he carefully pointed out that this share came through the warrantor: "He [the warrantor] distributes wages out of the aggregate capital." Stressing the direct, paternal nature of the head of the household's care for his dependents, Hughes argued that warrantors had an obligation to distribute sufficient "wages" to all members of the household, regardless of their ability to produce. "It is their [warrantors'] duty to see that the wages of all, whether efficient or inefficient, are duly received, and that none are ever in want." Distribution entailed, primarily but not exclusively, the rightful compensation of warrantees for their labor, but what form this compensation took affected the character of the household. As Hughes pointed out, wages did not necessarily consist of cash payments: "Currency wages are not the only kind. Wages in an economic system, may be paid in consumables." [14]

The form of wages warrantees received was no small matter for Hughes. In southern warranteeism, with the warrantor conducting mar-

---

from the land and the subsequent rise in a market for labor power, in effect the transformation of labor power into a commodity, characterize a capitalist society.

14. Hughes, *Treatise,* 251, 214, 145.

ket transactions and warrantees cut off as much as possible from market contacts, the payment of wages in "consumables" further isolated the warrantees in particular and the household in general from the market. "The process of exchange by the laborer, may be eliminated. He may not buy; he may earn and receive the immediate means of living." The warrantee thus did not come into contact with the market; what he received came directly from the warrantor. Although Hughes used the term *wages* to describe the goods warrantees received from warrantors, and although he advocated statutory enforcement of "minimum wage laws," the day-to-day process of work and compensation remained under the direction and control of the warrantor. The warrantee received his "pay" more as a gift bestowed by the warrantor than as an agreed-upon wage. Hughes did not focus on this aspect of warrantee-warrantor relations, which illustrates the psychological as well as material power of the warrantor. He instead sought to demonstrate that the personal allocation of "the immediate means of living" by the warrantor to the warrantee effectively realized the basic subsistence of all members of the household. His analysis of the free labor household, which related differently to the larger economy and thus the "immediate means of living," demonstrated the failure of that household, and therefore of that society, to realize the subsistence of all its members. And that failure damned the entire social system.[15]

Hughes held that the composition of a free laborer's household differed fundamentally from that of a warrantee's. The warrantee's household included the warrantor, for whom he produced and from whom he received his "wage." Although the free laborer had a similar economic relation to his employer, he did not include the employer as part of his household. In free labor society, Hughes argued, "the laborer and capitalist are free from each other. . . . [They] are not affamiliated. The economic household is not instituted."[16] Warrantees, "efficients and inefficients," as members of a warrantor-controlled household, were "economic constituents" of the warrantor; all depended on him for a share of the income the household produced. And the warrantor was bound by law to ensure that each warrantee received his or her share. But in free labor, only the employees themselves were "economic constituents" of the cap-

15. *Ibid.*, 145.
16. *Ibid.*, 114.

italist. The free laborer had dependents or "economic constituents" of his own; they depended directly on him, not the capitalist, for their income. Together, the free laborer and his dependents constituted a household. The "economic household" was not "instituted"; for the free laborer, in fact, the "economic household" did not exist. Instead, biological, not productive, relations established the household's boundaries. Production occurred outside the household, but income pooling and distribution took place within it. The income pool consisted of the wages received by laboring members from their employers.

Distribution in free labor society was thus a two-stage process: the capitalist paid a laborer a wage, and the laborer then distributed this wage among the members of the household. "The capitalist distributes on contract to the laborer: the laborer; to those he represents, or works for. These are his family. The free laborer's economic constituency, may be his wife, children and inefficient parents. What he earns he divides with them. These are not his co-distributees, but his sub-distributees. Their share from society, comes through him." In free labor society, nonworking members of a household depended on those who could obtain wages through participation in a market for labor power. "In the free labor system, the distribution to a class, is through the efficients. What the inefficients get; come [sic] through them. This is payment to a part, for the whole of a class."[17]

Hughes saw this process of distribution and the system of which it was part as inherently unjust because it imperfectly ensured universal subsistence. By separating the nonworking members of a laborer's household from direct dependence on a capitalist, the system forced those members to rely on the worker's wage (or workers' wages if more than one member of the household labored for a wage). Yet this wage, Hughes argued, was not determined by the needs of the family but by the impersonal market. "Wages . . . ," he stated, "vary. In this [free labor] system, they are free. They increase or decrease. Both the increment and decrement are unlimited and accidental." The unlimited character of wage variation ("in the free-labor system, there is no limit to these variations") threatened to result in distribution that failed to meet what Hughes termed a "minimum standard of justice": a "comfortable sufficiency of

17. *Ibid.,* 149.

necessaries" to every member of society.[18] The fluctuations of the market directly affected a worker's wage and, consequently, his ability to provide a "comfortable sufficiency of necessaries" to his "economic constituents." Because his wage bore no relation to the household's particular needs, it did not guarantee the members' survival. This, Hughes claimed, proved the economic and therefore moral bankruptcy of free labor. "The distribution is unjust. The share of a representative with a large inefficient constituency, may be the same as that of a representative with a smaller constituency. A free laborer with a large and helpless family, gets no more for himself and them; than a laborer with a small family or no family. This is not just; it is wrong. . . . It does not discriminate. It is blind sharing. It is distribution in derogation of subsistence."[19]

If a free labor household proved incapable of sustaining all its members, the fault lay not with the household *per se* but with the system that tied household maintenance to wages earned by laborers in the market. Hughes considered starvation the worst but not the only negative result produced by such a system. Inadequate wages led to crime and disease. While other defenders of slavery and critics of capitalism voiced similar objections about the vagaries of the market and their impact on free laborers and their families, Hughes also alluded to the internal dynamics of family life and how free labor, as a social system, negatively affected them.

Hughes recognized the free labor household as not only the site of income pooling and distribution but of reproduction as well. He argued that reproduction consisted of both birth and maintenance—that, in effect, human beings must be constantly "produced." "Their continuous production is their continuous existence." Such reproduction required flexible sustenance to allow for the maintenance of existing members of a household and to provide for new births and their subsequent needs. But the "blind" wages earned in the market took no account of any exigency that might occur. Thus in the free labor household, reproduction posed potentially serious problems. What was adequate income for a husband and wife might have proven inadequate if they added a child

18. *Ibid.,* 146, 144. Hughes uses these terms, or slight variations of them, throughout those sections of the *Treatise* in which he discusses wages and distribution. See, for examples, 141–42, 144, 152, and 154.

19. *Ibid.,* 149–50.

to their household: "Laborers, on sufficiency, may marry, breed, and make deficiency." This "deficiency" affected the entire family: "If inefficient children divide with parents, wages sufficient for the health and strength of them only; this is to all of them, the want of health and strength."[20]

The free labor household thus placed children, and children placed the household, in unstable, even dangerous situations. The isolation of the free laborer's family, especially the children, from the direct, paternalistic control of capital left it open to the possibility of want: "The child may be supported either by, the (1), parents, or by (2), other persons. These may be capitalists. Parental support is the method of the free-labor system. . . . This method is imperfect. . . . The child's subsistence is precarious."[21] Yet though Hughes wrote primarily of the material disadvantages free labor caused the laborer's household, he implied that material want, with its accompanying vices, was only part of the problem. He also wanted to suggest that free labor households encountered difficulties in familial relations, caused by their dependence on the market, that warrantee families did not. These contrasts emerge most fully in Hughes's examination and analysis of the warrantee family.

Hughes considered the warrantor to be the "head of the family," by which he meant the household or farm/plantation. All who resided in the household saw the warrantor, who controlled the unit's income, as the direct provider of the necessities of life. Unlike free labor, in which a laborer's family received its sustenance through its working members, warranteeism provided for the immediate distribution of sustenance from the warrantor to each and every warrantee. The biological parents of a child were therefore not the primary providers of their child's needs. "The warrantee association is composed of both efficients and inefficients. All are warranted. Every warrantee is an economic constituent of the capitalist. In the distribution, efficients and inefficients are coordinate. They both receive directly, their share of the produce. Payment is first hand to all; and second hand to none."[22] "Inefficient" children related to

20. *Ibid.,* 148, 150.

21. *Ibid.,* 160.

22. *Ibid.,* 154. James Henry Hammond was especially sensitive to the value of personally provisioning his slaves each week. "They should be brought into that contact with the master at least once a week of receiving the means of subsistence from him" (quoted

the warrantor in the same way as did their parents; whether producers or not, Hughes argued, all warrantees received the same attention and care from the warrantor. The market in free labor society, conversely, attended only to those who worked; "inefficients" received nothing directly from it.

But Hughes did not use his examination of the warrantee family to focus exclusively on the material failings of free labor. In the following passage he comments on the character of warrantee parent-child relations and, by implication, on those relations in free labor households: "What warrantee parents earn; they keep. They do not share bread with their sons and daughters. . . . In warranteeism, the relation of parent and child is not economic. It is relieved from that. The father does not sustain the child: the child sustains himself." Hughes maintained that such a parent-child relation eased familial tensions caused by financial concerns. "Children thus, are no privation to parents. The father in nature, is not also the father in art. Sons share their parents' affections, but not their parents' earnings. The filial and parental relations are not economic. They have no economic qualification: they are separated; they are disencumbered of that." [23] Hughes clearly believed that the "economic" dimension of parent-child relations in free labor placed considerable stress on a family's ability to live harmoniously. He in effect argued that warrantee families, "relieved" from economic relations between members, fostered a greater degree of affection.

As a defender of slavery, we should expect Hughes to depict strong affections among warrantee family members. But his comments about familial relations consist of more than a simple attempt to promote the image of happy, loving warrantee families, although that attempt certainly occupied a large part of his argument. He also sought to point out that the tensions free labor households faced grew directly out of their immediate relation to and dependence on the market. Although the entire household depended on the market for sustenance, only working members of the family received wages, which Hughes frequently pointed out took no account of the household's needs. The household's depen-

---

in Faust, *James Henry Hammond,* 103). For more contemporary discussions of food provisioning, see James O. Breeden, ed., *Advice Among Masters: The Ideal in Slave Management in the Old South* (Westport, Conn., 1980), 89–113.

23. Hughes, *Treatise,* 154–55.

dence on its working members, Hughes argued, resulted in tensions that qualified feelings of affection between working and nonworking members in general and parents and children in particular. Hughes did not devote much attention to the specific consequences of these tensions, but his general point regarding the difficulty of sustaining loving relations in the face of impersonal market pressures reveals a subtle insight of the free labor household.

Warrantee families did not suffer from these same tensions, Hughes maintained, because the family did not depend on its working members to support it. Rather, the warrantor allocated "wages" to each warrantee regardless of age or ability. Hughes argued that this process represented advance payment for future services. "Their [children's] wages run from birth. A part of what they may earn during future efficiency is advanced during present inefficiency. Every child supports himself." Whereas children in free labor looked to their natural parents for sustenance, warrantee children looked to the warrantor. The free labor household was separated from capital, but the household in warranteeism constituted a productive as well as a residential unit. The warrantor, as head of that unit, related to warrantees as more than an employer. As coresident and controller of all income, the warrantor occupied a position unknown in free labor. Hughes recognized not only the unique character of the warrantor but also of the household over which he presided in the following brief passage: "For the warrantee association is an economic family. . . . The associates, efficient and inefficient, are civilly affamiliated. The capitalist is the economic head of the family. He is the economic father of all the children." The "economic family," the household, contained within it individual warrantee families; but Hughes forcefully demonstrated the secondary character of those families within the household. The members of those warrantee families did not relate to the master through family units but as undifferentiated individuals. All warrantees, men and women, parents and children, were but "all the children" of the "economic father" of the household.[24]

Although Hughes focused on this dependence and paternalism to strengthen his defense of warranteeism, his analysis thus raises significant observations regarding the nature of the slave family. Hughes's reference

24. *Ibid.*

to all warrantees as "children" underscores the subordinate status not only of warrantees but also of their families within the warrantor's household. Elizabeth Fox-Genovese has argued that the power antebellum planters exercised within the plantation household effectively prevented the development of independent slave households.[25] Her argument does not deny that slaves actively shaped their own personal and family lives in innumerable ways, but it does suggest that the conditions under which they did so were established, for the most part, by slavery and slaveholders. Families could be established and, as Herbert Gutman and other historians have shown, these families provided slaves with an extended kin network that linked them with family members across time and space.[26] But as Hughes well knew, families and households are different things. African-American slaves built families, but they could not, with a few exceptions, build households. The master's control over property, over work, and over mobility circumscribed slaves, denying them, as Fox-Genovese states, "the margin of autonomy or choice that would permit them to constitute anything but fragmentary or truncated households."[27]

Hughes appropriately considered warrantees as members of the warrantor's household. He emphasized the warrantor's crucial role in controlling all aspects of life in his household. The authority Hughes placed in the warrantor served directly and significantly to limit the ability of warrantees to construct their own households. In particular, Hughes's insistence that the warrantor prevent warrantees' participation in market transactions, which constituted one of the few ways slaves accumulated income in the antebellum South, aimed at reinforcing warrantees' de-

25. See Fox-Genovese, "Antebellum Southern Households," 238–49, and *Within the Plantation Household,* 93–99.

26. Herbert G. Gutman, *The Black Family in Slavery and Freedom, 1750–1925* (New York, 1976). For other works on slave families, see George Rawick, *From Sundown to Sunup: The Making of the Black Community* (Westport, Conn., 1972), 77–94; John Blassingame, *The Slave Community: Plantation Life in the Antebellum South* (2nd ed.; New York, 1979), 149–91; Genovese, *Roll, Jordan, Roll,* 443–535; Robert Fogel and Stanley Engerman, *Time on the Cross: The Economics of American Negro Slavery* (Boston, 1974), 127–44; A. J. R. Russell-Wood, "The Black Family in the Americas," *Societas,* VIII (1978), 1–38; Shepard Krech III, "Black Family Organization in the Nineteenth Century: An Ethnological Perspective," *Journal of Interdisciplinary History,* XII (1982), 429–52; Deborah Gray White, *Ar'n't I a Woman? Female Slaves in the Plantation South* (New York, 1985).

27. Fox-Genovese, *Within the Plantation Household,* 94–95.

pendence on the warrantor for necessary provisions. Even if slaves produced as much of their sustenance as some historians claim, the master's
control over this production could effectively subvert autonomous slave
subsistence.[28] Hughes did not refer directly to warrantees' gardens or
traps, but he maintained that all "property rights" warrantees had, such
as shelter, food, and clothing, were "association rights." He could thus
claim that "the right of property, is warranted to warrantees" and then
add, "but warrantees are associates. Their property-right is in its forms,
therefore, qualified by the fact of association. . . . Hence, the warrantee-
associate's right of property, must be associationally exercised."[29] Since
the warrantor, as administrator of the association, retained authority over
all its property, he in effect controlled even warrantees' "personal property." Warrantees owned nothing, and what they possessed was at the
warrantor's pleasure. The power and position of the warrantor simultaneously undermined any possible development of an independent economic basis for warrantee households and reinforced warrantees' identification with the warrantor's household as their own.

In detailing warrantees' "property rights," or the lack thereof, Hughes
sought primarily to highlight the paternalistic and organic nature of
southern warranteeism in contradistinction to the callous and atomized
character of free labor society. He therefore saw the dependence of warrantee families on warrantors as an illustration of the superior quality of
warrantee family life. He especially desired to demonstrate the lack of
those tensions free labor families suffered as a result of their dependence
on an indifferent, impersonal market. Receiving their "wages" from birth
through death from a benevolent warrantor who could adjust to changing
circumstances within the household, warrantees, Hughes argued, faced
none of the "privations" free laborers encountered in trying to distribute
their "blind" wages among all household members. For Hughes these
differences provided ammunition for his larger argument, but they also
posed difficulties for that argument's internal consistency. By seeking to
use the warrantee family's relation to the warrantor as a basis of both his
defense of warranteeism and his critique of free labor, Hughes found

28. On slave food production, see Genovese, *Roll, Jordan, Roll*, 535–40; Rawick, *Sundown to Sunup*, 69–72; Sam Bowers Hilliard, *Hog Meat and Hoe Cake: Food Supply in the
Old South, 1840–1860* (Carbondale, Ill., 1972).

29. Hughes, *Treatise*, 230–31.

himself enmeshed in the contradictions of a slave society embedded in a capitalist world.

Hughes analyzed households in free labor society and warranteeism and their internal relations, but he only partially placed them in broader contexts. He anchored his critique of free labor in the market for labor power that characterized not only capitalist society but also the nature of the household in that society. Hughes underscored the essentially impersonal relation between worker and capital and the material and emotional consequences it had on a laborer's household. By removing production from the home and forcing the laborer to sell his labor power for whatever the market would bear, capitalism affected even the most personal of family relations as wage earners struggled against the vagaries of the market and the demands of providing for dependent family members. Hughes's analysis of the free labor household effectively pointed out the relentless pressure capitalism exerted on all aspects of life. But whereas the market dominates his analysis of free labor households, it remains conspicuously absent from his analysis of households in warranteeism.

Hughes focused much attention on the relations between warrantor and warrantee, which he correctly saw as qualitatively different from those between capitalist and free laborer. Warrantor-warrantee relations developed within the household and outside of direct market forces. These relations, and the household in which they were rooted, formed the basis of a unique southern social order that blocked the full development of capitalist labor relations and their attendant values. Yet these very developments in the South occurred within and as part of an emerging capitalist world market to which the South in general and the plantation in particular were inextricably tied. While the internal relations of production remained outside of capitalism's direct influence, the household, as a unit of production, did not.

Hughes did not acknowledge the South's dependence on external markets, but neither did his analysis suggest some form of autarky. The household existed to sell a surplus in the market and, as a consequence, fluctuations in the market affected the household. Hughes admitted as much. Yet he maintained that even in the event of an individual warrantor's inability to provide the basic needs for one or more of his warrantees, warranteeism could still ensure a warranted subsistence to all. His solution, which he termed the "systematic quantitative adaptation of labor to capital," consisted of a warrantor who could no longer maintain a warrantee "transferring" that warrantee's labor obligation to a warrantor who could. In other words, a master who could no longer afford to provide for a slave's continued existence had to sell him to one who could.

The transfer of warrantees from households that could not ensure subsistence to ones that could theoretically allowed warranteeism to meet the primary goal of any society: universal subsistence. Yet Hughes's notion of a network of households resulted in a problem that echoes one of the fundamental contradictions of antebellum southern society. Hughes praised warranteeism as a system composed of harmonious households in which labor and capital related to one another as members of a common family outside of market interference. The stability and security that Hughes attributed to warranteeism resulted from this internal isolation from market forces. But the warrantor household engaged in market activities, and the household could not remain isolated from market fluctuations. If a warrantor took a beating in the market, he might have to liquidate some or all of his holdings of labor obligations. At this point, Hughes brought in the "systematic quantitative adaptation" of labor and capital to restore the ordered, familial character of warranteeism. What he failed to discuss, for good reason, was that "systematic quantitative adaptation" depended on a market to function properly, a market of labor obligations, a market of human beings.

Hughes's warrantors maintained their households by selling surplus warrantees in an external market. The warrantee family, free from the market in labor power, remained vulnerable to the market in labor. Hughes's emphasis on the household's need to provide subsistence to all its members necessarily subordinated the warrantee family and each of its individual members to the demands of the larger household. Thus, although Hughes stated his disapproval of the breaking up of warrantee marriages through the sale of one of the partners, the logic of his argument forced him to permit dissolution of marriage through sale. "Sundering of husband and wife, *except for subsistence,* is a public wrong, and to be remedied, if needful" (emphasis added). Hughes maintained essentially the same position concerning warrantee children: "Warrantors have no power to separate families, except [when] such separation is essential to the subsistence of all."[30]

30. *Ibid.,* 258, 220.

The "instituted household" of warranteeism could neither remain outside of market influences nor, as a consequence, provide warrantee families with bucolic, isolated security. What it could do, Hughes asserted, was provide individual warrantees with assured subsistence. For him, at least, guaranteed universal subsistence was worth the price of some sundered marriages and separated families. In warranteeism, the maintenance of the warrantee family mattered far less than the larger society's goal of subsistence for each individual. In that sense, warranteeism recognized warrantees first and foremost as members of society and only secondarily, if at all, as members of families. That Hughes's focus on households in free labor society and warranteeism failed to achieve his desired aims can only partly be attributed to his own shortcomings. In a large sense, the failure was not so much Hughes's as the South's. As a slave society, its dominant relations of production fostered a society whose values and institutions, such as the household, set it apart from the capitalist world. But though the relations within the household resisted the intrusion of the market, the society as a whole emerged and flourished as part of the expanding capitalist world economy. The South, and Hughes, found themselves unable to reconcile the contradictions produced in a society whose internal social relations fundamentally differed from the relations of the external markets in which it was inextricably embedded.

The contradiction in Hughes's program for the maintenance of an organic, ordered household through market mechanisms revealed the inherent contradictions of southern slave society and his inability to transcend them. But his examination of households also reveals important contradictions within his own theory of warranteeism.

Conspicuously absent from Hughes's discussion and analysis of households is any sustained mention of the state. Indeed, his depiction of the household in warranteeism represents nothing so much as the quintessence of paternalism, complete with the benevolent warrantor personally attending to the needs of his family, black and white. Yet, as the preceding chapter demonstrated, Hughes rejected the basis of paternalism, the master who exercised direct authority over his slave, who looked to him as absolute provider and protector, in favor of a statist social order in which the state created and controlled all social relations. Hughes made it clear again and again that between warrantor and warrantee stood the state, which could modify the relation between warrantor and warrantee as it saw fit. But when discussing the merits of southern versus northern households, Hughes retreated from his bold vision of warranteeism to the comfortable claims of southern paternalism.

By embracing paternalism and denying the state an active role in the household and its internal relations, Hughes revealed how difficult it was for him to reject those ideas, arguments, and material realities that surrounded him in the antebellum South. Once again he encountered the difficulties inherent in his desire to defend slavery and the South while simultaneously advocating a new statist society. Although he developed a sophisticated and remarkably elaborate alternative social order, he could not dispense entirely with the familiar notions that slavery as a social system engendered among its defenders. Hughes did indeed propose drastic, fundamental transformations in southern society. But he remained a pragmatic defender of slavery as well. As such, he combined, albeit awkwardly and inconsistently, the near-omnipotent state of warranteeism with the benevolent paternalism of southern slavery. The abstractions of warranteeism, as much as they reflected genuine needs and developments of southern society, could not fully displace the appeal of proslavery paternalism that remained grounded in the actual social relations of the slave South. In the years that followed the publication of the *Treatise on Sociology,* Hughes would continue to try to resolve the dilemma of defending southern slavery while concurrently advocating "progress" toward warranteeism.

5

⸙

THE SOCIOLOGIST CONFRONTS THE WORLD
1854–1862

The *Treatise on Sociology* placed Hughes in the public arena, where he remained for the rest of his life. Although he never again published a book-length work, he wrote a significant number of wide-ranging essays, articles, and speeches during the last eight years of his life. He also became an active political presence in Mississippi, endorsing and in some cases initiating proposals ranging from levee laws to the reform of the English language. But the great bulk of his post-*Treatise* activity concerned slavery and the deepening crisis of southern society and politics in the 1850s. His work during these years continued to reflect the contradictory and conflicting tendencies in his thought revealed in the *Treatise* but also demonstrated the application of the principles expressed in the *Treatise* to specific legislative proposals and social policies. Although Hughes never resolved the fundamental contradictions in his thought, during these years he did advocate a course for southern social and political development that unmistakably pointed toward a new social order. Although warranteeism as an internally consistent and fully developed system remained an unrealized vision, Hughes never abandoned his attempt to incorporate its most notable features into southern life: a powerful regulatory state and ordered, stable social relations.

The *Treatise* did not bring Hughes the fame and glory he had hoped it would. In fact, the initial reaction to the *Treatise* was mixed at best. In the scrapbook in which he kept newspaper clippings by or about him, Hughes preserved several contemporary reviews. One reviewer termed the *Treatise* a "curiosity" and suggested that Hughes "ought to have [had] an interpreter." Struggling through the dense, maddeningly idiosyncratic prose of the *Treatise* like many subsequent readers, this reviewer boldly challenged "any plain man to understand the book." But it was not only Hughes's style that this reader found wanting. He also believed that Hughes labored and strained "to demonstrate what nobody denies," and thus "the reader is put to the utmost trouble to find out that he is stating what every body knew before."[1]

Other reviewers, however, though not disputing the peculiar character of Hughes's writing style, did find other aspects of the *Treatise* worthy of praise. An article in the New Orleans *Delta* in April, 1856, nearly eighteen months after the *Treatise*'s publication, noted that Hughes's argument "is framed upon the assumption that the only true aristocracy in the world is the aristocracy of mind." The reviewer termed Hughes's style "scientific . . . aiming not to entertain or relax, but to exhibit 'knowledge classified' truth in order." As for the content of the *Treatise,* the *Delta* writer only pointed out Hughes's call for replacing northern free labor with warranteeism without the "ethnical" qualification.[2]

While both of these reviews concentrated on Hughes's style and the form of his argument, a review by noted southern man of letters William Gilmore Simms virtually ignored these aspects of the *Treatise* and focused instead on the intellectual and political character of its author. In his review, which appeared in the Charleston *Mercury* and was reprinted in several Mississippi papers, Simms praised the *Treatise* as a "profound, searching investigation" that "demands and deserves the careful perusal not only of Southern politicians, but of philosophers in general." But Simms's most lavish praise was for Hughes himself. "This volume," Simms wrote, "fully establishes the claims of Mr. Hughes as one of the most logical and complete reasoners upon the subject [of slavery], of all who have striven in its investigation." Simms, acutely conscious of the need for a respected southern intelligentsia, posited that "in justice to

1. "Treatise on Sociology, Theoretical and Practical," original source unknown, clipping, Hughes Scrapbook, Hughes Papers.
2. "Sociology of the South: Slave Labor, or the Warrantee System, Vindicated," New Orleans *Delta,* April ?, 1856, clipping, *ibid.*

itself, the intellect of the South should be put in possession of this production." He closed his glowing notice trusting that the "people of Mississippi will take early occasion to put [Hughes and his abilities] to their
proper uses." The Port Gibson *Reveille* echoed his sentiment in a brief
article that accompanied a reprint of Simms's review. "We know of no
man," the *Reveille* stated, "who would represent the views of the
Southern people in Congress with more ability and fidelity than Mr.
Hughes."[3]

Simms's and the *Reveille*'s suggestion that Hughes be elevated to a
position of public authority by virtue of the *Treatise* did not find much
support in Mississippi. The limited success of the *Treatise,* even in the
Port Gibson area, prompted Zebulon Butler, minister of Port Gibson's
First Presbyterian Church, to write a letter to the Port Gibson *Herald
and Correspondent* on December 15, 1854. Arguing that the *Treatise* "richly
merits every attention that the papers and public can bestow upon it,"
Butler worried that Hughes's efforts might be ignored even in his home-
town. "Shall this gifted young author have the extinguisher placed on
the flame of his genius by the hands of those coetaneous with his uncle
... or his father?" Butler acknowledged Hughes's difficult style, but he
urged the readers of the *Correspondent* to give the *Treatise* its due. "It is
a great mistake to proclaim the *Treatise* a failure, because of its unique-
ness. . . . It requires reperusal and much mental exercise, but in this there
is pleasure." Butler suggested that such "reperusal" would help southern
readers recognize the persuasiveness of Hughes's argument. "When the
mind of the reader acts in sympathy with the mind of the author, there
will be a full appreciation of his peculiar style, and a repose of soul in the
rightfulness of our 'Warranteeism,' and the prospect of its ultimate results, which few now enjoy."[4]

Butler's final point touched on an aspect of the *Treatise* to which other
commentators also drew attention. His claim that "few now enjoy" the
"rightfulness" and "ultimate results" of warranteeism suggests that in

3. William Gilmore Simms, Letter to Charleston *Mercury,* reprinted in Port Gibson
Southern Reveille, December 30, 1854, and in Port Gibson *Herald and Correspondent,* December 29, 1854, *ibid.* Simms's letter was also reprinted in the Woodville (Miss.) *Republican,* January 23, 1855.

4. "Z. B." [Zebulon Butler], Letter to Port Gibson *Herald and Correspondent,* December 15, 1854, clipping, *ibid.*

1854 many southerners needed to overcome lingering reservations about their social system. The publication of George Fitzhugh's *Sociology for the South* in 1854 led some writers to see a healthy movement of southern thought in the near simultaneous release of two major defenses of slavery in the abstract. "The coincidence of time, subject and title, between these works of those authors is remarkable," wrote one Virginia journalist, "and proves better than anything else can do that the South is rapidly discarding her halfway, namby pamby defence of slavery on grounds of temporary expediency, and preparing to vindicate her institutions upon principles that embrace all time, all latitudes, all races and all conditions."[5]

Another writer, in an article commenting on the advertising prospectus of the *Treatise,* readily endorsed Hughes's abstract defense without having read it. To Hughes's claim that unfree labor constituted the basis of proper social order the writer asserted that to "this pregnant fact the South is becoming alive. . . . Intelligent minds are hastening to the conviction that Slavery is desirable upon higher grounds than mere expediency." For this writer, Hughes's *Treatise* and the ideas it contained helped combat a tendency in southern sentiment that weakened the South's resolve and undermined its struggle against those hostile to slavery. "To admit that slavery is 'an evil in the abstract,' as many Southern men are unfortunately in the habit of doing, by a sort of quiet acquiescence in an arrogant assumption of its enemies, is to concede away the main pillar upon which we should rely." Rather than doubt the moral legitimacy of slavery, this writer suggested that "it is the duty of Philanthropists to propagate [slavery] as a blessing and to disapate [*sic*] the delusion which exists in the minds of the ignorant and fanatical."[6] Hughes's arguments provided fresh ammunition in the battle between slavery and abolition.

Hughes's *Treatise* was thus seen as almost exclusively a defense of southern slavery and of slavery in the abstract. Of all the surviving reviews, none mentions his elaborate theory of the state or its concomitant restrictions on the power of the master. Rather, southern journalists seized upon Hughes's unflinching defense of unfree labor as evidence of

5. "Sociology of the South; or, The Failure of Free Society," original source unknown, clipping, *ibid.* The writer identified Fitzhugh as "of this State," and as a result I have identified the writer as a Virginian.

6. "A Mississippi Book," original source unknown, clipping, *ibid.*

the increasingly uncompromising position of southern proslavery thought. Hughes's attempt to establish a new theory of unfree labor received no attention. Although Simms commended the intellectual sophistication of Hughes's argument, even he did not examine it critically. The *Treatise* remained little read and even less analyzed. Hughes himself would never again write such an abstract and ambitious work. Instead, he turned his attention to the more mundane and practical task of local, state, and regional political action. Yet he did not abandon his vision of a dramatically different social order. Even as he worked and wrote in support of short-term, pragmatic measures, he revealed a continuing attraction to and belief in an ordered, systematic, and centralized society in which a strong and rational government exercised control over fundamental aspects of social, political, and economic life.

Simms implied that Hughes should serve in some public capacity, and the *Reveille* explicitly recommended that he should, but Hughes never held elected office.[7] A "Cotton Planter and Negro Holder" in a letter to the Natchez *Free Trader* of June 20, 1855, did follow Simms's advice and nominated Hughes for Congress as a states'-rights Democrat.[8] That year the Democrats nominated John A. Quitman. As a supporter of Quitman throughout the 1850s and author of a glowing eulogy of him in 1858, Hughes most likely willingly deferred to him, and Hughes's name never surfaced again as a potential candidate. But he remained a fixture in Claiborne County Democratic activities, giving speeches, serving as a delegate to state conventions, and sitting on and chairing various committees. He also became a frequent and active delegate to the Southern Commercial Conventions of the late 1850s. In these capacities Hughes put forth his ideas on a wide assortment of issues. No issue occupied as much of his time or prompted him to write as extensively as the movement to reopen the African slave trade.[9]

7. Several historians have erroneously stated that Hughes was a state senator in Mississippi. A check of the senate membership lists establishes that Hughes never served in that body. For references to Hughes's "senatorship," see Takaki, *Pro-Slavery Crusade,* 20; Faust, ed., *Ideology of Slavery,* 239; and Wyatt-Brown, *Yankee Saints and Southern Sinners,* 174.

8. Cotton Planter and Negro Holder, "Congressional Nomination—Henry Hughes," Natchez *Free Trader,* June 20, 1855.

9. For references to Hughes's political activity, see Natchez *Free Trader,* August 1, 29, 1855, March 3, April 5, September 13, 1858, May 12, June 23, August 29, September

Sentiment in favor of reviving the African slave trade in the latter half of the 1850s grew for a number of reasons. Ronald Takaki, the most thorough historian of the movement, has demonstrated that the slave trade argument constituted a response to several crises in southern society. The increasing price of slaves led some to fear that slaveholding was becoming too narrowly concentrated and that the nonslaveholders' support for slavery would decrease as their chances of becoming slaveholders declined. The importation of Africans would lower the price of slaves and consequently allow more southerners to become slaveholders and defenders of slavery. The growing fear of the South's minority position in the national government led others to support the efforts to reopen the trade to help increase the southern population and, consequently, southern representation in Congress. Concern over foreign competition in cotton cultivation prompted some to advocate an expansion of the slave labor force to increase production and thereby allow the South to maintain its position in the world market. Some southerners believed that an increased supply of slaves would encourage the expansion of southern industry and consequently lessen the region's dependence on the North. The internal slave trade's drain of slaves from upper South states, especially Maryland and Virginia, convinced some slave trade supporters that only new imports could stem this flow and preserve slavery in the upper South. Others saw the trade as a moral issue. To defend slavery but to condemn the trade seemed inconsistent at best and insidious at worst. As the militant proslavery argument developed, more and more southerners recognized that if southern slavery represented the best system of social relations, to weaken it or prevent its expansion by denying it a steady supply of new slaves constituted an immoral act. And if, as most believed, Africans were barbaric, heathen, and incapable of self-advancement, then the African slave trade would be a moral, Christian endeavor that would benefit all concerned.[10]

5, 1859; Vicksburg *Whig,* September 8, 1855, March 13, May 26, October 15, 20, 22, November 30, December 4, 1858; Jefferson (Miss.) *Journal,* January 22, 1858; Port Gibson *Reveille,* November 22, 1858; Natchez *Daily Courier,* August 24, 1858; Jackson *Mississippian and State Gazette,* September 8, 1858; Jackson *Semi-Weekly Mississippian,* April 13, 1855, January 18, 1856, March 26, September 3, November 16, 29, December 1, 1858, May 13, 20, 1859.

10. Takaki, *Pro-Slavery Crusade, passim.* Takaki tends to dwell far too extensively on

To isolate these various strands of the slave trade argument is not meant to suggest that each strand had its own clearly defined constituency. Most slave trade advocates embraced several or all positions at one time or another. Hughes was no exception. In fact, Hughes's writings on the slave trade provide an excellent introductory primer on the various arguments employed by slave trade supporters. But they also reveal Hughes's distinct vision of social organization. Even as he echoed others' arguments, he presented them within a framework that remained clearly his own. In his writings on the slave trade, Hughes attempted to combine the polemical skills of an agitator with the theoretical inclination of a sociologist.

Both Hughes's contemporaries and modern students of the agitation to reopen the African slave trade have rightly seen him as one of the foremost advocates of the revival of the trade.[11] As such, he occupied a minority, extremist position in the South. Majority opinion, even in Mississippi, Louisiana, and South Carolina, where pressure for reopening the trade was strongest, remained opposed to it. Ministers in particular overwhelmingly opposed it and pointed out that although the Bible sanctioned slavery *per se,* it condemned "man stealing." Yet notwithstanding this resistance, Hughes embraced what he termed the "African labor supply" movement with vigor and saw in it the solution to nearly all the South's worries. A list of all the blessings Hughes believed the slave trade would bestow upon the South would fill several pages. Essentially, for Hughes the slave trade provided a platform to advocate reforms designed to remedy certain flaws in the South's economic and political situation and to convey broader notions of the proper development of southern society in general.

---

what he believes was a crisis of guilt over slaveholding and even suggests that the "proslavery argument was to an important extent a response to the psychological need of Southern society to overcome an anxiety based on a feeling of guilt, a feeling that slavery was 'a sin against God'"(78). See Takaki's Chapter 3 for a succinct discussion of the major goals of the slave trade advocates.

11. For contemporary references to Hughes's role in the effort to reopen the trade, see Vicksburg *Whig,* March 13, October 15, 1858, in which the *Whig* refers to "Mr. Henry (African slave trade) Hughes." For historical works noting Hughes's role, see Takaki, *Pro-Slavery Crusade;* Dorfman, *Economic Mind in American Civilization,* II, 935–36; and Wyatt-Brown, *Yankee Saints and Southern Sinners,* 178–79.

In early November, 1857, Hughes began a series of articles for the Jackson-based *Mississippian and State Gazette.* The series of nine major pieces, some of which were divided into several articles, appeared irregularly until April, 1860. In this series Hughes continued to develop some of the themes of the *Treatise,* notably the attack on free labor and the praise of southern warranteeism. He articulated at greater length and detail other views that received less attention in the *Treatise,* especially his thoughts on race and the expansion of the southern labor system. Looming large behind these articles and their subjects was the sectional conflict to which Hughes continually drew the reader's attention. He clearly saw the need to mobilize southern opinion against free labor as a social system and against the concentration of political power by the free labor North. Hughes remained convinced of free labor's essential flaws, and he pointed them out whenever the opportunity presented itself. But he was more immediately concerned with the threat that free labor as a political movement posed to southern unfree labor. Thus his series on the slave trade, like most of his post-*Treatise* writings, focused less on warranteeism as an abstract system than on the necessity of preserving southern society from hostile attack.

In the fourth number of the series, which appeared in December, 1857, Hughes characteristically boasted that "the South is, in the whole world, the only country secure against its laboring class." The potential danger laboring classes posed to social order served as one of his major tests of a society's performance. "The laboring class of every government," he wrote, "is more or less dangerous, and so will be until all governments are perfect, because all the suffering of imperfect society, falls on the laborer." Building on the contention he first made in the *Treatise* that laborers in the South never suffered from want, Hughes argued that the "South, therefore, has the most manageable, because the least miserable of mobs. Its laboring class are the least dangerous because the most comfortable."[12] In an earlier article that focused on the question of "Penitentiary Punishment for Slaves," Hughes had similarly argued: "In England, and in all free-labor countries, the vast majority of crimes less than capital are crimes against property. They are in short such crimes as would not

---

12. "St. Henry" [Henry Hughes], "'Reopening of the African Slave Trade—Sectional and State Security Argument' Number IV," Jackson *Mississippian and State Gazette,* December 2, 1857.

have been committed if the criminal had been in comfort." The "true theory of the penitentiary," he continued, "is to prevent crimes against property." These crimes resulted "from idleness and want." But since "our labor-system eliminates both idleness and want," it "therefore, eliminates the innumerable and enormous crimes against property" that plague free labor societies.[13] Hughes thus turned the argument that slavery invited rebellion on its head, arguing that free labor promoted disorder because by tying wages to market forces it failed to ensure adequate comfort to laborers. "Rebellion, therefore, is sooner or later, the issue of the free-labor system, because in that system wages will, sooner or later, be under the standard of subsistence, and the starvelings become insurgents for the sake of a living."[14] Hughes's use of the phrase "sooner or later" twice in this sentence suggests that, like other contemporary critics of free labor, he focused not on actual conditions in the North but on the supposedly logical outcome of free labor systems.

In addition to reiterating the *Treatise*'s claim that free labor could not guarantee sufficient wages to all members of the laboring class, Hughes's slave trade articles also extended the *Treatise*'s discussion of warranteeism's superior ability to "adapt" the quantity of laborers to the amount of work in a given area. Commenting on the relation between markets for labor in the North and South, he maintained that since labor obligations in warranteeism inhered in capitalized laborers, they circulated like capital to find their highest value. "In the Southern system, capital is interested or economically enforced to circulate labor because labor is capital, and capital hunts the place of its highest appreciation."[15] The cost of providing for a warrantee encouraged masters who held more labor obligations than they could support to "transfer" those obligations to masters who needed additional laborers. As he had in the *Treatise*, Hughes based his analysis on the assumption that masters would exercise

13. Henry Hughes, "Penitentiary Punishment for Slaves," Port Gibson *Reveille*, December 20, 1856.

14. "St. Henry" [Hughes], "'Reopening of the African Slave Trade—Sectional and State Security Argument' Number IV," Jackson *Mississippian and State Gazette*, December 2, 1857.

15. "St. Henry" [Hughes], "'Re-opening of the African Slave Trade—Security Argument—Balance of Antagonisms' Number I." Jefferson (Miss.) *Journal*, November 6, 1857.

a certain degree of cost analysis in their relations with their warrantees. The self-interest of masters ensured the proper balance of workers and work. "Excess mothers misery, but our system warrants the regular circulation of laborers in relief of excess and in supply of scarcity."[16] Through this circulation, warranteeism eliminated the basis for both the property crime and the social unrest that inevitably disrupted free labor societies.

Free labor's inability to circulate laborers adequately from areas of excess to areas of scarcity constituted for Hughes, as it had in the *Treatise,* one of the system's greatest weaknesses. "The free labor system does not [provide circulation]. In that, above all things, this system is a failure."[17] By placing the burden of circulation on the laborer rather than on the capitalist, free labor practically prevented a balance of workers and work, for laborers often lacked the desire, knowledge, or means to circulate "regularly." Surplus labor drove wages down and created the potential for want. For Hughes, these tendencies were hardly accidental. The free labor system "permanently encourages just less than rebellious excess of population to make wages cheap and workmen submissive. It institutes misery."[18]

Hughes saw in free labor's "tendency to crowd together and make an excess of population" the process by which it would realize its ultimate and essential disorder. "This is sooner or later," he wrote, "the defect of all free labor states."[19] Although capitalists desired "just less than rebellious excess of population," Hughes claimed that "sooner or later" a reduction of wages below subsistence would turn submissive workers into "insurgents." Since capitalists could not circulate laborers, and laborers could not or would not circulate themselves, Hughes asserted that the nature of the system led to inevitable conflict. The struggle between labor

16. "St. Henry" [Hughes], "'Reopening of the African Slave Trade—Sectional and State Security Argument' Number IV," Jackson *Mississippian and State Gazette,* December 2, 1857.

17. *Ibid.*

18. "St. Henry" [Hughes], "'Re-opening of the African Slave Trade—Abolition of Antagonisms' Number II," Jefferson (Miss.) *Journal,* November 20, 1857; "St. Henry" [Hughes], "'Reopening of the African Slave Trade—Sectional and State Security Argument' Number IV," Jackson *Mississippian and State Gazette,* December 2, 1857.

19. "St. Henry" [Hughes], "'Re-opening of the African Slave Trade—Abolition of Antagonisms' Number II," Jefferson (Miss.) *Journal,* November 20, 1857.

and capital in free labor society could only produce "despotism if the capitalists govern, and agrarianism if the laborers govern."[20]

Hughes's bleak vision of the future of free labor society focused, as it had in the *Treatise,* on the antagonism and conflict between social classes. He continually appealed to what he saw as the "harmony" and "syntagonism" of warranteeism as evidence of its superiority over free labor. Hughes remained convinced that the goal of social harmony could be achieved only if material needs—universal subsistence—were constantly met. Any system that failed to ensure the fulfillment of those material needs invited social conflict, which Hughes viewed with almost as much horror as he did starvation. In fact, Hughes tended to see the two as parts of a single phenomenon; social conflict was almost always caused by material want. Only by systematically eliminating such want could a society remain permanently harmonious, free of social disorder. But if free labor, as a system, could not eliminate want, it could, through political means, temporarily minimize the degree of social disorder.

Free labor's crisis, Hughes argued, could be delayed, if not eliminated, only if some means were found either to prevent the concentration of surplus laborers or to furnish those laborers with subsistence. The North therefore had to adopt a policy that Hughes labeled "centrifugal." Such a policy consisted of measures "which relieve surplus population. They are any measures which supply work to workmen in excess. They are any measures which procure subsistence for supernumerary subsistees."[21] Yet while the North's policy was necessarily centrifugal, the South's was "centripetal." Whereas the North wanted to encourage dispersion of population, the South, Hughes argued, suffered from a "natural tendency ... to affusion, to a too-rapid circulation from old states to new ... to move and clear new lands, rather than remain and improve old lands." This tendency toward "centrifugalism" constituted "the defect of the Southern labor system as it is." It resulted in large part from the high price of slaves that made it "profitable to transfer labor from old land in old states to new land in the new states, provided the new lands are

20. "St. Henry" [Hughes], "Re-opening of the African Labor Supply—Number Seven—Wealth Argument," Jackson *Semi-Weekly Mississippian,* October 4, 1859.

21. "St. Henry" [Hughes], "Re-opening of the African Slave Trade—Wealth Argument. Number V," Jackson *Mississippian and State Gazette,* February 17, 1858.

cheap."[22] The reopening of the slave trade, Hughes asserted, would reduce the price of slaves and thus both slow down the "transfer" of domestic slaves from old to new states and encourage slaveholders in older states to improve their lands, for the trade "will enable us to expend less for labor and therefore more for fertilizing."[23]

Hughes's pat solution to the problems of land exhaustion and the drain of slaves from older slave states to new lands in the West was hardly convincing. One might ask, for example, how cheap African slaves would provide a Virginia tobacco planter with more money to invest in fertilizer.[24] But Hughes did not elaborate on the differences between the North's policy of centrifugalism and the South's policy of centripetalism only to justify the need for new importations of Africans, although that clearly constituted his main goal. He also sought, and much more successfully one might add, to establish the essential differences between the northern and southern social systems and to demonstrate in particular the ways in which the North's political policy grew out of its labor system and adversely affected the ability of the southern system to survive.

Hughes insisted in his slave trade writings, as he had in the *Treatise,*

22. "St. Henry" [Hughes], " 'Re-opening of the African Slave Trade—Abolition of Antagonisms' Number II," Jefferson (Miss.) *Journal,* November 20, 1857.

23. "St. Henry" [Hughes], "African Labor Supply—Wealth Argument—No. 9. Land Repair," Jackson *Semi-Weekly Mississippian,* April 24, 1860.

24. Hughes reasoned that the three "elements of cost" were land, labor, and fertilizing, and that a decrease in one element would allow greater investment in another. But in a slave-based economy like that of the Old South, a decrease in the cost of labor, which a reopened trade would produce, would not necessarily provide masters who already owned slaves with more liquid capital for investment. Unlike wage labor, which permitted capitalists with the flexibility to divert capital saved from decreased wages to other investments almost immediately, slavery tied up a master's capital in slaves and prevented him from transforming a decline in the prices of those slaves into increased investment capital, unless, of course, he sold them. Thus the sale of slaves provided a Virginia tobacco planter with much of the capital to invest in fertilizer. A drop in slave prices, therefore, would require planters in slave-exporting states to sell even greater numbers so they could acquire capital for agricultural improvements that were needed to maintain productivity on marginal lands. For these planters, a reopened trade would undermine the already tenuous condition of slavery in slave-exporting states. Hughes may have been thinking that a lower price for slaves would have provided new masters with more capital for land and fertilizer, but, for the social system as a whole, a decrease in the price of slaves would not have made significant amounts of investment capital available.

that the North and South differed in fundamental ways, including in their policies regarding population movement. "The radical difference between the Northern and Southern States is this. The defect of the free-labor states is centripetalism and their policy is centrifugalism, but the defect of the slave-labor states is centrifugalism, and their policy, centripetalism." But these differences in policy evolved out of differences in labor systems. "We thus see that the two sections are in antagonism because their policies are in antagonism, and their policies are different because their labor systems are different. Different systems make different policies." For Hughes, such fundamental dissimilarities produced incompatible interests. "Indeed," he claimed, "it may be asserted that now any domestic measure if policy for the North is not policy for the South."[25]

Hughes used the example of a protective tariff to illustrate how a centrifugal measure benefited the North at the expense of the South. A "protective tariff is a measure of centrifugal policy, because such a tariff appropriates the money of the agricultural or exporting section of the Union to employ the surplus labor of that section whose system sooner or later realizes a surplus."[26] Similarly, while "a homestead law is the policy of the free-labor states, because it encourages population to diffuse to the West and thus relieves the excess in the East," it "is not now the policy of the slave states, because it would encourage diffusion, and our population already diffuses so rapidly as to exhaust the older slave states."[27] Both protective tariffs and homestead laws relieved the surplus labor of the North, the former by stimulating domestic industry and the latter by encouraging migration of surplus labor to the West. And both adversely affected the South.

The centrifugal policy of the North included measures such as protective tariffs and homestead laws, but Hughes cited an entire catalog of additional measures, which for years most southern Democrats had op-

25. "St. Henry" [Hughes], "'Re-opening of the African Slave Trade—Abolition of Antagonisms' Number II," Jefferson (Miss.) *Journal,* November 20, 1857.

26. "St. Henry" [Hughes], "Re-opening of the African Slave Trade—Wealth Argument. Number V," Jackson *Mississippian and State Gazette,* February 17, 1858.

27. "St. Henry" [Hughes], "'Re-opening of the African Slave Trade—Abolition of Antagonisms' Number II," Jefferson (Miss.) *Journal,* November 20, 1857.

posed in Congress and to a large extent on the state level as well.[28] Examples of centrifugal measures included "internal improvements by the State, acts to make labor, such as canal enlargements, railroads, parks ... National work-shops, public buildings ... acts for the increase of the army, navy, and all public offices ... poor laws, tax exemptions of laborer's consumables, bread and meat ordinances, government eating-houses, discouragements of immigration, [and] debasing the coin." But the policy itself, Hughes argued, could never succeed because the basic problem inhered in the system itself. "All these are decreed measures which either temporarily or indefinately [sic] and for better or worse, relieve the evils of surplus population, evils which cannot be abolished, except by abolishing the labor-system which realizes them."[29]

Such a condemnation of free labor and its inability to reform itself echoes Hughes's claims in the *Treatise*. But in his slave trade writings Hughes was not and could not be content with simply writing off free labor as a doomed system. He recognized that, however unavoidable the ultimate failure of free labor, in the late 1850s it represented a powerful political force that could, through the very measures Hughes enumerated, delay its ultimate fate for some time. Meanwhile, the South and its labor system, Hughes alleged, would pay for free labor's delaying tactics.

The growth of northern population would eventually precipitate a crisis of subsistence, which would in turn produce open rebellion. Hughes believed that such an eventuality did not lie far in the future. "It is in short, not improbable, not extravagant at least," he wrote in December, 1857, "that before the very next freeze shall thaw, the awful yell of blood

---

28. Although southern states did contribute to railroad construction and other internal improvements, and, as Gavin Wright has pointed out, southern states sponsored a higher percentage of railroad mileage than did northern states, they rarely adopted well-financed programs of internal improvements. See Wright, *Old South, New South: Revolutions in the Southern Economy Since the Civil War* (New York, 1986), 21–24. For southern opposition to federal aid for internal improvements, see George Rogers Taylor, *The Transportation Revolution, 1815–1860* (New York, 1951), who notes that even in 1817 John C. Calhoun could not "command a majority of southern votes in favor of his internal improvements measure" (21). The Confederate Constitution explicitly prohibited federally sponsored internal improvements, although the exigencies of war permitted the government to ignore this prohibition.

29. "St. Henry" [Hughes], "Re-opening of the African Slave Trade—Wealth Argument. Number V," Jackson *Mississippian and State Gazette*, February 17, 1858.

or bread, shall ring from the throats of thirty thousand starvelings mustered in order and under arms in Broadway."[30] To prevent such a calamity, Hughes claimed, the "surplus population of the North must therefore be subsisted at the expense of either the North or the South." Hughes never doubted that the North would use its political power to make the South bear this expense. Arguing that the cost of providing subsistence to the growing number of surplus laborers "must sooner or later impoverish one section or the other," Hughes concluded that "it is of course the North's policy and interest to pauperize the South for the subsistence of Northern paupers." The South would thus become a figurative "poorhouse, garden, and smokehouse" for the North because southern wealth would be expropriated to pay the costs of free labor society's inability to feed its members.[31]

This scenario of northern domination and exploitation of the South would come about, Hughes asserted, through the increasing power of the North in national politics. The "organ" of the North's policy, he claimed, "is the Federal Government, and a majority in the Government make practicable the policy." Such a policy could take several forms but would produce similar results. The policy could be implemented through "indirect taxation which is statutory agrarianism and indirect robbery." Or the North could choose to "disorganiz[e] our labor-system, in order to colonize our lands and provincialize our section." Hughes foresaw the South becoming the North's colony unless the slave trade were reopened and the South could regain a balance of power with the North. Without a reopened trade, he suggested, the South's "relation to the North will be that of Ireland to England, of Hungary to Austria, or of Norway to Sweden." In short, the "South will be a dependency, and we dependents, a province and we provincials."[32]

Hughes argued that the "colonization" of the South would produce far greater evils than dependency. If "Federal power is northernized," the resulting policy would "disorganize our labor-system and thus ruin

30. "St. Henry" [Hughes], "'Re-opening of the African Slave Trade—International Security Argument' Number III," Jackson *Mississippian and State Gazette,* December 2, 1857.

31. "St. Henry" [Hughes], "Re-opening of the African Slave Trade—Wealth Argument. Number V," Jackson *Mississippian and State Gazette,* February 17, 1858.

32. *Ibid.*

the property of the South and its means of reproduction. Then Northern ambition will with federal honors and emoluments, aggrandize Northern States and citizens, and practice on us knee-benders of the lick-spittle section, the monopolies of monarchs."[33] Hughes thus combined his analysis of the inherent crisis of free labor with an appeal to southern notions of liberty and honor. The slave trade could not prevent the inevitable collapse of free labor, but it could shield the South, through a balance of political power, from becoming the subjugated colony whose wealth would delay that collapse. Hughes recognized that the question of the superiority of unfree over free labor meant little compared to the realities of political power. The slave trade became a political necessity to prevent federal authority from becoming "northernized." Here one sees clearly that Hughes did not fear political power *per se*—as a thoroughgoing statist he could and would not—but the wielding of political power by the South's enemies who sought to destroy the South's social order.

Hughes urged southerners to avoid allowing a "deluded, despotic and meddling mob of another section fast growing into an overpowering and aggressive majority" to "tell us in insult to our sacred honor" that "our negro labor system is a moral evil soon to be ended" and the proposed "negro labor supply is a malignant felony never to be begun." For Hughes, the slave trade became both a point of honor and the means of survival; for southerners not to support it reflected the prevalence of a "lickspittle policy" in the South. "Our past policy has been to lick the spittle squirted on our beards and kiss the polluted boot which kicks our cringing bodies."[34] Such behavior on the part of southerners was especially ignominious because by failing to import African slaves, not only would the North reduce the South to abject dependence, but the lack of plentiful slaves would force southern white women to perform menial labor. Hughes forcefully employed the powerful cultural icon of the southern lady in his efforts to arouse southern support for the slave trade.

In the slave trade writings Hughes underscored the intimate relation between slavery and the position of women in southern society, although he did not always do so consistently. In an article from December, 1857, he asserted that in "the South alone, the Caucasian woman is not a cook

33. *Ibid.*
34. "St. Henry" [Hughes], "Re-opening of the African Labor Supply—Number Seven—Wealth Argument," Jackson *Semi-Weekly Mississippian,* October 4, 1859.

and chambermaid but a queen."[35] But his assertion reflected the ideal, and in the later numbers in the series he acknowledged that reality contradicted this ideal, to the shame of southern men. In an October, 1859, article Hughes argued that although "menial service does not degrade," it was also true that "if the menial servant's talents fit him for a higher grade, then menial service is a degradation." Hughes incorporated into this discussion a rather unsophisticated but interesting Aristotelian notion of human nature. "Nature's grades must be respected, . . ." he wrote, "and social status should be proportioned to natural grades." In language reminiscent of the *Treatise,* he concluded, "and the State should graduate like nature." It was the state's responsibility somehow to follow the law of nature in affixing status as well as ensuring subsistence. "But," he warned, "if grades are natural, and the people contradict nature, then the people lie, and a State lie is always the mother of miseries." He lamented that the current position of southern white women "contradicted nature." "Such a flagrant wrong the ladies of our land now suffer. Our menials are our mothers, sisters, wives and daughters." He then returned to his notion of natural grades. "Are they fitted for higher duties? Who asserts that they are not?" Yet "in sixty-nine out of seventy families we make our household angels cook and scrub. That is hardly the Caucasian woman's mission." The southern state, by allowing southern white women to perform menial labor, not only violated southern cultural ideals but also contradicted "holy nature's true law of toil."[36]

Hughes focused on the "degradation" of southern white women, as he had on the nature of free labor's tendency toward surplus labor and domestic rebellion, both to alert southerners to the necessity of reopening the slave trade and to demonstrate the irreconcilable nature of northern and southern social systems. By refusing to reopen the trade, southerners meekly accepted northern domination and willingly condoned the degradation of southern white women. In both cases, Hughes emphasized, southerners shamed themselves. "We are a gallant people," he suggested,

35. "St. Henry" [Hughes], " 'Reopening of the African Slave Trade—Sectional and State Security Argument' Number IV," Jackson *Mississippian and State Gazette,* December 2, 1857.

36. "St. Henry" [Hughes], "Re-opening of the African Labor Supply—Number Seven—Wealth Argument," Jackson *Semi-Weekly Mississippian,* October 4, 1859.

"but are we gallant enough to relieve our ladies?"[37] Regarding the impending "northernization" of federal power and the subsequent "colonization" of the South, Hughes wrote contemptuously that there "shall be noted in indignant history, three crouching commonwealths, three bastard people or Spaniel States, whose citizens or subjects deemed the sons of illustrious sires, could not hold their own, but kissed the cowhide and danced to their father's clinking castanets.... Then shall modern Greeks, modern Romans, and modern Southerners be reckoned kindred peoples."[38] In his discussion of the degradation of women, he was, if anything, more impassioned. Violating a law of nature was odious, but the South's shame was compounded by its violating that law out of subservience to the North: the South's "servility is doubly base because we are submissive not to a sage and soldier king worthy of our loyalty ... but to an insulting, usurping and ravenous rabble, who are our fellow-citizens in all but fellowship and our brothers in all but brotherhood."[39]

In his slave trade writings, Hughes thus condemned the South first and foremost for bowing to northern opinion and pressure. Although the slave trade would help solve the problems of southern "centrifugalism" and the degradation of white women, Hughes used the issue primarily to draw southern attention to the political and ideological struggle with the North and to the South's need to recognize and resist northern threats to southern society. The fundamental antagonism between the North and South, which Hughes always asserted resulted from different labor systems, had developed to such a degree that in February, 1858, he concluded "that our country is no longer homogeneous." The North's ability and intent to use its superior political strength to thwart the South's only hope for political equilibrium—the slave trade—proved to Hughes that "our sections are not fragments, pieces or segments, but in themselves, integers, units or crystals." Hughes expressed this growing sense of southern nationalism simply: "We are two peoples."[40]

37. *Ibid.*

38. "St. Henry" [Hughes], "Re-opening of the African Slave Trade—Wealth Argument. Number V," Jackson *Mississippian and State Gazette,* February 17, 1858.

39. "St. Henry" [Hughes], "Re-opening of the African Labor Supply—Number Seven—Wealth Argument," Jackson *Semi-Weekly Mississippian,* October 4, 1859.

40. "St. Henry" [Hughes], "Re-opening of the African Slave Trade—Wealth Argument. Number V," Jackson *Mississippian and State Gazette,* February 17, 1858.

Hughes proposed reopening the slave trade as a cure for the South's troubles, which included a labor shortage that prevented adequate workers for new manufacturing, the exhaustion and desertion of older lands, and the degradation of white women. He hoped to mobilize southern opinion in favor of the trade and interpreted southern opposition to the trade as the product of shameful capitulation to northern domination. Hughes evoked Greece and Rome not to compare their glory to that of the South but to warn his fellow southerners of the fate of those two peoples in the modern world. Unless the South recognized the danger posed by the free labor North and acted decisively to alleviate its inferior position in national politics by reopening the trade, only secession could prevent the South from sharing the fate of modern Greeks and Romans: political domination and humiliation.

To overcome northern dominance and avoid historical infamy, Hughes urged southerners to develop attitudes that would prove equal to the challenge before them. Since only unequivocal opposition to northern aggression could protect southern society, southern children had to be raised to "make them masters of their country's emergency and defenders against their country's ruin." Let us hope that he meant to be satirical or to shock when he advised that "the babies whose blood is thin and face is white, be sweetly and piously smothered with wet towels; or strangled between the thumb and finger for such pale imps make compromisers." But he was deadly serious in suggesting that children "play most with the rod that they may long for the rifle, and most with the scabbard that they may prize the sword." He concluded: "Soon swords only can save us, and if the spirit of compromise still is the spirit of our citizens, soon the sword will be no savior."[41] Hughes's claims that the slave trade would eliminate all of the South's problems fade in contrast to these desperate pleas for southern militancy against northern encroachment.

Hughes repeated these pleas for southern mobilization against the northern threat in writings that did not relate to the slave trade. In one of his most forceful and succinct post-*Treatise* articles, "New Duties of the South," which appeared in the November 18, 1854, Port Gibson *Reveille,* he argued that since "the slavery discussion has been puffed and

41. "St. Henry" [Hughes], "Re-opening of the African Labor Supply—Number Seven—Wealth Argument," Jackson *Semi-Weekly Mississippian,* October 4, 1859.

blown from a few sparks and splinters into a flame ... we must now fight the fire, or be burnt up." After noting that "that namby pamby twaddle about the 'moral evil of slavery,'" was "the tap-root of all our evil," because "many of the best and sincerest men adopt it," Hughes defiantly declared "*We want, and now must have, a new verdict of the world on the slavery question.*" To achieve this new verdict required a wide dissemination of knowledge about slavery's true character. "Let the home institution be known," Hughes proclaimed, "and we challenge any man, rising from the study of it, to call one of its essentials 'a moral evil.'" [42]

Although the spread of knowledge about slavery outside the South was necessary, Hughes argued that within the South southerners themselves had to become better advocates of slavery in order to overcome "the old opinion against us." And since many of the "best and sincerest" southerners believed that slavery was immoral, the internal climate of opinion also needed drastic reform. Hughes understood that the struggle for slavery first required that southerners thoroughly master the proslavery argument so they could then combat the enemies without. Education was central to this task. "The schools must help. The young men must be taught to reason the matter. They must learn why our home system is not wrong; why it is right; and be able to give the reasons for it." The only way to respond to the "agitators" who "have by threats and fraud, actualized abolition every where upon the continent" was to prepare a generation with the proper knowledge and will to meet and defeat those who threatened southern society. [43] Hughes did not doubt that knowledge would defeat those enemies as effectively as would combat. In another article he wrote, "Let us respond. Let us answer back. Let us be patient. Let us teach and explain, quietly argue and completely prove. The time has come." [44]

Hughes thus used his post-*Treatise* writings to warn the South of the immeasurable dangers posed by free labor's growing political and ideological strength. And though his arguments for the reopening of the slave trade were not particularly original, they did express new dimensions to

42. Henry Hughes, "New Duties of the South," Port Gibson *Southern Reveille,* November 18, 1854, clipping, in Hughes Scrapbook.

43. *Ibid.*

44. Henry Hughes, "A Law Is Not Its Legislation, But Its Execution," Port Gibson *Reveille,* n.d., clipping, in Hughes Scrapbook.

the political and social thought he had outlined in the *Treatise*. Just as his analysis of North-South relations reflected a heightened concern over immediate political developments, so too did this analysis reveal Hughes's increased sensitivity to the practical realities of southern society in the late 1850s.

One of the most intriguing manifestations of this increased sensitivity is the emphasis on race in the slave trade writings. Race occupied a secondary position within the larger framework of the *Treatise*. And although Hughes employed racial arguments more frequently in his slave trade writings, they remained peripheral to his essential purpose: the mobilization of southern opinion against northern domination. Nevertheless, Hughes's use of race indicated a heightened appreciation of its powerful presence in southern thought and an increased willingness to appeal to it. Although he did not abandon his claim that the racial character of southern warranteeism was "accidental" and "not essential to theoretical or abstract warranteeism," his shift in focus from abstractions to contemporary realities led him to articulate his thoughts on race and its relation to southern development to a much greater extent than he had in the *Treatise*.[45]

The continuity between the racism of the *Treatise* and that of the slave trade writings is evidenced most clearly in Hughes's discussion of race mixing. In the *Treatise* Hughes vehemently denounced miscegenation as "heinous" "degeneration" and a violation of a law of nature; in the slave trade writings he extended these sentiments and widened their application to peoples of various ethnic and racial backgrounds. Unquestionably his strongest statement regarding race appeared in a December, 1857, article. Displaying his strong support for slavery's expansion, Hughes claimed that "if the African slave trade shall be reopened, all Mexico, all Central and South America may be reckoned wild land." He clarified

---

45. Hughes, *Treatise*, 207. Although Hughes unquestionably placed greater emphasis on race in his later writings as compared with the *Treatise*, it is unreasonable to claim, as John McCardell has, that Hughes's writings as a whole "vividly reveal the transformation of Southern proslavery thought from paternalism to racism." As will be argued below, Hughes's increased emphasis on race did not entail the wholesale rejection of the nonracist, authoritarian thrust of his thought, as McCardell suggests. See McCardell, *The Idea of a Southern Nation: Southern Nationalists and Souther Nationalism, 1830–1860* (New York, 1979), 358.

his meaning of "wild" by adding that "they may be esteemed not only uncultivated but unpeopled lands." Hughes argued that although populated, these areas contained "either pure blood or mixed." He then boldly asserted that "if mixed blood, extinction by degeneration or sagacious and benevolent extermination for the purity of races is a certainty and perhaps an ethical duty." To believe that mixed bloods would eventually prove unable to reproduce was a commonplace in antebellum America, but Hughes's call for "extermination" represented a dramatic departure in racial thought. Since the "purity of races" constituted a natural law, he saw no alternative to the "ethical duty" of extermination.[46]

Hughes separated the "pure blood" inhabitants of Latin and South America into three groups: Caucasians, Africans, and Indians. He did not discuss what was to be done to Caucasians because "there [were] virtually none." But the racial character of the other groups determined their destinies. Not surprisingly, he proposed that the Africans "will be elevated into slavery." Such "elevation," he explained, was necessary "to prevent, amongst other atrocities, that of sexual amalgamation."[47] As it had in the *Treatise,* the prevention of miscegenation remained one of slavery's most important functions. Unlike the *Treatise,* however, Hughes here called for the "elevation" of Africans into slavery purely to prevent an atrocity, not to realize a more just and efficient social order. He thus moved closer to justifying slavery as an effective method of racial control rather than as the ideal system of social relations for all societies regardless of their racial composition.

"And as to the pure blooded Indians," Hughes concluded, "they will not be civilized, and therefore must, directly or indirectly, be benignly

46. Hughes, *Treatise,* 239–40; "St. Henry" [Hughes], " 'Reopening of the African Slave Trade—Sectional and State Security Argument' Number IV," Jackson *Mississippian and State Gazette,* December 2, 1857. For a discussion of several antebellum advocates of the idea that mulattoes could not reproduce over several generations, see William Sumner Jenkins, *Pro-Slavery Thought in the Old South* (1935; rpr., Gloucester, 1960), 264–68. Also see Josiah C. Nott, one of the foremost advocates, "Two Lectures on the Natural History of the Caucasian and Negro Races," in Faust, ed., *Ideology of Slavery,* 208–38, esp. 228–32.

47. "St. Henry" [Hughes], " 'Reopening of the African Slave Trade—Sectional and State Security Argument' Number IV," Jackson *Mississippian and State Gazette,* December 2, 1857.

slaughtered." Unlike his earlier advocacy of extermination of mixed bloods, which grew directly out of his notion of "purity of race," this statement demonstrated that Hughes believed that some races, although "pure," were nonetheless so naturally inferior that extermination was their ultimate fate. And since Indians faced inevitable extinction, southern Caucasians would civilize the "wild" lands "from the head waters of the Red River to the highlands of Patagonia." The language Hughes used to depict this process explicitly reveals his gendered and sexually charged conception of nature and its subjugation. These vast lands, he wrote, may "be deemed . . . a young virgin soil hot flushed, leering, and in a languish smile, and pant for the impetuous ardor and prolific charge of the Caucasian deflowerers."[48] Such images of Caucasian virility reveal his sense of the power of white men to transform ("deflower") nature through domination. Civilization required the extermination of some inferior peoples, the enslavement of others, and the rape of "virgin soil" by Caucasians, for "Caucassians [sic] are the world's governing class."[49] No Caucasians, Hughes maintained, were better suited for these tasks than white southerners.

Hughes praised southerners as "the quintessence of Caucassianism [sic]." Unlike other Caucasian peoples, southerners were not "heterogeneous RACES incestuously amalgamated" but "the rare, the racy, refined, unconquerable and magnificent mingle of homogeneous breeds." Hughes extolled the unique blending of French, Norman, Spanish, Welsh, Irish, Teutonic, and Scot "bloods" that resulted in southerners being "the first of the first race." An examination of "our people's stud book," he boasted, would convince anyone that the "blood of Rome was dishwater to our people's."[50]

This concern with "breeding" prompted Hughes to advocate what might best be termed an unrefined policy of eugenics. As some of the passages quoted above, such as his recommendation that "babies whose blood is thin and face is white, be sweetly and piously smothered," suggest, Hughes proposed exercising control over reproduction so that only "proper" children were raised to adulthood. Although various societies

48. *Ibid.*
49. "St. Henry" [Hughes], "African Labor Supply—Wealth Argument, No. 8. Manufactures," Jackson *Semi-Weekly Mississippian,* February 3, 1860.
50. *Ibid.*

throughout history have practiced some form of euthanasia on sickly or deformed infants as a method of population control, Hughes advocated a far different practice. One of the clearest expressions of this tendency in his thought appeared in a speech he gave on March 4, 1857, at a rally for the Port Gibson Riflemen, a local unit in which he served as lieutenant.

In a manner reminiscent of the interest in heroes Hughes had expressed in his diary, the speech focused on the need for a "New Washington" to lead the South and ultimately the world. Hughes posited that "all progress is either the commencement, continuance or close of revolution" and that "we ourselves, are in a revolution, and . . . this revolution . . . must have a hero or Washington." The tasks of the "New Washington" entailed not only political and military responsibilities but also a "duty . . . to promote the health of humanity." The paramount goal in fulfilling this duty was the birth of what Hughes termed "the Thorough-bred Generation."[51]

This "Thorough-bred generation" represented the physical perfection of humanity. Contrasting its men with "the dwarfing city's pale abortions," Hughes envisioned them as "wondrous men of nearly giant stature, their forms all symmetry, their faces all beauty, and motions all grace, their sinews like steel, their locks all silk, and looks all love."[52] Hughes's fascination with the ideal male form reflected but one part of his larger belief in the perfection of humanity and its institutions. In the final pages of the *Treatise* he had asserted that the "consummation of its [warranteeism's] progress, is the perfection of society."[53]

Hughes's interest in "progress" and "perfection" surfaced in all of his writings—political, personal, and scientific. In fact, the desire to perfect all aspects of human existence constituted one of the most constant elements of his thought. He filled his diary, as we have seen, not only with prayers and wishes for personal greatness but also with the conviction that both personal and societal perfection were possible through knowl-

51. [Henry Hughes], Untitled clipping ["New Washington"], in Hughes Scrapbook. An earlier clipping from the Port Gibson *Herald and Correspondent* mentions the date of Hughes's speech and the occasion. From that article I have concluded that the untitled clipping is the text of the speech mentioned.

52. *Ibid.*

53. Hughes, *Treatise*, 291.

edge and will. The *Treatise,* in large part, sought to establish the proper model and principles for social perfection. Similarly, Hughes devoted his scientific essays to the search for perfection. For instance, in an unpublished lecture titled "Theory of Capillarity," Hughes claimed that "because it is a science, agriculture is progressive. It goes on to perfection." Capillarity, he posited, "is an agricultural process. It is an element of farming. If therefore agriculture is perfect, the theory of capillarity must be perfect." Hughes again emphasized, in good Baconian fashion, that the ultimate goal of intellectual activity was social utility. "For if agricultural theories are not perfect, agricultural practice cannot be. But if practice is not perfect, production cannot be." Even in this essay, Hughes eventually returned to the paramount social questions that informed nearly all his work. "And if agricultural production is not duly perfected, men sooner or later will starve." The control of nature, like the control of the self and of society, would ultimately yield perfection. "With her poetic eye, Science looks forward to the perfection of agriculture and medicine. She looks to see plenty everywhere, and no starvation." Hughes's romanticized view of scientific progress matched his vision, best expressed at the end of the *Treatise,* of a future utopia: "She [science] looks for the rise of new patriarchs, whose hale, hearty length of life shall span and measure all time's furlongs, from the budding of new republics to their full bloom. She looks toward the new Eden."[54]

Just as agriculture could be perfected through study and application, so too, Hughes insisted, could language. In an essay titled "The New Science: Aristology, or that Branch of Philology whose end is the Perfection of the English Language—Aristologic Formulas," which Hughes delivered on March 8, 1858, before the New Orleans Academy of Science, he asserted that because languages change, "the changes must be either proper, and therefore progressive; or improper and therefore regressive." But how could changes be controlled so that the language progressed rather than regressed? Not surprisingly, Hughes maintained that only public regulation could ensure progress. "The changes of language," he wrote, "may be regulated. Its regulator is of course the philological umpire. This may be systemized as in France, where the Academy arbitrates all changes; or it may be free as in the United states, where popular usage

54. Henry Hughes, "Theory of Capillarity, January 1, 1855," in Folder 4, Box 1, Hughes Papers.

is the arbitrator." Hughes's evaluation of these two methods once again reveals his repudiation of freedom in favor of control. Only ordered, controlled processes could effect progress. "Progress in the regulation is of course progress in the regulator, and the systemized philological umpire is as much better than the free philological umpire, as association is better than dissociation, or system better than disorder."[55] The progress of language, like the progress of society, could not result from freedom but from systematic, expert control; disorder, whether in language or in society, was the greatest of evils.

Hughes's general idea that progress "goes on to perfection" received further elaboration in a lecture titled "Hebe or Hygienic Worship" that he delivered to the young women of the Port Gibson Academy in June, 1855, and later incorporated into a series of "Woman in Sociology" lectures that he presented in New Orleans and Vicksburg in 1856. Acknowledging that "none are all perfect; that is impossible," Hughes nonetheless reminded his young audience that "God's service is religion and that is not to be perfect, but to approach it as nearly as possible. Going on to perfection is piety. Man's progress is God's praise." After noting and detailing the different kinds of progress humanity pursues, he concluded that "God's service is to go on to perfection, and this is progress either ethical esthetic or educational, economic, political or hygienic," and though these "are technical terms," Hughes assured his listeners that "in the new movements of humanity, they will become as common as household words." His concern for health led him to declare that "perfect health is the law of nature, and the law of nature is the law of God. . . . Sickness is sin." Yet, as we would expect, the perfection of health was not to be attained for its own sake. "If we praise God by perfect health, we are then more fit to go on to other perfections."[56] Progress took many forms, but all brought humanity closer to complete perfection.

55. Henry Hughes, "The New Science: Aristology; or, That branch of Philology whose end is the Perfection of the English Language—Aristologic Formulas," New Orleans *Sunday Delta*, n.d., clipping, Hughes Scrapbook. This essay can also be found in Lyman, ed., *Selected Writings of Hughes*, 197–205. Hughes was one of the founding members of the academy and its first treasurer. See Reinders, *End of an Era*, 145.

56. Henry Hughes, "Hebe or Hygienic Worship," in Folder 4, Box 1, Hughes Papers. For references to this lecture in the "Woman in Sociology" series, see Natchez *Free Trader*, April 8, 1856, for the New Orleans presentation and Vicksburg *Whig*, May 16, 1856, for the Vicksburg appearance. The types of progress listed here—the ethical, aesthetic, ed-

Thus progress toward human perfection included perfecting the body through "esthetic" and "hygienic" progress. In his speech on the "New Washington" Hughes maintained that this new leader "must therefore be the Esculapius [the ancient Roman god of medicine and healing] of the new health." The New Washington need not be a practicing doctor but rather "the great medical jurisprudent." Hughes conceived of this "medical jurisprudent" as a supervisor of social health, one who assured that "progress" continued in the best interest of the race. The New Washington had to know "how to direct and administer the skill and knowledge of others not merely to the cure nor to the prevention of disease but to the scientific and systematic, bodily, blood-progress of the race."[57] The application of science to the "blood-progress" of the race would help produce perfect humans and thereby realize God's will. But to neglect or violate this "blood-progress" threatened such perfection and transgressed God's will.

Hughes's preoccupation with the superior character of white southern "blood" and its relation to the perfect race led him to view with horror any possible "pollution" of that blood. In an article called "Right to African Contract Labor," which appeared in *De Bow's Review* in 1858, Hughes contended that to deny the South the right to import African contract laborers was to help realize "a whole people degenerated by helpless amalgamation with filthy blood of blacks freed by the unbalanced increase of anti-slavery States." In contrast, to permit and commence the labor supply would ensure "the victorious regeneration of our own pure and excelsior blood, preserved by unabolished caste, and made even more fine and heroic by thorough breeding."[58]

Hughes reiterated these themes at the Southern Commercial Convention of 1858 in Montgomery, Alabama, where he introduced a resolution regarding the possible introduction of Chinese laborers into the South. According to the New Orleans *Delta*'s report from the convention,

---

ucational, economic, political, hygienic, and religious—correspond to six of the seven "bodies" or systems of the "heptarchy" that Hughes discussed in "Theoretical Sociology" in the *Treatise*. The only "body" missing is the religious.

57. [Hughes], ["New Washington"].

58. Henry Hughes, "State Liberties; or, The Right to African Contract Labor," *De Bow's Review*, n.s., 1 (o.s. XXV), No. VI (December, 1858), 626–53. The article originated as a pamphlet published by the office of the Port Gibson *Southern Reveille*.

Hughes's resolution called for a committee to report to the next convention "whether amalgamation between the Anglo-American and Chinese races will be a desirable progress or a degeneration." Hughes's concern over white-Chinese "amalgamation" demonstrated the degree to which his ideas of race and class had intertwined. Race, in a racially diverse society, to a large extent determined class. The *Delta's* correspondent expressed Hughes's reasoning: "If the amalgamation of the Chinese with our white race is a degeneration, then there must be 'caste for the purity of the races.' But if there is caste, then our Chinese laborers must be subordinated, or made warrantees." The Chinese, like Africans and African Americans, had to be denied political rights because "political amalgamation realizes sexual amalgamation." Hughes thus argued that any race that would "degenerate" whites had to made subordinate to whites so as to preserve racial purity. In short, as Hughes explained in Montgomery, "the quality of the coolies' blood will affect the quality of the coolies' status."[59]

In those writings that dealt with other races, Hughes presented the outlines of a theory of race relations that linked progress with Caucasian racial preservation and the subordination and/or extermination of "inferior" peoples. By endorsing eugenics and raising the specter of race mixing Hughes sought both to elevate the self-image of all whites in the South and to convince them that only slavery and the reopened slave trade could preserve that which made them superior: their "blood."[60] Although this effort reflected an awareness and response to the powerful racism of the antebellum South, it threatened to add to the contradictions and inconsistencies in Hughes's thought. Although he maintained that

59. "Clear as Mud!," article taken from Montgomery correspondent of New Orleans *Delta* and published in Vicksburg *Whig*, May 26, 1858. Although Vicki Vaughn Johnson discusses the Montgomery convention in her *The Men and the Vision of the Southern Commercial Conventions, 1845–1871* (Columbia, Mo., 1992), 146–54, she mentions neither Hughes nor the debate over Chinese labor.

60. Hughes's ideas on eugenics were not systematic, and he never returned to them in his later writings. Eugenics, as Mark Haller has demonstrated, did not develop significantly in the United States until after 1870. Hughes's ideas thus constitute an early expression of what would become, by the first few decades of the twentieth century, a widespread concern about "breeding" and its relation to "human progress." For more on the development of American eugenic thinking, see Haller, *Eugenics: Hereditarian Attitudes in American Thought* (New Brunswick, 1963).

southerners were the "first of the first race," his emphasis on "Caucasianism" seemingly weakened his critique of other white societies; judging a society by its ability to maintain racial purity might have allowed for social systems other than warranteeism to be acceptable. His dire warnings about the fate of white southerners if slavery were ever abolished narrowed his focus by making slavery a matter of specific racial policy, not of universal social organization. In one article, Hughes approved of the wider application of a Georgia law that barred slaves from being public skilled laborers for then "everywhere negroes [will] be brute laborers only and not craftsmen; for that is the true theory of our social organization."[61] In passages like this, warranteeism as a model system of social relations appears to have been set aside and racial subordination has become the "true theory" of the South's labor system.

But the seeming contradiction between Hughes's praise of slavery as an effective means of preserving racial purity and his advocacy of warranteeism for all societies regardless of racial composition actually represented no contradiction to Hughes. The "ethnical qualification" of southern warranteeism required southerners to respect natural laws regarding racial purity. But as the term suggests, such respect for race constituted but a "qualification" to warranteeism and its primary goal, universal subsistence. A society that maintained racial purity but failed to provide subsistence was still a flawed social system. Only warranteeism could provide universal subsistence. Racial policy, although vitally important, could not and in Hughes's view did not in the South take precedence over ensuring that the system provided subsistence. The racial composition of the South required that specific measures be taken to preserve racial purity. But all societies faced the challenge of providing subsistence. What made the South's social system superior to all others was its ability to meet that challenge. That it also prevented miscegenation and thus promoted racial "progress" contributed to but did not in itself make that social system the model for all others to emulate.

Hughes's racial thoughts elicited no apparent criticism in the South; their general thrust probably found widespread support, although his more specific eugenicist ideas may have been less popular. What is clear

61. "St. Henry" [Hughes], "'Reopening of the African Slave Trade—Sectional and State Security Argument' Number IV," Jackson *Mississippian and State Gazette,* December 2, 1857.

is that when he devoted more of his thought to racial matters his work displayed a clear orientation toward the politically expedient tactic of appealing to southerners' racism to unite them in defense of their society. Nevertheless, Hughes did not retreat from the defense of slavery in the abstract. His descent into racist demagoguery did not prevent him from continuing to advocate the expansion of state authority in the South as well as the universal overthrow of free labor and the implementation of unfree labor in all societies, regardless of racial composition.

In the *Treatise,* Hughes had distinguished between warranteeism and slavery. His post-*Treatise* writings did not so rigidly observe that distinction, and many times Hughes used the term *slavery* positively. But he returned to the question of the differences between slavery and warranteeism several times after 1854, usually to emphasize the "progress" of the South's labor and social system. In his "Report on the African Apprentice System" presented at the May, 1859, Southern Commercial Convention at Vicksburg, Mississippi, Hughes noted that "when the Constitution of the United States was formed, our negro-labor system, was in theory and practice, Slavery," and thus "was . . . a system of inhumanity and injustice." The source of this inhumanity and injustice and the basic characteristic of slavery was the "master's private power." Although there may have been "some statutes prohibiting the wanton slaughter of slaves," Hughes alleged that "the master's powers were sovereign, irresistible, unlimited, and irresponsible."[62] The process by which the state limited these powers and extended to the slave "all the rights justly due him" represented the progress of slavery into warranteeism.

In language almost identical to that in the *Treatise,* Hughes noted that the "State to whom economic allegiance for the subsistence of all is as well due as political allegiance for the security of all, associates, adapts and regulates the master's powers, rights, duties and responsibilities." It also "entrusts to the masters [the] capitalized labor-obligations" of laborers and regulates "the negroes' hours of service, holidays, and food, raiment, habitation and peculium, and other elements of their wages." Hughes admitted that some "may deny that our labor system has so

62. Henry Hughes, "A Report on the African Apprentice System, Read at the Southern Commercial Convention by Henry Hughes. Held at Vicksburg, May 10th, 1859," in Lyman, ed., *Selected Writings of Henry Hughes,* 168–82. Also see the discussion of the convention and Hughes's role in it in Johnson, *Men and Vision,* 154–59.

rapidly progressed as to be now pure warranteeism," but he maintained that "the negro labor system of the United States South either is now warranteeism, or by progress may become such."[63]

Hughes reiterated his claim that slavery had progressed into warranteeism in large part because he wanted to demonstrate that the writers of the Constitution had not and could not have conceived of warranteeism. He then concluded that the introduction of African "apprentices" and their "elevation" into warrantees would "be against neither the letter nor the spirit of the United States Constitution and laws, because never contemplated, and therefore, never prohibited."[64] He even urged the passage of an "organic law" in which "our negro labor system shall be held, taken and adjudged to be warranteeism."[65] But his claims that warranteeism rather than slavery best described the South's social system were not mere legal maneuvers. As all his writings attest, Hughes believed in the use of state power to achieve social goals, whether they be limits on the master's authority or measures to increase the labor supply. His frequent calls for state action showed a consistent desire for the expansion of state authority as the best means to realize both the immediate needs and ultimate perfection of southern society.

Hughes never systematically developed his ideas on the proper nature and role of the state. They usually appear throughout his writings in reference to specific problems or concerns. One of the more explicit and detailed expressions of his views is a lengthy letter he wrote to Robert H. Purdom, the fire-eating editor of a short-lived Jackson-based newspaper the *Eagle of the South,* that appeared in the October 9, 1858, edition of the paper. Purdom had been the editor of the Port Gibson *Herald and Correspondent* in the mid-1850s and had solicited the letter from Hughes

63. Hughes, "Report on African Apprentice System," in Lyman, ed., *Selected Writings of Henry Hughes,* 176–77, 179, 181.

64. *Ibid.,* 181–82.

65. Untitled, original source unknown, clipping, in Hughes Scrapbook. The full text of the "organic law" included in this clipping reads: "Be it enacted—That hereafter, our negro labor system shall be held, taken, and adjudged to be warranteeism in which the masters shall be magistrates, property in man shall be abolished, labor obligations shall be capitalized, caste shall be maintained for the progress and purity of races, the negroes never shall be citizens, the rule of distribution as of the system shall be justice, the agent of the distribution shall be the State, and [means] of distribution shall be the ordinance of work and wages."

after the two of them had discussed what measures the Mississippi leg-islature "ought promptly but deliberately to adopt."[66] Hughes responded with the letter that outlined nine laws he felt should be passed. Although the nine proposals cover a wide range of topics and hardly amount to a complete exposition of his thought, they nonetheless contain some valu-able indications of the direction Hughes wanted state legislation to pursue.

Hughes saw the principles underlying his proposals as "the platform of a new State policy" that would help the "bold and inexorable progress" that was "now the highest duty of the State." Echoing sentiments found in other writings, Hughes observed that "as now propagandism is self-preservation," and since "editors are the propagandists . . . the defenders and extenders of our peculiar institutions," they "ought to enjoy a more liberal call to the honors and emoluments of the State." Hughes's praise of editors and their role as propagandists, a topic he had developed at greater length in a lecture titled "The New Governing Class," reflected his recognition of the ideological battle the South was engaged in, the importance of printed media in that battle, and the state's need to support and honor those engaged in it. After acknowledging the importance of the press, Hughes proceeded to use his access to it and presented his "new Platform."[67]

Not surprisingly, Hughes first advocated enactment of the African Contract-labor Immigration Bill. His second proposal, the "Georgia Stat-ute Against Negro Mechanics," called on the state to prohibit the em-ployment of slaves as "public mechanics." This statute limited the mas-ter's ability to hire out his slaves on public projects, thereby preserving such work for white laborers. While Hughes noted that the "policy of the statute is the harmony of the ruling classes," the law also embodied the principle that the state could restrict masters in the marketplace. By prohibiting the hiring out of skilled slave laborers, the state in effect regulated the labor market. Although hardly creating the powerful state advocated in the *Treatise,* such legislation would have expanded the role of the state in southern society, limited masters' freedom to dispose of

66. R.[obert] H. Purdom, "Letter to Henry Hughes," August 19, 1858, in Lyman, ed., *Selected Writings of Henry Hughes,* 144.

67. Henry Hughes, "Letter to R. H. Purdom," October 9, 1858, *ibid.,* 145; Hughes, ["The New Governing Class"], in Folder 3, Box 1, Hughes Papers.

their slaves' labor, and sanctioned the notion that it was the state's responsibility to address social problems arising in the marketplace, in this case the competition between white and slave laborers.[68]

Another proposal in the letter to Purdom related to an issue Hughes had specifically discussed in the *Treatise:* emancipation. Hughes had long opposed emancipation as contrary to warranteeism because it created the possibility of starvation by separating workers from masters. He now maintained this position and recommended that "the Legislature ought to expel or economically subordinate the free negroes, and declare that emancipation is against the negroes' subsistence and true liberty."[69] This suggestion thus contained both a practical action, the expulsion or economic subordination (reenslavement) of free blacks, and a declaration of principle, opposition to emancipation. Hughes considered both dimensions significant. The former would have used state authority to realize a desirable social end, thereby demonstrating the state's power and purpose. On this particular question, Hughes believed the state's prerogative to "subordinate or elevate" free blacks was absolute. Less than two months later, in a letter to Ethelbert Barksdale, editor of the *Mississippian,* Hughes reiterated this belief: "The power to fix or change [every black's] status is a State right.... The State has the power to decree what shall be the status of every free negro in the State."[70]

The second aspect of the antiemancipation proposal, the declaration that emancipation was contrary to black subsistence and "true liberty," represented an attempt to help reverse what Hughes termed the "judicial slander" of the 1818 case of *Harry* v. *Decker & Hopkins.* In that case, the Mississippi Supreme Court had asserted that slavery was "condemned by reason and the law of nature" and that in cases regarding questions of a black's freedom courts should lean " 'in favorem et libertatis.' " Hughes thus wanted the state to affirm "the morality, the perpetuity and the progress of our laboring system," by both proclaiming "our labor-system ... reasonable and natural" and exercising its authority to eliminate an element in society—free blacks—that contradicted that labor system's

---

68. Hughes, "Letter to Purdom," in Lyman, ed., *Selected Writings of Henry Hughes,* 149.

69. *Ibid.*

70. Henry Hughes to Ethelbert Barksdale, Jackson *Mississippian and State Gazette,* January 13, 1858.

logic. The exercise of legitimate state action would thus rectify social and ideological inconsistencies and mold society into its proper shape.[71]

Hughes's other proposals in his letter to Purdom dealt with such questions as penitentiary punishments for slaves, the governor's pardoning power, the consolidation of chancery, circuit, and probate courts, the adoption of the federal basis of representation of slaves on the state level, and the need for a levee law. In none of these proposals did Hughes develop his ideas of the state to the extent he did in the two proposals discussed above.[72] But in his other writings he presented views that reaffirmed and expanded the critical role the state played in his thought.

Not surprisingly, the slave trade writings contained some of Hughes's most significant references to the state. He devoted considerable attention to the question of how a reopened trade would affect the ratio of whites to blacks. Responding to those whites who feared a dramatic increase in the number of slaves, Hughes turned to the use of state power to allay those concerns. In an early article, he observed that upon reopening "the proportion of blacks to whites will be a variable." But this variable was not located entirely in the market, beyond social control. Instead, Hughes suggested, "Legislation can systematically make it [the proportion] more or less. For when the slave population shall have reached some certain limit, a tax on slaves introduced will regulate the introduction." State needs will

71. *Harry* v. *Decker & Hopkins,* Walker (Mississippi) 36 (1818); Hughes, "Letter to Purdom," in Lyman, ed., *Selected Writings of Henry Hughes,* 149–50.

72. It is interesting to note that, in his letter to Purdom, Hughes modified his position regarding the role of penitentiaries in the South. In his earlier article from December, 1856, Hughes had asserted that the "penitentiary is a free labor institution." He further stated that "the penitentiary is the college of crime. . . . [It], indeed, is the Devil's workshop." He then argued that the "penitentiary for slaves is against the spirit of our labor-system" and unnecessary because "our labor system eliminates both idleness and want, and, therefore, eliminates the innumerable and enormous crimes against property." In his letter to Purdom, however, Hughes endorsed "penitentiary life-punishment" for slaves. Such punishment, he suggested, would "be both an example and a disability of the Criminal, and as the punishment is for life the vicious negro will never be turned loose to corrupt his fellows and wreak new felonies, but will serve the State and do no harm." Hughes may have simply decided that prison was appropriate for serious slave criminals, who threatened life and limb, but not for slave thieves, whom he would not admit existed. See Hughes, "Penitentiary Punishment for Slaves," Port Gibson *Reveille,* December 20, 1856, and Hughes, "Letter to Purdom," in Lyman, ed., *Selected Writings of Henry Hughes,* 150.

determine state policy, and state action will implement state policy. Hughes's interest in the use of the taxing power to achieve state ends, first mentioned in his diary and developed further in the *Treatise,* here became part of practical policy. "Thus taxation will be regulation, and each State can adapt to its need the number of its laborers." Hughes also argued that "the number of whites may be systematically regulated." Noting the laws already existing in some states providing for a minimum ratio of whites to blacks, Hughes wrote that the "proportion is, of course, arbitrary and perfectly variable to the exigency. If need be, the law can as efficiently ordain one white to every five as well as one to every fifty blacks."[73] These passages reflect Hughes's conception of the state as social architect, using its powers of legislation and taxation to regulate "systematically" and "efficiently" the class and racial composition of society. His almost casual reliance on state action to remedy or prevent social uncertainties, such as a dangerous imbalance of black slaves to whites, demonstrates his support of the extension of state authority so that it could effectively control real or potential social problems.

Hughes advocated state regulation not only of the number of slaves to be imported but also of their actions once imported. Responding to the argument that an increase in slaves would lead to an increase in cotton production and a subsequent decline in price, Hughes asserted that newly imported slaves could be restricted from performing field labor and serve only as menials. "Can the African Labor Supply," Hughes asked rhetorically, "be so restricted that only menials be introduced and our cotton force not directly or indirectly increased? Nothing is easier." The ease of solving this potential problem lay with using the means of the state. "Only judicious legislation is needed. A statutory proviso that all Africans and their descendants here shall be restricted to menial service or extra labor, and shall not directly, indirectly or by substitution become cotton hands" would prevent the feared increase in production and decrease in price. Those who violated this proviso could be punished through "either a forfeiture of the negroes['] service or any condign damage of the master's purse or person."[74]

73. "St. Henry" [Hughes], "'Reopening of the African Slave Trade—Sectional and State Security Argument' Number IV," Jackson *Mississippian and State Gazette,* December 2, 1857.

74. "St. Henry" [Hughes], "Re-opening of the African Labor Supply—Number Seven—Wealth Argument," Jackson *Semi-Weekly Mississippian,* October 4, 1859.

Hughes recognized that a law that merely forbade masters from employing imported Africans and their descendants in cotton fields would prove hard to enforce. The new laborers "might be merely substituted for our menial American negroes and ... these would become cotton hands and increase the crop." To avoid this potentiality Hughes proposed that the state conduct a sweeping process of "Classification, Registration and Identification" of all blacks. "Each negro by this method," Hughes posited, "is in law, first identified, then classified as a cotton hand or an extra hand, and then duly registered." To support this dramatic reform, which would have provided the state with the means to achieve vast economic regulation, Hughes appealed to contemporary licensing of tradesmen as an example of the practicality of such a system. Just as "no baker can without [a] license be a brewer," so no registered "extra hand" could work the fields without the master running the risk of punishment.[75]

Although Hughes did not detail all the means of implementing and enforcing this system, he did discuss how the state could conduct the identification of the slaves. He assured his readers that the "identification of our negroes will not be difficult" and then proceeded to describe a possible method of identifying slaves that combined his desire for an expanded bureaucracy to fulfill state objectives with his seething contempt for free labor critics of slavery. "Public officers," he suggested, "if necessary may be ordained and sworn to identify. If necessary bloody letters may by State authority, be branded on the negroes['] cheeks or chins." Although this may have appeared brutal, Hughes insolently and sarcastically recommended even harsher techniques if this proposition elicited criticism from the North:

Let us in hard and staunch protest against what is philanthropy in design but misanthropy indeed; let us in humorous contempt, in delightful and deliberate detestation of sanctimonious meddlers ... mark them [slaves] like hogs and brand them like beeves; let us slit their nostrils; let us pinch in their bleeding ears ... or with hot and salted irons, fry on their brows and breasts, lasting letters, forbidding the negro to be a cotton picker. Then let freedom shriek till her face is red, and her voice is as cracked as her skull.[76]

75. *Ibid.*
76. *Ibid.*

Hughes's audacious proposals, which echoed his outrage at southern submission to northern notions of morality, should not prevent us from
recognizing their relation to his vision of the state. The "public officers"
he mentioned and the "State authority" they were to carry out represent
two features of a significantly modified southern social order, one in
which the state, through its agents, ensured the proper functioning of
society.

In Hughes's conception, the state would have limited the type of labor
workers could have performed, and that their masters could have made
them perform, so as to control cotton production and regulate the economy generally. But in one of his last slave trade articles, published in
February, 1860, he argued that, in fact, increased production would benefit the South. He maintained that a decline in cotton prices would expand consumption and result in a larger net profit. "Our true economy
. . . is to double our crops, because we more than double the consumers
at more than half the price." But such a policy had to be accompanied
by state actions that would help guarantee its desired outcome. "Preparation must be proportioned to production," Hughes advised, "our crops'
expected increase, therefore, must be duly estimated." Hughes suggested
that this estimation could be conducted by "the agricultural bureau,
through the tax-assessors, the road overseers, the members of the police
boards, or special reporters." [77] From this list it is clear that who estimated
the size of the crop mattered less to Hughes than that it be a public
agency. But the state's role did not end with estimating the crop's size.
The state also had to aid the movement of the crop to markets.

"Transportation," he urged, "must be facilitated; the money of Government must be not needlessly hoarded, but judiciously liberated, and
the markets must be duly extended." [78] Hughes thus endorsed publicly
funded internal improvements not as a "centrifugal" measure because it
did not aim at relieving excess labor but as a means of improving the
performance of the state's economy. Once again, we see that Hughes, like
other southerners, could voice opposition to specific actions of the federal
government, such as internal improvements, without being opposed in
principle to government-funded internal improvements or to state eco-

77. "St. Henry" [Hughes], "African Labor Supply—Wealth Argument. No. 8. (continued)," Jackson Semi-Weekly Mississippian, February 7, 1860.
  78. Ibid.

nomic aid and regulation in general. Together with the public estimate of crop production, Hughes's proposals looked to the state to foster and guide economic development.

Hughes knew that the state he envisioned—especially in its estimation of crop production, classification and registration of slaves, expulsion of free blacks, and general regulation of economic activity—required an efficient (and greatly enlarged) bureaucracy. Some of his most interesting and innovative ideas regarding the state concern the establishment of a "scientific" basis for the state. The application of scientific methods to the study and solution of social problems would enable qualified and informed state agencies to perform their roles efficiently and responsibly. The state would thus oversee society and administer it according to the dictates of science. True to his understanding of sociology as the "science of societary organization," he conceived of a state run, in large part, by sociologists, scientists like himself who understood society's needs and what the state had to do to meet them.

In "New Duties of the South" (October, 1854), Hughes urged that southern schools teach southern men how to defend and propagate their "home system." But he also believed that as a critical part of the ideological struggle against free labor "the Southern States should commence the collection of SLAVERY STATISTICS." Characteristic of his Baconian and positivist tendencies, Hughes saw statistics as a valuable weapon in the South's effort to establish the morality and efficiency of its social system to a disbelieving world. And it was a belief that Hughes thought needed to be debunked. "The old opinion against us," he argued, "is founded on belief only. The new [opinion] must be bottomed on both *knowledge and belief.*" The dissemination of "knowledge" would thus remedy false beliefs. "People abroad must be informed," he pleaded, and "statistical information is the very best." Its utility and value resided in its "objectivity." Statistical information "is received without prejudice. It impresses. It is reliable." Although Hughes stated that this information could be collected either by "statistical associations" or "the state," his subsequent comment that the one "whose collection shall be more copious in detail and more classic in arrangement" would prove more beneficial suggests he favored state collection.[79] His later writings confirm this deduction.

79. Hughes, "New Duties of the South."

Indeed, in his later writings, especially those on the slave trade, Hughes made the collection and use of statistics a central aspect of the state's progress. In an article in which he detailed the process of classification, registration, and identification of slaves, Hughes concluded that such a process would not only facilitate state regulation of labor but also provide valuable information for other state actions. In language that came directly out of the *Treatise,* he asserted that "information must always precede reformation, and statistics ought to be the basis of all legislation." Through the classification and registration of slaves, he maintained, "the State . . . will always be informed of the conditions, the proportions and the progress of its negro laborers . . . such information is essential to right legislation."[80] It is worth noting the identification Hughes made between the state and "*its* negro laborers." Hughes continued to claim that the primary responsibility toward laborers rested with the state. To care for and supervise "its" laborers efficaciously required the state to collect whatever information it considered relevant to its tasks. The acquisition of statistical information and the application of this information to state policies were legitimate, indeed necessary, state functions. The state would thus act in accordance with the statistics it possessed; the more "copious in detail" the statistics, the more "right" the state's actions.

Hughes's argument on the applicability of statistical information to legislation and social planning implied the vast expansion of state authority and bureaucracy. In another slave trade article published in February, 1860, he further delineated his views on how statistics provided the basis for solving nearly every social problem that plagued society.

Although Hughes's main argument in the article concerned the relation between cotton production, prices, and consumption, it eventually led him into a discussion of the wonders of statistics. He noted that "the solid of consumption is an upright cone broadening upwards" because the poor constituted the largest stratum, "and narrowing downwards," as the rich numbered few. For Hughes, the intriguing question was "what curve shall with its co-ordinate and abscissa, precisely represent

80. "St. Henry" [Hughes], "Re-opening of the African Labor Supply—Number Seven—Wealth Argument," Jackson *Semi-Weekly Mississippian,* October 4, 1859. In the *Treatise,* 72, Hughes wrote: "There ought, therefore, to be information before reformation; instruction before destruction or construction; statistics before legislation."

the relation of Consuming Numbers to Consuming Ability," the answer
to which, he acknowledged, was "not yet known." Of course, he observed,
"different communities will show different ratios," for the composition
of strata and their "consuming abilities" would vary. Clearly, Hughes
was concerned not so much with the actual ratios in different communities as with the models that could be constructed to determine the ratios
"precisely."[81]

Hughes marveled at the possibilities such models held for understanding a full array of social ills. "When known," he wrote, "such ratios will
show uniform and startling relations to disease, crime, malformation,
idiocy, celibacy, intemperance, under-growth, suicide, fatal accidents, su-
perstitions, mobs, ignorance and war." The ratios would, in effect, allow
one to develop a science of society. "The ratios will show enlightening,
suggestive and most exciting correspondences in all quantitative sciences,
from astronomy and meteorology to anatomy and pathology." Even
though social ills were not purely material, Hughes alleged that they
nonetheless could be examined and analyzed scientifically through their
"correspondences" in the quantitative sciences. "For whatever is spiritual," Hughes argued, "is sooner or later variable by whatever is material,
and whatever is material is sooner or later mathematical, that is, its
changes are capable of expression in numbers or ratios." Thus a ratio
expressing the mathematical relation of consuming numbers to consuming ability also demonstrated the relation of that material reality to the
immaterial, "spiritual," social ills enumerated above.[82]

Hughes knew that applying mathematics and science to social phenomena was an as yet unrealized hope. Again commenting on the in-
adequacies of southern thought and practice, he lamented that what
"these momentous ratios" were "we now can scarcely suspect." The reason for this ignorance was not impracticality but negligence. Knowledge
of the ratios "is and must be statistic, and such knowledge is neglected."
Hughes concluded this article with an impassioned plea for the recognition of the immense value of statistical analysis of social phenomena

81. "St. Henry" [Hughes], "African Labor Supply—Wealth Argument, No. 8. (continued)," Jackson *Semi-Weekly Mississippian,* February 4, 1860. The articles from the February 4, 1860, and February 7, 1860, editions of the *Semi-Weekly Mississippian* share the
same title but are different articles.
82. *Ibid.*

and the prompt implementation of such analysis. After noting the neglect of statistical knowledge, he informed his readers that "the science of statistics is the science of humanity, the invaluable science, the chart of our progress." The acquisition and study of statistical knowledge would demonstrate the course of social development and would "chart . . . our progress." Repeating his oft-stated maxim that "information must precede reformation," Hughes happily predicted that "sooner or later the census-book will be the second volume of the Bible."[83] Just as the Bible provided the indispensable and unquestioned guide to spiritual progress, so the census book would be the indispensable and unquestioned guide to social progress. Faith in the Bible would be matched by faith in statistics.

To realize this vision of a "scientific" polity required an ambitious and concerted effort to collect and analyze all the information the state would need to execute its duty. "Let us, then," Hughes proclaimed, "have in our Universities great professorships of statistics; let the census be frequent; let the tax-assessor be a truth-collector; let everything be counted, recounted, and ratiocinated."[84] The science of statistics would, and in Hughes's mind had to, lead to "truth." He had no doubt that this "truth" would keep the South—and ultimately make the world—unfree.

In this article Hughes expressed some of the unique dimensions of his thought, most of which he had been developing for years. In the combination of unfree labor and the modern "scientific" state, Hughes en-

83. "St. Henry" [Hughes], "African Labor Supply—Wealth Argument, No. 8. (continued)," Jackson *Semi-Weekly Mississippian,* February 4, 1860.

84. *Ibid.* Hughes's ideas regarding the application of mathematical methods to the solution of social problems bear striking resemblance to those of Condorcet. Both Condorcet and Hughes looked forward to the removal of politics from the arena of conflicting interests and its elevation into an empirical, objective science. Both also emphasized the need to educate the masses to accept as "right" the decisions of the scientific state. The question of the nature of political power and structure in which this objective political science would function is, however, another matter. Keith Michael Baker has persuasively argued that Condorcet "intended to provide the basis for a liberal social science oriented towards a conception of rational individual conduct in an open society." Hughes provided no evidence to suggest that warranteeism resembled an "open society" or that the masses were to understand the decisions of the state as opposed to recognizing their obligation to accept them as the product of scientific reason. On Condorcet see Manuel, *Prophets of Paris,* Chap. 2, and Keith Michael Baker, *Condorcet: From Natural Philosophy to Social Mathematics* (Chicago, 1975). The above quotation is from page 339.

visioned the pinnacle of progress, the model social order. This combination represented the culmination of his efforts, first apparent in his diary, to use modern social thought in the defense of southern society. Such efforts led him to criticize certain aspects of that society and to advocate reforms that would help achieve the harmony, order, and justice of warranteeism. His criticisms of the underregulated powers of the master must be seen as a piece along with his call for a statistical basis for social legislation. Both constituted parts of a broader conception of a social order in which individuals would act "as they ought," according to that which the state, through science, determined to be proper. Hughes's dizzying faith in statistical social analysis reveals the degree to which he understood society to be a mechanism, subject to repair or even rebuilding by trained experts. In his embrace of statistics and the correct interpretation of them, he brought together the ambitious self of the diary and the vigilant defender of slavery. He would realize his destiny of greatness and preserve unfree labor by demonstrating how the South, by obeying his "science of societary organization," would prove to the world the superiority of unfree labor.

Hughes approached perfect consistency in his thought no more closely than others. But he did maintain throughout his writings a firm belief in the efficacy and morality of a statist social order that subordinated individual freedom to social necessity. Slavery provided the basis, if not always the exact form, of his notions of social relations. But his interest in and study of contemporary social and scientific thought contributed to his ideas of the state as the agent and embodiment of progress. Hughes made a case for the progressive character of unfree labor, urging his fellow southerners to join him in defying the contemporary convention of equating progress with ever-expanding freedom. In doing so, he hoped to achieve a "new verdict of the world on the slavery question." As the South moved toward a war that would pronounce through force a different verdict, Hughes, and the South, became ever more convinced of the righteousness and superiority of a society based on order, unfree labor, and hierarchy.[85]

85. For more on the relation between antebellum southern intellectuals and the notion of progress, see Genovese, *Slaveholders' Dilemma*. Genovese briefly but incisively discusses Hughes on pages 55–58. See also Hughes, "New Duties of the South."

CONCLUSION:
THE MAN FOR TIMES COMING

The last "African Labor Supply" article appeared on April 24, 1860. Hughes would never publish again. Within a year he would be in uniform, preparing to fight for a new southern nation. In October, 1862, at the age of thirty-three, he died of a war-related illness at his home in Port Gibson. His old friend the Reverend William D. Moore preached a funeral sermon on October 26, which was subsequently published in 1863 at the request of the officers of "Hughes' Battalion" stationed at Port Hudson, Louisiana. In their request to Moore, the officers expressed hope that the publication of Moore's sermon would "go forth to work its mission of arousing all Southrons to the desire of reading and studying the writings of him who has piled Pelion upon Ossa in proof of the justice of their cause and the sacredness of their institutions: so that even other generations may,

> 'To such a name,
> Preserve a broad approach of fame,
> And ever-winging avenues of praise'"[1]

Hughes would have appreciated the gesture of his fellow officers and shared their hope that perhaps in death his ideas would gather the following they had failed to attract in life. In 1862 some, like Moore and Hughes's fellow officers, could still entertain the vain hope that his writings would be read by future generations. The defeat of the Confederacy assured Hughes's obscurity, yet the ideas he espoused and articulated did not die with him. He and his writings have largely been forgotten, but his vision of a statist, authoritarian social order found expression, albeit in muted form, during the war and beyond. The war killed Hughes,

---

1. J. M. Magruder *et al.,* Letter to Professor William D. Moore, in Moore, *Life and Works of Col. Henry Hughes,* preface.

slavery, and the Old South, but it did not kill the principles that united them: order, hierarchy, human interdependence, and hostility toward free labor and its attendant ideology of freedom and the marketplace version of individualism.

Hughes had prepared for war and through his writings had urged the South to do the same. His affiliation with the Port Gibson Riflemen and his call for mothers to encourage militaristic habits in their male children represented but two aspects of this preparation. In a November 16, 1859, letter to Mrs. S. E. Vertner, Hughes further revealed his expectation of impending military struggle. Writing of his desire to have Major Earl Van Dorn promoted to general, Hughes noted that "Quitman is dead, Jefferson Davis is in feeble health, and Earl Van Dorn is the only soldier patriot around whom, we could in coming difficulties, rally."[2] Hughes continued to emphasize the need for a "New Washington" in passages such as this; a heroic figure had to guide the coming revolution. War would thus offer the South an opportunity both to break free of northern dominance and to find the hero who could lead the South into the future.

After the secession of Mississippi in January, 1861, Hughes volunteered for duty and was elected captain of the Claiborne Guards in April, 1861. He and the Guards were ordered to Virginia in July, 1861, where he was made colonel of the Twelfth Regiment of Mississippi Guards. He helped construct fortifications at Second Manassas and then returned to the Port Gibson area in the summer of 1862 to raise a regiment of "Partizan Rangers" for the defense of the area around Vicksburg. Inflammatory rheumatism, which he had first acquired in Virginia, cut short these efforts and eventually took his life.[3]

Although the Reverend Mr. Moore's glowing eulogy of Hughes remains valuable for the many insights it provides into Hughes and his life, a brief and rather hastily drawn portrait of a few years earlier captures much of Hughes's essential character. In 1859, during the Southern Commercial Convention in Vicksburg, a writer for the Yazoo *Democrat* penned descriptions of Hughes and some other members of the conven-

2. Henry Hughes to Mrs. S. E. Vertner, November 16, 1859, Roll 2, J. F. H. Claiborne Collection, MDAH.

3. This paragraph relies primarily on Moore, *Life and Works of Col. Henry Hughes.*

tion. Hughes preserved the sketch of himself in his scrapbook, perhaps somewhat amused by its critical perception of him and his talents. For the *Democrat*'s writer grasped the uneasy tension in Hughes between the abstract theoretician and the pragmatic polemicist and the ways in which the former limited the effectiveness of the latter. "The great difficulty in his way," the unknown journalist wrote, "is that the mass of antiquated information in which he buries his ideas, renders it uncertain and doubtful whether the people—the great lever of power, will ever understand him."[4] Hughes never did gain a large following in Mississippi, let alone the South. Perhaps, as the *Democrat*'s correspondent suggested, the people never understood him. But it may have been less a lack of understanding than a lack of relevance that kept Hughes and his ideas on the margins of southern politics and social thought. Hughes's vision of a vigorous, activist state and a planned social order might well have appeared foreign to white southerners accustomed to the limited government and extensive personal freedom that characterized both southern society and the mainstream of proslavery thought. Yet as foreign as such a vision may have seemed in 1859, southern society would soon incorporate many of its fundamental features into a new political order forged in war.

As the Confederate States of America undertook the immense task of fighting its war for independence, a remarkable transformation occurred in southern society. A war of the magnitude of the Civil War was bound to transform both South and North.[5] But the transformation within the Confederacy deserves special attention, in part because of the dramatic use of state power to achieve desired social, economic, and military ends. The incredible expansion of state authority in a region long committed to limited government constitutes one of the most significant developments of the Civil War. To a significant and unprecedented extent, the wartime South recognized the benefits and developed the machinery of a strong, interventionist centralized state.

The growth of state power in the Confederacy and in the individual

4. Untitled, Yazoo *Democrat,* clipping, in Hughes Scrapbook.

5. See, for example, Bensel, *Yankee Leviathan;* Philip Shaw Paludan, *"A People's Contest": The Union and the Civil War, 1861–1865* (New York, 1988); George M. Fredrickson, *The Inner Civil War: Northern Intellectuals and the Crisis of the Union* (New York, 1965); and Ralph Andreano, ed., *The Economic Impact of the Civil War* (2nd ed.; Cambridge, Mass., 1967).

Confederate states was neither planned nor always welcomed. Although government authority largely resulted from wartime exigencies, it became a force that many southerners accepted as legitimate and necessary. This is not meant to claim that southerners became staunch advocates of statist policies in peace as well as war; most undoubtedly did not. But the degree to which southerners approved of the exercise of state power over their lives and activities represented an accommodation to limits on their freedom in return for the benefits of independence. Those limits imposed by the Confederate and state governments for the good of society distinctly echoed Hughes's assertion that the state "is the economic sovereign, or lord-paramount. All are its lieges. It has in the premises, supreme executive[,] legislative[,] and judicial powers. Justice is its only limit; and it is the judge of that."[6] During the war, the state began to resemble Hughes's vision.

The particular measures adopted by the Confederate government and the governments of the individual states to aid the war effort covered a wide range of economic and social activity. Every state except Louisiana and Texas imposed limits on cotton production in efforts to increase grain production. As Hughes had suggested in all his works but especially in his slave trade writings, most states employed taxes to compel planters and farmers to shift production. Others, like Georgia, limited the acreage planters could devote to cotton. Most states prohibited the distillation of grains to increase food supplies. The pressing necessity of maintaining adequate salt supplies led states such as Virginia to authorize the governor to seize real and personal property for salt production, while Mississippi and Texas constructed state salt wells on state-owned land. Some states participated directly in the manufacture of necessary items. Louisiana owned and operated a cloth factory, turpentine stills, and an iron foundry, as well as lesser concerns. Other states, again as Hughes had suggested, expanded penitentiary production to meet wartime needs. Most states also regulated and in some cases conducted the distribution of state-produced items. In short, throughout the Confederacy state governments invoked traditional powers, such as taxation, and developed new ones, like ownership of factories and stores, to aid the war effort. In doing so, they demonstrated the efficacy of public over private control of economic

6. Hughes, *Treatise*, 166.

activity. Remarkable as these measures were, the actions of the Confederate government dwarfed them both in scope and achievement.[7]

The Confederate government's intervention in and direction of economic activity have led several scholars to label its policy "state socialism."[8] During the course of its existence, the Confederacy constructed one of if not the largest nationally operated economies in the world. The government owned and operated foundries, shipyards, armories, lead smelting factories, leather works, machine factories, gunpowder mills, meatpacking plants, and cloth, button, and shoe factories. By the end of the war the South's transportation system, including all railroads, was under direct government control. Laws passed in 1863 and 1864 placed almost all foreign trade under national control with fixed and compulsory freight rates. Perhaps the most effective tool the government employed was its control of labor through the conscription laws of 1863 and 1864. By threatening to remove skilled and nonskilled laborers from privately owned factories that did not agree to contract a certain share of output to the government, the state exercised a near monopoly on production, gearing it almost totally to its own purposes. By controlling labor it controlled economic activity. The government also bought out private firms that could not or would not perform as the government dictated. In addition, the Confederacy created government agencies and bureaus, such as the Bureau of Conscription, the Ordnance Bureau, the Niter and Mining Bureau, and the Bureau of Foreign Supplies, to coordinate and implement its economic policies. More than seventy thousand civilians

7. On state-level activities see Charles W. Ramsdell, *Behind the Lines in the Southern Confederacy* (Baton Rouge, 1944); May Spencer Ringold, *The Role of the State Legislatures in the Confederacy* (Athens, Ga., 1966), esp. Chap. 4; Curtis Arthur Amlund, *Federalism in the Southern Confederacy* (Washington, D.C., 1966); Ella Lonn, *Salt as a Factor in the Confederacy* (New York, 1933); and Mary A. DeCredico, *Patriotism for Profit: Georgia's Urban Entrepreneurs and the Confederate War Effort* (Chapel Hill, 1990). For Hughes's advocacy of penitentiary production, see Hughes, "Penitentiary Punishment for Slaves," Port Gibson *Southern Reveille,* December 20, 1856, clipping, Hughes Scrapbook.

8. The earliest use of the term *state socialism* in reference to the Confederate experience is Louise Biles Hill, *State Socialism in the Confederate States of America* (Charlottesville, 1936). Others who have since employed it include Raimondo Luraghi, *The Rise and Fall of the Plantation South* (New York, 1978), and Richard E. Beringer, Herman Hattaway, Archer Jones, and William N. Still, Jr., *Why the South Lost the Civil War* (Athens, Ga., 1986).

worked for the Confederate government, making its bureaucracy larger in proportion to the South's population than that of the United States during the war. This incredible expansion and exercise of state authority in the economy of the Confederacy represented, in the words of Raimondo Luraghi, "the most sweeping experience in state socialism to that time." It placed the state at the center of society, limiting market activity and individual freedom in the name of social necessity. As Richard Bensel has written, "Confederate direction of railway operations, taxation, and conscription conferred upon the central government almost absolute control over the southern economy." Although some government policies, notably the impressment of necessities by the military, aroused deep resentment and even open defiance, the vast majority of state actions met with acceptance.[9]

The actions of the Confederate government did not result in the creation of a state like the one Hughes discussed in the *Treatise* and his other writings. Nor did there develop a discernible tendency among large numbers of southerners to see the state as the repository and embodiment of justice, sovereignty, and progress. Most southerners understood and accepted the statist policies and actions of the government as wartime necessities, not as permanent conditions. But by 1865 the leviathan state that had been created had grown to such a point that perhaps only defeat ensured its demise. "It is hard to see how," Luraghi has argued, "had the Confederacy survived the war, it could have been spared from wholesale economic planning, more and more centralism, bureaucracy, and finally

---

9. Luraghi, *Rise and Fall of the Plantation South,* 137; Bensel, *Yankee Leviathan,* 137. On the activities of the Confederate government, see Ramsdell, *Behind the Lines;* Ramsdell, "The Control of Manufacturing by the Confederate Government," *Mississippi Valley Historical Review,* VIII (1921), 231–49; Luraghi, *Rise and Fall of the Plantation South;* Luraghi, "The Civil War and the Modernization of American Society: Social Structure and Industrial Revolution in the Old South Before and During the War," *Civil War History,* XVIII (1972), 230–50; Hill, *State Socialism in the Confederate States;* Lonn, *Salt as a Factor;* Amlund, *Federalism in the Southern Confederacy;* Bensel, *Yankee Leviathan;* Bensel, "Southern Leviathan," 68–136; Albert Burton Moore, *Conscription and Conflict in the Confederacy* (New York, 1924); Paul D. Escott, *After Secession: Jefferson Davis and the Failure of Confederate Nationalism* (Baton Rouge, 1978); Emory M. Thomas, *The Confederacy as a Revolutionary Experience* (Englewood Cliffs, N.J., 1971); Thomas, *The Confederate Nation, 1861–1865* (New York, 1979); Frank Vandiver, *Ploughshares into Swords: Josiah Gorgas and Confederate Ordnance* (Austin, 1952); and DeCredico, *Patriotism for Profit.*

complete take-over of all economic activity (indeed, of the national economy as a whole) by the government."[10] The achievements of the state may well have been celebrated after southern independence to justify the preservation and extension of the state's role in a Confederacy that had a weak private manufacturing sector and indigenous bourgeoisie. Just as wartime necessity had legitimated the exercise of state power, social and economic necessity might have been invoked to warrant the continued use of that power. Hughes's ideas might well have found a more receptive audience in such a society that, although unaware of him, had adopted many of his fundamental notions of social organization and development.

Such speculation can do no more than suggest a possible course an independent Confederacy might have taken. But the state actions undertaken during the war also suggest that Hughes's ideas were neither totally detached from reality nor foreign to southern sensibilities. Hughes articulated a particular strain in antebellum southern thought that combined contemporary positivist notions of progress and the scientific study of social development with the reality of southern slavery. The result was a distinct defense of unfree labor that looked to the future and to change rather than to a changeless past or present. Hughes built this defense on a concept that few other southerners viewed as a logical defender of their interests: the strong, interventionist state. Hughes recognized the enormous potential that state power presented to southerners anxious over the fate of their hierarchal, interdependent, and unfree social order in a world increasingly dominated by free labor social relations and ideology. Under state supervision and guidance, the imperfect warranteeism known as slavery would be perfected, and social change would be planned, implemented, and evaluated by state statisticians and sociologists who would maintain order and stability by ensuring subsistence to all. Propaganda would educate and inform through the use of statistical information and logical argument. Warranteeism would be recognized as the most rational, moral, and progressive social organization humans could devise. Its triumph would vindicate unfree labor by making it the central component of a system based on science, morality, and the law of universal subsistence.

Hughes thus embraced state power as both means and end. It would

10. Luraghi, *Rise and Fall of the Plantation South,* 152.

be the means toward universal subsistence, human progress, and social perfection. It would be an end in itself, the embodiment of knowledge and justice. The state would enable the South to realize the goal of war-ranteeism; it would be the instrument of perfection, the guarantor of progress. Southerners recognized during the war something remarkably similar to the vision Hughes had projected years earlier and sustained throughout his life: crisis required centralized, effective state action that subordinated freedom to duty, the individual to society. For Hughes the permanent crisis was the need for universal subsistence; the more im-mediate crisis was the struggle between free and unfree labor. For the South, the crisis was the armed struggle between northern free labor and southern slavery. Hughes may have recognized the crisis and its solution too early to win widespread support; the South recognized its crisis too late to win the war for its own survival.

Hughes did not represent a dominant tendency in antebellum south-ern thought. His vision contained too many innovations for most south-erners to accept. But to dismiss him and his ideas as deviant prevents us from seeing in him and his ideas an inclination among southern intellec-tuals and other cultural leaders, especially among the clergy, toward what might best be termed the modern authoritarian state. As Eugene Gen-ovese has reminded us, white southern conservatives have usually looked upon the state with suspicion if not outright hostility. But as Genovese points out, this southern tradition of antistatism did not totally silence those southerners who believed that a strong state provided the best means of protecting southern interests, especially unfree labor. "Strong voices within the proslavery camp," Genovese writes, "uttered serious reservations about state rights and suggested that the survival of a slave society in the modern world of contending nation-states required a con-siderable centralization of power in a national government."[11] Hughes's was the strongest, if not the most widely heard, of these voices. His appeals to his fellow southerners sought to overcome their biases against concentrated state power, biases that resulted, in large part, from northern domination of the central government from the time of the Missouri Compromise down to the Civil War. Hughes worried less about the necessary, and to his mind desirable, restraints that a strong state would

11. Eugene D. Genovese, *The Southern Tradition: The Achievement and Limitations of an American Conservatism* (Cambridge, Mass., 1994), 58 and *passim*.

place on individuals and more about the ability of the southern social order to survive without a considerable expansion of state authority. In an important sense, he did differ from most southerners in his conviction that only the state could save the South. Hughes's embrace of the authoritarian state was no mere tactical maneuver. More so than any other defender of slavery, to say nothing of subsequent southern conservatives, Hughes looked to the state as the moral as well as political center of social existence. In doing so, he demonstrated the extent to which the crisis of southern slave society led him away from both American and southern political traditions and toward a modern alternative to the rule of the market, possessive individualism, and the limited state.

Hughes, like many nineteenth-century European corporatist theorists, envisioned the proper society as one in which individual freedom, human equality, democracy, and the market were all subordinated to or eliminated by individual dependence on others and society, inequality, hierarchy, and a state-controlled economy. He thus represented one response to the "social question" that plagued nineteenth-century men and women and has continued to plague many in the twentieth. A product of the intermingling of the social context of the Old South, whose social relations literally rested on inequality and authoritarian command, and contemporary Western social thought, Hughes's solution to the "social question" would appear in different forms in the years after his death, as the desire for state-supervised social order and the forcible subjugation of the working class confronted the fears of social instability and worker revolution.

Appendix: Henry Hughes's Readings, 1848–1853

These are the works, arranged by subject, that appear in Hughes's diary. The titles are given as Hughes wrote them; I have not corrected his spelling or punctuation and have used [*sic*] only if confusion would otherwise result. The dates that immediately follow the titles refer to the diary entry in which Hughes first mentioned the reading. Where appropriate and possible, I have included additional bibliographic material in brackets, including date of publication or the edition that Hughes likely read. For cases in which determining the edition is impossible, such as classic works or poems, I have included the author's birth and death years.

History

Hallam's View of the Middle Ages (January 1, 1848). [Henry Hallam, *View of the State of Europe During the Middle Ages,* 6th ed. (1847)]

Hallam's Constitutional History of England (January 1, 1848). [Henry Hallam, *The Constitutional History of England from the Accession of Henry VII to the Death of George II* (1829)]

Gibbon's History of the Decline and Fall of Rome (January 1, 1848). [Edward Gibbon (1737–94), *The History of the Decline and Fall of the Roman Empire*]

Bancroft's history of the United States (February 6, 1848). [George Bancroft, *History of the United States of America* . . . (1846)]

Eliot's [*sic*] Debates on the Constitution (June 4, 1848). [Jonathan Elliot, *The Debate in the Several State Conventions on the Adoption of the Federal Constitution* . . . , 2nd ed. (1836)]

the "Madison Papers" (December 3, 1848)

Life of Lord Bacon in the Edinburgh Encyclopedia (July 1, 1849). [Hughes read a number of articles in *The Edinburgh Encyclopedia,* an eighteen-volume work "conducted by David Brewster, with the assistance of gentlemen eminent in science and literature." It was published in Philadelphia in 1832.]

Robertson's Charles the 5th (July 22, 1849). [William Robertson, *The History of the Reign of the Emperor Charles the Fifth* (1846)]

Macaulay's History of England (August 5, 1849). [Catherine Macaulay (1731–91), *The History of England* ...]

Hallam's History of Literature (September 16, 1849). [Henry Hallam, *Introduction to the Literature of Europe in the Fifteenth, Sixteenth, and Seventeenth Centuries* (1841)]

Lord Brougham's Sketches of Eminent men (January 13, 1850). [Henry Peter, Lord Brougham and Vaux, *Historical Sketches of Statesmen Who Flourished in the Time of George III* (1842)]

Turnbull's "Genius of Scotland" (September 15, 1850). [Robert Turnbull, *The Genius of Scotland* (1848)]

"Carlyle's Letters & Speeches of Cromwell" ("first volume," "250 pages about") (September 29, 1850). [Thomas Carlyle, ed., *Oliver Cromwell's Letters and Speeches,* 3rd ed. (1849)]

Hero as Divinity, as Prophet & as Poet (December 29, 1850). [These are the first three chapters of Thomas Carlyle's *On Heroes, Hero-Worship, and the Heroic in History* (1840)]

Garland's "Life of John Randolph" (October 26, 1851). [Hugh A. Garland, *The Life of John Randolph of Roanoke* (1850)]

Kennedy's Life of Wirt (November 23, 1851). [John Pendleton Kennedy, *Memoirs of the Life of William Wirt* (1850)]

Macaulay's Essay on Bacon (June 27, 1852). [Thomas Babington, Lord Macaulay, *The Life and Writings of Francis Bacon* (1837)]

"Cuba and the Cubans" (February 20, 1853). [Richard B. Kimball, *Cuba, and the Cubans* (1850)]

Macfarlane's Japan (March 13, 1853). [Charles MacFarlane, *Japan* (1852)]

LAW

Blackstone's Commentaries (January 1, 1848). [William Blackstone (1723–80), *Commentaries on the Laws of England*]

Story on the Constitution (December 17, 1848). [Joseph Story, *Commentaries on the Constitution of the United States* ... (1833)]

Kent's Commentaries (February 11, 1849). [James Kent, *Commentaries on American Law,* 6th ed. (1848)]

"Vattels Law of Nations" (March 11, 1849). [Emmerich de Vattel (1714–67), *The Law of Nations; or, Principles of the Law of Nature, Applied to the Conduct and Affairs of Nations and Sovereigns* (1829)]

Justinians Institutes (March 18, 1849).

"Pothier on Obligations" (March 25, 1849). [Robert Joseph Pothier, *A Treatise on Obligations, Considered in a Moral and Legal View* (1802)]

"Greenleaf on Evidence" (April 22, 1849). [Simon Greenleaf, *A Treatise on the Law of Evidence* (1842)]

"Story on Promissory Notes" (June 10, 1849). [Joseph Story, *Commentaries on the Law of Promissory Notes and Guaranties of Notes* ... (1845)]

"Chitty on Bills" (June 18, 1849). [Joseph Chitty, *A Practical Treatise on Bills of Exchange* ... (1840)]

Story on Partnership (July 1, 1849). [Joseph Story, *Commentaries on the Law of Partnership* (1841)]

Smiths Leading Cases (July 8, 1849). [John William Smith, *A Selection of Leading Cases on Various Branches of the Law* (1838)]

American Leading Cases (July 15, 1849). [John Innes Clark Hare, *American Leading Cases: Being Select Decisions of American Courts* ... (1847–48)]

Phillips on Insurance (August 12, 1849). [Willard Phillips, *A Treatise on the Law of Insurance,* 2nd ed. (1840)]

Abbot on Shipping (September 2, 1849). [Charles Abbott, Baron Tenterden, *A Treatise on the Law Relative to Merchant Ships and Seamen,* 5th American ed. (1846)]

Stephen's Pleading (September 9, 1849). [Henry John Stephen, *A Treatise on the Principles of Pleading in Civil Actions* ... , 5th ed. (1843)]

Conkling's Treatise (September 16, 1849). [Alfred Conkling, *A Treatise on the Organization and Jurisdiction of the Supreme, Circuit and District Courts of the United States* ... 2nd ed. (1842)]

Civil Code of Louisiana (September 23, 1849). [Probably *Civil Code of the State of Louisiana* (1838)]

Bullard & Curry's Digest (September 30, 1849). [Henry Adams Bullard (Thomas Curry, reporter), *A New Digest of the Statute Laws of the State of Louisiana* ... (1842)]

"Story on Agency" (November 18, 1849). [Joseph Story, *Commentaries on the Law of Agency as a Branch of Commercial and Maritime Jurisprudence,* 2nd ed. (1844)]

"Barton's Suit in Chancery" (November 18, 1849). [Charles Barton, *An Historical Treatise of a Suit in Equity* ... (1796)]

Jeremy's "Law of Carriers" (December 2, 1849). [Henry Jeremy, *The Law of Carriers, Inn-Keepers, Warehousemen, and Other Depositories of Goods for Hire* (1816)]

Story on "Bailments" (December 2, 1849). [Joseph Story, *Commentaries on the Law of Bailments,* 4th ed. (1846)]

Story on "Bills of Exchange" (December 2, 1849). [Joseph Story, *Commentaries on the Law of Bills of Exchange* ... , 2nd ed. (1840)]

Story on "the Conflict of Laws" (December 9, 1849). [Joseph Story, *Commentaries on the Conflict of Laws* ... , 2nd ed. (1841)]

Curtis' Rights & duties of Merchant Seamen (December 16, 1849). [George Ticknor Curtis, *A Treatise on the Rights and Duties of Merchant Seamen* ... (1841)]

"Angell & Ames on Corporations" (December 24, 1849). [Joseph K. Angell, *A Treatise on the Law of Private Corporations,* 3rd ed., rev., corrected, and enlarged by Samuel Ames (1846)]

Code of Practice of Louisiana (January 6, 1850). [Probably *Code of Practice of the State of Louisiana, Containing Rules of Procedure in Civil Actions* ... (1844)]

Domat's Civil Law (February 17, 1850). [Jean Domat, *The Civil Law in Its Natural Order* (1720, 1737); 2nd London ed. (2 vols.; 1850)]

Curtis' Admiralty Digest (March 3, 1850). [George Ticknor Curtis, *A Digest of Cases Adjudicated in the Courts of Admiralty of the United States* ... (1839)]

Betts Admiralty Practice (March 10, 1850). [Samuel Rossiter Betts, *A Summary of Practice in Instance, Revenue and Prize Causes* ... (1838)]

Russel on Crimes (March 10, 1850). [Sir William Oldnall Russell, *A Treatise on Crimes and Misdemeanors,* 3rd American ed. (1836)]

Story's Equity (April 21, 1850). [Joseph Story, *Commentaries on Equity Jurisprudence as Administered in England and America,* 4th ed. (1846)]

"Reformation of the Law" (November 2, 1851). [Possibly Daniel Magenise, *The Reformation of the Law, Physic and Divinity.* . . . Although the second edition of this pamphlet was published in London in 1778, a copy is in the Tulane University Library, suggesting that it may have been in New Orleans in 1851.]

Sedgwick on Damages (December 21, 1851). [Theodore Sedgwick, *A Treatise on the Measure of Damages* . . . (1847)]

Philosophy

Logic in the Edinburgh Encyclopedia (January 1, 1848)

Whately's Logic (February 6, 1848). [Richard Whately, *Elements of Logic* (1832)]

Locke [no title provided] (July 23, 1848).

Bacon's Works (July 22, 1849). [In this entry, Hughes recorded that he had "received Bacon's Works." He again mentioned having "Bacon's Works, by Montague [*sic*]" on July 11, 1852, adding, "I expect soon to attack them." I believe that he did not seriously read Bacon until 1852. Basil Montagu's edition of Bacon's works, *The Works of Francis Bacon, Lord Chancellor of England,* was first published in 1825. A three-volume edition was published in Philadelphia by Carey and Hart in 1844.]

Life of Immanuel Kant in the Edinburgh Encyclopedia (July 29, 1849)

Kant's "Critic of Pure Reason" ("about 113 pages") (December 24, 1849). [Hughes mentioned that he had "begun again" Immanuel Kant's (1724–1804) *Critique* on December 19, 1852, although he again referred to it as the "Critic."]

Locke's Essay on the Conduct of the Understanding (September 15, 1850). [John Locke (1632–1704), *The Essay Concerning Human Understanding*]

Whewell's "Elements of Morality" ("first two chapters") (October 13, 1850). [William Whewell, *The Elements of Morality, Including Polity* (1847)]

Mill's Logic (June 6, 1851). [John Stuart Mill, *A System of Logic, Ratiocinative and Inductive* . . . (New York, 1850)]

"Philosophy of Mathematics" (June 29, 1851). [Auguste Comte, *The Philosophy of Mathematics.* In an entry from August 17, 1851, Hughes noted that he "finished

'Compte's Philosophy of Mathematics' by 'Gillespie.'" William Mitchell Gillespie edited an edition of Comte's *Philosophy of Mathematics*. It was published in 1851 in New York by Harper.]

North British Review's paper on "The Recent Extension of Logic" (September 21, 1851)

"Passions of the Human Soul" by Charles Fourier (February 29, 1852). [Hughes most likely read the two-volume edition of *The Passions of the Human Soul* translated by John Reynell Morell and published by H. Bailliere in New York in 1851. Hughes mentioned finishing Volume I on May 2, 1852, and continuing, apparently in Volume II, on May 9, 1852.]

"History of the Course of Modern Philosophy," by Cousin (April 13, 1852). [Victor Cousin, *Course of the History of Modern Philosophy* (1852)]

Macintosh's "View of Ethical Philosophy" (June 7, 1852)

"Influence of Authority in Matters of Opinion" (June 13, 1852). [Hughes read James Chesnut, Jr.'s, critical review of George Cornwall Lewis' *Influence of Authority in Matters of Opinion* (London, 1849). Chesnut's review appeared in the *Southern Quarterly Review,* N. S. 5 (April, 1852), 341–72.]

Bentham on Legislation by Dumont translated by Neal ("I wish I had all Bentham's published works.") (September 12, 1852). [Hughes read Etienne Dumont's edition of Bentham's *Principles of Legislation,* which was translated by John Neal and published in New York and Boston in 1830 by several publishers, including Wells and Lilly and G. & C. H. Carvill.]

Emerson's Essays (November 28, 1852). [Ralph Waldo Emerson. It is not clear from the diary whether Hughes read the first or second series of Emerson's Essays.]

CLASSICS

Cicero's Essay on the character of an Orator (January 23, 1848)

Demosthenes' orations (January 30, 1848)

Cicero's Oration for Milo (February 4, 1849)

"Dryden's Eneid" (April 22, 1849). [Probably John Dryden's 1697 edition of Virgil's *Aeneid*]

the Odyssey (December 16, 1849)

Horace's Odes ("Anthon's Edition, first book; began the second") (November 3, 1850). [Charles Anthon, ed., *The Works of Horace* (New York, 1840)]

PLAYS

Milman's tragedy Fazio (November 26, 1848). [Henry Hart Milman, *Fazio: A Tragedy* (1815)]

Shakespeare [no specific titles] (January 7, 1849)

King Lear (February 4, 1849). [William Shakespeare (1564–1616)]

"Romeo & Juliet" (April 1, 1849). [William Shakespeare]

Midsummer Nights Dream (December 2, 1849). [William Shakespeare]

Bulwer's Money (December 2, 1849). [Edward Bulwer, Lord Lytton, *Money: A Comedy in Five Acts* (1845)]

Shakespeare's Henry the Eighth (December 2, 1849)

Troilus & Cressida (December 16, 1849). [William Shakespeare]

Shakespeare's "Much Ado About Nothing" (March 20, 1853)

"Twelfth Night" (March 27, 1853). [William Shakespeare]

RELIGION

The Literature of the Scriptures (March 11, 1849)

Young's Night Thoughts (November 4, 1849). [Edward Young (1683–1765), *The Complaint and Consolation; or Night Thoughts on Life, Death, and Immortality*]

Isaiah (November 18, 1849)

Pilgrim's Progress (December 2, 1849). [John Bunyan (1628–88), *The Pilgrim's Progress*]

Bible ("several pages on Sundays") (January 6, 1850)

"Horne's Compendious Introduction." (May 12, 1850). [Thomas Hartwell Horne, *A Compendious Introduction to the Study of the Bible* (1833)]

Lewis' Restoration of the Jews (April 27, 1851). [Seth Lewis, *The Restoration of the Jews* ... (1851)]

Borrow's "Bible in Spain" (July 20, 1851). [George Henry Borrow, *The Bible in Spain* ..., 2nd ed. (1843)]

Keble's "Christian Year" (July 11, 1852). [John Keble, *The Christian Year; Thoughts in Verse for Sundays and Holydays* ... 1st American ed., from the 18th Oxford ed. (1851)]

POETRY

Dyers "Grongar Hill" (February 4, 1849). [John Dyer (1700?–58), *Grongar Hill*]

Hudibras (March 18, 1849). [Samuel Butler (1612–80), *Hudibras*]

"Lady of the Lake" (March 25, 1849). [Sir Walter Scott (1771–1832), *The Lady of the Lake: A Poem*]

Cowper's Task (June 24, 1849). [William Cowper (1731–1800), *The Task, A Poem in Six Books*]

Mathew Greens "Spleen" (September 16, 1849). [Matthew Green (1696–1737), *The Spleen: An Epistle to Mr. C. Jackson*]

Cadenus & Vanessa (September 16, 1849). [Jonathan Swift (1667–1745), *Cadenus and Vanessa. A Poem*]

Paradise Regained ("Paradise Lost I read at College—Oakland") (September 16, 1849). [John Milton (1608–74), *Paradise Regained*]

poem entitled "Cider" by Phillips (September 23, 1849)

"Eloisa to Abelard" (September 23, 1849). [Alexander Pope (1688–1744), *Eloisa to Abelard* (1720)]

Swift on Poetry (October 14, 1849). [Jonathan Swift, *On Poetry, A Rhapsody*]

Somerville's Chase (October 21, 1849). [William Somerville (1675–1742), *The Chase*]

Pollock's Course of Time (October 29, 1849). [Robert Pollok (1798–1827), *The Course of Time; A Poem*]

the Endymion, of Keats (November 18, 1849). [John Keats (1795–1821), *Endymion, A Poetic Romance*]

"Eve of St Agnes" (December 2, 1849). [John Keats, *The Eve of St. Agnes*]

Shelley's "Queen Mab" & "Adonais" (December 2, 1849). [Percy Bysshe Shelley (1792–1822), *Queen Mab: A Philosophical Poem* and *Adonais: An Elegy on the Death of John Keats*]

Shelley's "Prometheus" (December 9, 1849). [Percy Bysshe Shelley, *Prometheus Unbound: A Lyrical Drama in Four Acts*]

the Dunciad (December 16, 1849). [Alexander Pope, *The Dunciad: An Heroic Poem in Three Books*]

"Festus" (December 1, 1850). [Philip James Bailey, *Festus, A Poem* (1839)]

Thompson's "Castle of Indolence" (March 7, 1852). [James Thompson (1700–1748), *The Castle of Indolence*]

Scott's "Rokeby" (March 9, 1851). [Sir Walter Scott, *Rokeby: A Poem*]

"The Lay of the Last Minstrel" (March 9, 1851). [Sir Walter Scott, *The Lay of the Last Minstrel, A Poem*]

"Rime of the Ancient Mariner" ("re-perused") (March 16, 1851). [Samuel Taylor Coleridge (1772–1834), *The Rime of the Ancient Mariner*]

Tennyson's "Poems" (July 25, 1852). [Alfred, Lord Tennyson (1809–1892)]

Browning's—Elizabeth Barrett—Poems (November 28, 1852)

Natural Sciences

"Page's Geology" (April 22, 1849). [David Page, *Elements of Geology* (1849)]

Trimmer's Geology & Mineralogy (August 5, 1849). [Joshua Trimmer, *Practical Geology and Mineralogy* (1842)]

Davies' Shades Shadows and Linear Perspective (August 5, 1849). [Charles Davies, *A Treatise on Shades and Shadows, and Linear Perspective* (1848)]

Zoology from the Edinburg Encyclopedia (August 12, 1849)

Carpenter's Physiology (October 7, 1849). [William Benjamin Carpenter, *Principles of Human Physiology,* 3rd American ed. (1847)]

Reese's Vegetable Physiology (November 18, 1849). [David Meredith Reese, *Rudiments of Vegetable Physiology* (1846)]

Brougham's "Review of Cuvier's Researches" (December 9, 1849). [Henry Peter, Lord Brougham and Vaux, probably reviewing the work of George Cuvier on the natural history of animals.]

Brougham on Instinct (December 16, 1849). [Henry Peter, Lord Brougham and Vaux, *Dialogues on Instinct; with Analytical View of the Researches on Fossil Osteology* (1845)]

Almstead's Natural Philosophy (magnetism) (March 24, 1850)

"Elements of Zoology" (April 21, 1850). [Possibly David Meredith Reese, ed., *Elements of Zoology; or, Natural History of Animals* (1849)]

Davies Descriptive Geometry (September 15, 1850). [Charles Davies, *Elements of Descriptive Geometry,* 2nd ed. (1840)]

Conchology (November 24, 1850)

Brocklesby's "Elements of Meteorology" (June 29, 1851). [John Brocklesby, *Elements of Meteorology*, 2nd ed. (1849)]

Liebigs "Agricultural Chemistry" (June 29, 1851). [Justus Freiherr von Liebig, *Professor Liebig's Complete Works on Chemistry: Comprising His Agricultural Chemistry* (1850)]

Loomis' Differential Calculus (July 6, 1851). [Elias Loomis, *Elements of Analytical Geometry and of the Differential and Integral Calculus* (1851)]

Loomis'"Recent Progress of Astronomy" (September 28, 1851). [Elias Loomis, *The Recent Progress of Astronomy: Especially in the United States* (1851)]

"Randal on Sheep-Husbandry" (September 12, 1852). [Henry Stephens Randall, *Sheep Husbandry in the South* (1848)]

Edinburgh Encyclopedia on Hydrodynamics (September 26, 1852)

Political Economy

Article on the Organization of Labor in July number of *Electic* Magazine ["explanation of schemes of Fourier and St Simon"] (August 19, 1849). [*The Electic Magazine of Foreign Literature, Science and Art*]

Carey's papers on the tariff (June 23, 1850). [Possibly Mathew Carey, *Cursory Views of the Liberal and Restrictive Systems of Political Economy*, 4th ed. (1826)]

Carlyle's Latter Day Pamphlets, the 3rd, 4th, 5th, & 6th—Parliaments. (September 1, 1850). [Thomas Carlyle, *Latter-Day Pamphlets* (Boston, 1850)]

Mill's Political Economy (September 22, 1850). [Although Hughes did not specify whether this was James Mill's or John Mill's *Political Economy*, he does mention reading two volumes, which strongly suggests that it was John Stuart Mill's *Principles of Political Economy*, which appeared as a two-volume work, 2nd ed. (1849)]

articles of Reviews on Southern manufactures (April 27, 1851)

Congressional Speeches on the Compromise Measures (June 22, 1851)

"Fletcher's Studies on Slavery" (July 25, 1852). [John Fletcher, *Studies on Slavery* (1852)]

Calhoun's Disquisition on Government (August 15, 1852)

Webster's Reply to Calhoun on the South Carolina Tariff Matter (August 22, 1852)

Redfields' "Men of the Times" (November 28, 1852). [Probably the encyclopedia *The Men of the Time: or, Sketches of Living Notables* (New York: Redfield, 1852)]

Montesquieu's "Spirit of Laws" (March 27, 1853). [Charles de Secondat, Baron de Montesquieu (1689–1755), *The Spirit of the Laws*]

NOVELS

Alphonse De Lamartine's "Raphael" (March 25, 1849) [*Raphael, or, Pages of the Book of Life at Twenty* (1849)]

"Vivian Grey" (December 9, 1849). [Benjamin Disraeli, *Vivian Grey,* 3rd American ed. (1833)]

Second volume of the "Caxtons" (April 7, 1850). [Edward Bulwer, Lord Lytton, *The Caxtons: A Family Picture* (1849)]

Walter Scott's Woodstock (June 23, 1850). [1826]

D'Israelis "Young Duke" (August 4, 1850). [Benjamin Disraeli, *The Young Duke* (1831)]

"Contarini Fleming" (August 4, 1850). [Benjamin Disraeli, *Contarini Fleming: A Romance* (1832)]

D'Israelis' Venetia (August 11, 1850). [Benjamin Disraeli, *Venetia* (1837)]

Scott's Monastery & Abbot (September 8, 1850). [Walter Scott, *The Monastery: A Romance* (1820) and *The Abbot: Being a Sequel to The Monastery* (1820)]

Bulwer's Last Days of Pompeii (September 22, 1850). [Edward Bulwer, Lord Lytton, *The Last Days of Pompeii* (1850)]

"Clinton Bradshaw" (September 29, 1850). [Frederick W. Thomas, *Clinton Bradshaw; or The Adventures of a Lawyer* (1835)]

"Genievieve" of Lamartine (December 29, 1850). [Alphonse de Lamartine, *Genevieve* (1850)]

David Copperfield of Dickens (December 29, 1850). [Charles Dickens, *The Personal History and Experience of David Copperfield the Younger* (1850)]

Scott's "Marmion" (March 2, 1851). [Sir Walter Scott, *Marmion: A Tale of Flodden Field* (1808)]

Dickens' Pickwick Papers (May 4, 1851). [Charles Dickens, *The Posthumous Papers of the Pickwick Club* (1837)]

Dumas' Fernande (May 4, 1851). [Alexandre Dumas, *Fernande* (1844)]

Rockingham (May 4, 1851). [Probably Philippe Ferdinand Auguste de Rohan-Chabot, comte de Jarnac, *Rockingham: or, The Younger Brother* (1849)]

"Adventures of an Attorney &c" (June 6, 1851). [Sir George Stephen, *Adventures of an Attorney in Search of a Practice, or A Delineation of Professional Life* (1839)]

"St. Ronan's Well" (June 15, 1851). [Sir Walter Scott, *St. Ronan's Well* (1824)]

"Old Mortality" (July 6, 1851). [Sir Walter Scott, *Old Mortality* (1816)]

"Alton Locke Tailor & Poet" ("glanced with delight, amazement, hope, pity") (June 6, 1851). [Charles Kingsley, *Alton Locke, Tailor and Poet, An Autobiography*, 1st American ed. (1851)]

"Chronicles of the Canongate" (August 10, 1851). [Sir Walter Scott, *Chronicles of the Canongate*. Hughes did not specify whether he read the first (1827) or second series (1828) of *Chronicles of the Canongate*, although his mention in the same entry of "St. Valentine's Day," which was part of the second series, suggests it was the latter.]

"Red Gauntlet" (August 10, 1851). [Sir Walter Scott, *Red Gauntlet: A Tale of the Eighteenth Century* (1824)]

"St. Valentine's Day" (August 10, 1851). [Sir Walter Scott, *The Fair Maid of Perth; or Saint Valentine's Day* (1828)]

"Legend of Montrose" (August 17, 1851). [Sir Walter Scott, *A Legend of Montrose* (1819)]

Scott's "Fortunes of Nigel" (September 7, 1851). [Sir Walter Scott, *The Fortunes of Nigel: A Romance* (1822)]

"Mordaunt Hall" (September 21, 1851). [Anne Marsh-Caldwell, *Mordaunt Hall; or, A September Night* (1849)]

Thackeray's "Pendennis" (September 28, 1851). [William Thackeray, *The History of Pendennis* (1850)]

"Uncle Tom's Cabin" by Mrs Beecher Stowe (August 15, 1852). [Harriet Beecher Stowe, *Uncle Tom's Cabin; or, Life Among the Lowly* (1851)]

"Pilgrims of the Rhine" (September 19, 1852). [Edward Bulwer, Lord Lytton, *The Pilgrims of the Rhine* (1843)]

Mrs Eastman's "Aunt Phyllis' Cabin" (October 10, 1852). [Mary H. Eastman, *Aunt Phillis's Cabin, or, Southern Life as It Is* (1852)]

Savage's "Reuben Medlicott" (October 31, 1852). [Marmion W. Savage, *Reuben Medlicott, or, The Coming Man* (1852)]

Randolph's tale about slavery (November 14, 1852). [Probably Charles Jacobs Peterson's *The Cabin and Parlor; or, Slaves and Masters*. This book was published under Peterson's pseudonym, J. Thorton Randolph (1852)]

Hawthorne's "Blithedale Romance" (November 21, 1852). [Nathaniel Hawthorne, *The Blithedale Romance* (1852)]

Faben's "Life on the Isthmus" (February 13, 1853). [Joseph W. Fabens, *A Story of Life on the Isthmus* (1852)]

"Vanity Fair" by Thackeray (March 20, 1853). [William Thackeray, *Vanity Fair, A Novel Without a Hero* (1847)]

Eugene Sue's "Wandering Jew" (January 16, 1853). [(1844)]

"Villette" (April 3, 1853). [Charlotte Brontë, *Villette* (1853)]

Miscellaneous

Whately's Rhetoric (December 17, 1848). [Richard Whately, *Elements of Rhetoric* (1847)]

Henry Siddons on Gesture (January 28, 1849). [Johann Jakob Engel (1741–1802), *Practical Illustrations of Rhetorical Gesture and Action,* ed. and trans. Henry Siddons]

Doctor Rush on the Human Voice (February 4, 1849). [James Rush, *The Philosophy of the Human Voice,* 2nd ed. (1833)]

Getty's Oratory (April 21, 1850). [John A. Getty, *Elements of Rhetoric* (1831)]

"Varley" (June 1, 1850)

"Alison on 'Taste' (September 1, 1850). [Archibald Alison, *Essays on the Nature and Principles of Taste* (1844)]

Elements of Drawing (November 24, 1850). [Possibly John Heaviside Clark, *Elements of Drawing,* 2nd American ed. (1849). This work was part of the Chambers' educational course series. Hughes read several volumes from the series, including David Page's *Elements of Geology* and David Meredith Reese, ed., *Elements of Zoology.*]

"Fernley Manor" (January 4, 1852)

"Lessons of Madevilles [*sic*] System of Elocution" (May 16, 1852). [Probably Henry Mandeville, *An Introduction to the Author's "Course of Reading" and "Elements of Reading and Oratory"* (1848)]

article on "Heraldry" (September 26, 1852)

Gillespie on "Roads and Railroads" (October 3, 1852). [William Mitchell Gillespie, *A Manual of the Principles and Practice of Road-Making . . .* (1852)]

"Mary the Star of the Sea" ("a tale of the Catholic Religion") (October 3, 1852)

Dix's "Winter in Madeira" (February 13, 1853). [John A. Dix, *A Winter in Madeira: and A Summer in Spain and Florence* (1850)]

"English Items" (April 3, 1853)

BIBLIOGRAPHY

UNPUBLISHED PRIMARY SOURCES

Louisiana State University Library, Special Collections, Baton Rouge, Louisiana
  Batchelor, Albert A. Papers.
  Seymour, William. Papers.
  Terry, William and Family. Papers.
Mississippi Department of Archives and History, Jackson, Mississippi
  Alcorn Family. Papers.
  Barksdale, Ethelbert. Papers.
  Claiborne, J. F. H. Collection.
  Claiborne County
      Land Deeds.
      Letters of Administrators and Guardians.
      Marriage Bonds.
      Minutes of Orphans' Court.
      Personal Tax Rolls.
      Probate Court Records.
  Daniell, Smith Coffee, IV. Collection.
  Ellett-Jefferies Family. Papers.
  First Presbyterian Church of Port Gibson. Records.
  Forbes, Alden Spooner. Diary.
  Hughes, Henry. Papers.
  Hughes, Mary Bertron. Letters.
  Hughes, William and Family. Papers.
  Humphreys, George Wilson and Family. Papers.
  Magruder, James Trueman. Papers.
  Maury, James H. Papers.
  Musgrove, Maggie Williams. Papers.
  Oakland College. Papers.
  Port Gibson Bank. Records.
  Port Gibson Female College. Papers.

Quitman, John A. Papers.
Wade, Walter. Plantation Diaries.
Wailes, Benjamin L. C. Diaries.
Wailes, Benjamin L. C. Letterbook.
Wailes, Benjamin L. C. Papers.
Wailes-Covington Family. Papers.
Whitehurst, William N. Papers.

CENSUSES

Seventh Census of the United States, 1850. Washington, D.C., 1853.
Eighth Census of the United States, 1860. Washington, D.C., 1864.

NEWSPAPERS

Baton Rouge *Daily Advocate,* 1854–60.
Fayette (Miss.) *Watch Tower,* 1856–57.
Jackson *Mississippian and State Gazette,* 1857–58.
Jackson *Semi-Weekly Mississippian,* 1855, 1857–60.
Jefferson (Miss.) *Journal,* 1857–59.
Natchez *Daily Courier,* 1857–60.
Natchez *Mississippi Free Trader,* 1843–61.
New Orleans *Crescent,* 1849–61.
New Orleans *Daily Picayune,* 1850–61.
New Orleans *Weekly True Delta,* 1858–61.
Port Gibson *Correspondent,* 1835–47.
Port Gibson *Herald,* 1846, 1848.
Port Gibson *Herald and Correspondent,* 1849–51.
Port Gibson *Southern Reveille,* 1852–54, 1858–59.
Vicksburg *Whig,* 1839–60.
Vidalia (La.) *Concordia Intelligencer,* 1858–60.
Woodville (Miss.) *Republican,* 1855.

PUBLISHED PRIMARY SOURCES

Bacon, Francis. *The Philosophical Works of Francis Bacon.* Edited by John M.
　　Robertson. Freeport, N.Y., 1970.
Baldwin, Joseph G. *The Flush Times of Alabama and Mississippi: A Series of*
　　Sketches. 1853; rpr. Baton Rouge, 1987.
Carlyle, Thomas. *The Works of Thomas Carlyle.* 30 vols. New York, 1903.
Catterall, Helen T., ed. *Judicial Cases Concerning American Slavery and the Negro.*
　　5 vols. Washington, D.C., 1926–36.
Claiborne, J. F. H. *Life and Correspondence of John A. Quitman.* 2 vols. New
　　York, 1860.

Cobb, Thomas R. R. *An Inquiry into the Law of Negro Slavery in the United States of America*. 1858; rpr. New York, 1968.

Davis, Reuben. *Recollections of Mississippi and Mississipians*. 1891; rpr. Hattiesburg, Miss., 1972.

Elliott, E. N., ed. *Cotton Is King and Pro-Slavery Arguments*. Augusta, Ga., 1860.

Faust, Drew Gilpin, ed. *The Ideology of Slavery: Proslavery Thought in the Antebellum South*. Baton Rouge, 1981.

Fitzhugh, George. *Cannibals All! or, Slaves Without Masters*. Edited by C. Vann Woodward. 1857; rpr. Cambridge, Mass., 1960.

———. *Sociology for the South; or, The Failure of Free Society*. 1854; rpr. New York, 1965.

Hughes, Henry. *Speech of Henry Hughes, on Our Administration of Justice; or, The New Bar and New Court.* . . . Port Gibson, Miss., 1860.

———. "State Liberties; or, The Right to African Contract Labor." *De Bow's Review*, N.s., I (1858), 626–53.

———. *Treatise on Sociology, Theoretical and Practical*. 1854; rpr. New York, 1968.

Hundley, Daniel R. *Social Relations in Our Southern States*. Edited by William J. Cooper, Jr. 1860; rpr. Baton Rouge, 1979.

Hurd, James Codman. *The Law of Freedom and Bondage in the United States*. 2 vols. Boston, 1858.

[Ingraham, Joseph H.]. *The South-West, by a Yankee*. 2 vols. 1835; rpr. New York, 1968.

Lenzer, Gertrud, ed. *Auguste Comte and Positivism: The Essential Writings*. Chicago, 1975.

Lyman, Stanford M., ed. *Selected Writings of Henry Hughes, Antebellum Southerner, Slavocrat, Sociologist*. Jackson, 1985.

McKitrick, Eric L., ed. *Slavery Defended: The Views of the Old South*. Englewood Cliffs, N.J., 1963.

Moore, William D. *The Life and Works of Col. Henry Hughes: A Funeral Sermon Preached in the Methodist Episcopal Church, Port Gibson, Miss., October 26th, 1862*. Mobile, 1863.

The Pro-Slavery Argument as Maintained by the Most Distinguished Writers of the Southern States. Philadelphia, 1853.

Rose, Willie Lee, ed. *A Documentary History of Slavery in North America*. New York, 1976.

Thornwell, James Henley. *The Rights and Duties of Masters*. Charleston, 1850.

Secondary Sources

Books

Amlund, Curtis Arthur. *Federalism in the Southern Confederacy*. Washington, D.C., 1966.

Atherton, Lewis E. *The Southern Country Store, 1800–1860.* Baton Rouge, 1949.

Baker, Keith Michael. *Condorcet: From Natural Philosophy to Social Mathematics.* Chicago, 1975.

Barney, William L. *The Secessionist Impulse: Alabama and Mississippi in 1860.* Princeton, 1974.

Bateman, Fred, and Thomas Weiss. *A Deplorable Scarcity: The Failure of Industrialization in the Slave Economy.* Chapel Hill, 1981.

Bensel, Richard Franklin. *Yankee Leviathan: The Origins of Central State Authority in America, 1859–1877.* New York, 1990.

Boles, John B., and Evelyn Thomas Nolen, eds. *Interpreting Southern History: Historiographical Essays in Honor of Sanford W. Higginbotham.* Baton Rouge, 1987.

Bonner, James C. *Milledgeville, Georgia's Antebellum Capital.* Athens, Ga., 1978.

Bozeman, Theodore Dwight. *Protestants in an Age of Science: The Baconian Ideal and Antebellum American Religious Thought.* Chapel Hill, 1977.

Brugger, Robert J. *Beverley Tucker: Heart Over Head in the Old South.* Baltimore, 1978.

Cash, W. J. *The Mind of the South.* New York, 1941.

Clinton, Catherine. *The Plantation Mistress: Woman's World in the Old South.* New York, 1982.

Conkin, Paul. *Prophets of Prosperity: America's First Political Economists.* Bloomington, 1980.

Coulter, E. Merton. *College Life in the Old South.* 1928; rpr. Athens, Ga., 1983.

Davis, David Brion. *The Problem of Slavery in the Age of Revolution.* Ithaca, 1975.

———. *The Problem of Slavery in Western Culture.* Ithaca, 1966.

———. *Slavery and Human Progress.* New York, 1984.

DeCredico, Mary A. *Patriotism for Profit: Georgia's Urban Entrepreneurs and the Confederate War Effort.* Chapel Hill, 1990.

Dobb, Maurice. *Studies in the Development of Capitalism.* New York, 1947.

Dorfman, Joseph. *The Economic Mind in American Civilization, 1606–1865.* 5 vols. New York, 1946–59.

Eaton, Clement J. *The Mind of the Old South.* Baton Rouge, 1964.

Escott, Paul D. *After Secession: Jefferson Davis and the Failure of Confederate Nationalism.* Baton Rouge, 1978.

Farmer, James Oscar, Jr. *The Metaphysical Confederacy: James Henley Thornwell and the Synthesis of Southern Values.* Macon, Ga., 1986.

Faust, Drew Gilpin. *The Creation of Confederate Nationalism: Ideology and Identity in the Civil War South.* Baton Rouge, 1988.

———. *James Henry Hammond and the Old South: A Design for Mastery.* Baton Rouge, 1982.

————. *A Sacred Circle: The Dilemma of the Intellectual in the Old South.* Baltimore, 1977.

Fede, Andrew. *People Without Rights: An Interpretation of the Fundamentals of the Law of Slavery in the U.S. South.* New York, 1992.

Fields, Barbara J. *Slavery and Freedom on the Middle Ground: Maryland During the Nineteenth Century.* New Haven, 1985.

Fox-Genovese, Elizabeth. *Within the Plantation Household: Black and White Women of the Old South.* Chapel Hill, 1988.

Fox-Genovese, Elizabeth, and Eugene D. Genovese. *Fruits of Merchant Capital: Slavery and Bourgeois Property in the Rise and Expansion of Capitalism.* New York, 1983.

Fredrickson, George M. *The Arrogance of Race: Historical Perspectives on Slavery, Racism, and Social Inequality.* Middletown, Conn., 1988.

————. *The Black Image in the White Mind: The Debate on Afro-American Character and Destiny, 1817–1914.* New York, 1971.

————. *The Inner Civil War: Northern Intellectuals and the Crisis of the Union.* New York, 1965.

Freehling, William W. *Prelude to Civil War: The Nullification Controversy in South Carolina, 1816–1836.* New York, 1965.

————. *The Reintegration of American History: Slavery and the Civil War.* New York, 1994.

Genovese, Eugene D. *In Red and Black: Marxian Explorations in Southern and Afro-American History.* 2nd ed. Knoxville, 1984.

————. *The Political Economy of Slavery: Studies in the Economy and Society of the Slave South.* New York, 1965.

————. *Roll, Jordan, Roll: The World the Slaves Made.* New York, 1974.

————. *The Slaveholders' Dilemma: Freedom and Progress in Southern Conservative Thought, 1820–1860.* Columbia, 1992.

————. *"Slavery Ordained of God": The Southern Slaveholders' View of History and Modern Politics.* Gettysburg, 1985.

————. *The Southern Tradition: The Achievement and Limitations of an American Conservatism.* Cambridge, Mass., 1994.

————. *The World the Slaveholders Made: Two Essays in Interpretation.* New York, 1969.

Gillespie, Neal C. *The Collapse of Orthodoxy: The Intellectual Ordeal of George Frederick Holmes.* Charlottesville, 1972.

Gray, Lewis Cecil. *History of Agriculture in the Southern United States to 1860.* 2 vols. 1933; rpr. Gloucester, 1958.

Greenberg, Kenneth S. *Masters and Statesmen: The Political Culture of American Slavery.* Baltimore, 1985.

Guarreri, Carl J. *The Utopian Alternative: Fourierism in Ninteenth-Century America*. Ithaca, 1991.

Gutman, Herbert G. *The Black Family in Slavery and Freedom, 1750–1925*. New York, 1976.

Hartz, Louis. *The Liberal Tradition in America: An Interpretation of American Political Thought Since the Revolution*. New York, 1955.

Hawkins, Richmond Laurin. *Auguste Comte and the United States (1816–1853)*. Cambridge, Mass., 1936.

———. *Positivism in the United States (1853–1861)*. Cambridge, Mass., 1938.

Headley, Katy McCaleb, comp. *Claiborne County, Mississippi: The Promised Land*. Port Gibson, Miss., 1976.

Hill, Louise Biles. *State Socialism in the Confederate States of America*. Charlottesville, 1936.

Hilliard, Sam Bowers. *Hog Meat and Hoe Cake: Food Supply in the Old South, 1840–1860*. Carbondale, Ill., 1972.

Holifield, E. Brooks. *The Gentlemen Theologians: American Theology in Southern Culture, 1795–1860*. Durham, 1978.

Horsman, Reginald. *Josiah Nott of Mobile: Southerner, Physician, and Racial Theorist*. Baton Rouge, 1987.

Jenkins, William Sumner. *Pro-Slavery Thought in the Old South*. 1935; rpr. Gloucester, 1960.

Johnson, Vicki Vaughan. *The Men and the Vision of the Southern Commercial Conventions, 1845–1871*. Columbia, Mo., 1992.

Johnston, James Hugo. *Race Relations in Virginia and Miscegenation in the South, 1776–1860*. Amherst, 1970.

Kaufman, Allen. *Capitalism, Slavery, and Republican Values: American Political Economists, 1819–1848*. Austin, 1982.

Kolchin, Peter. *Unfree Labor: American Slavery and Russian Serfdom*. Cambridge, Mass., 1987.

Kousser, J. Morgan, and James McPherson, eds. *Region, Race, and Reconstruction: Essays in Honor of C. Vann Woodward*. New York, 1982.

Kulikoff, Allan. *Tobacco and Slaves: The Development of Southern Cultures in the Chesapeake, 1680–1800*. Chapel Hill, 1986.

Laslett, Peter, ed., with Richard Wall. *Household and Family in Past Time: Comparative Studies in the Size and Structure of the Domestic Group over the Last Three Centuries in England, France, Serbia, Japan, and Colonial North America, with Further Materials from Western Europe*. Cambridge, Eng., 1972.

Lebsock, Suzanne. *The Free Women of Petersburg: Status and Culture in a Southern Town, 1784–1860*. New York, 1984.

Leiman, Melvin M. *Jacob N. Cardozo: Economic Thought in the Antebellum South*. New York, 1966.

Lonn, Ella. *Salt as a Factor in the Confederacy*. New York, 1933.

Loveland, Anne C. *Southern Evangelicals and the Social Order, 1800–1860*. Baton Rouge, 1980.

Luraghi, Raimondo. *The Rise and Fall of the Plantation South*. New York, 1978.

Manuel, Frank. *The Prophets of Paris*. Cambridge, Mass., 1962.

Mathews, Donald G. *Religion in the Old South*. Chicago, 1977.

May, Robert. *John A. Quitman: Old South Crusader*. Baton Rouge, 1985.

McCardell, John. *The Idea of a Southern Nation: Southern Nationalists and Southern Nationalism, 1830–1860*. New York, 1979.

McLemore, Richard A., ed. *A History of Mississippi*. Hattiesburg, Miss., 1973.

Moore, Albert Burton. *Conscription and Conflict in the Confederacy*. New York, 1924.

Moore, John Hebron. *Agriculture in Ante-Bellum Mississippi*. New York, 1958.

———. *The Emergence of the Cotton Kingdom in the Old Southwest: Mississippi, 1770–1860*. Baton Rouge, 1988.

North, Douglass C. *The Economic Growth of the United States, 1790–1860*. Englewood Cliffs, N.J., 1961.

Oakes, James. *The Ruling Race: A History of American Slaveholders*. New York, 1982.

———. *Slavery and Freedom: An Interpretation of the Old South*. New York, 1990.

O'Brien, Michael, ed. *All Clever Men Who Make Their Way: Critical Discourse in the Old South*. Fayetteville, 1982.

———. *A Character of Hugh Legaré*. Knoxville, 1985.

———. *Rethinking the South: Essays in Intellectual History*. Baltimore, 1988.

O'Brien, Michael, and David Moltke-Hansen, eds. *Intellectual Life in Antebellum Charleston*. Knoxville, 1986.

Phillips, Ulrich Bonnell. *American Negro Slavery: A Survey of the Supply, Employment, and Control of Negro Labor as Determined by the Plantation Regime*. Edited by Eugene D. Genovese. 1918; rpr. Baton Rouge, 1966.

———. *Life and Labor in the Old South*. New York, 1929.

———. *The Slave Economy of the Old South: Selected Essays in Economic and Social History*. Edited by Eugene D. Genovese. Baton Rouge, 1968.

Ramsdell, Charles W. *Behind the Lines in the Southern Confederacy*. Baton Rouge, 1944.

Rawick, George. *From Sundown to Sunup: The Making of the Black Community*. Westport, Conn., 1972.

Reinders, Robert C. *End of an Era: New Orleans, 1850–1860*. New Orleans, 1964.

Ringold, May Spencer. *The Role of the State Legislatures in the Confederacy*. Athens, Ga., 1966.

Rose, Willie Lee. *Slavery and Freedom*. Edited by William W. Freehling. New York, 1982.

Sellers, Charles Grier, Jr., ed. *The Southerner as American*. Chapel Hill, 1960.

Shore, Laurence. *Southern Capitalists: The Ideological Leadership of an Elite, 1832–1885*. Chapel Hill, 1986.

Simpson, Lewis P. *The Brazen Face of History: Studies in the Literary Consciousness in America*. Baton Rouge, 1980.

————. *The Dispossessed Garden: Pastoral and History in Southern Literature*. 1975; rpr. Baton Rouge, 1983.

————. *The Man of Letters in New England and the South: Essays on the Literary Vocation in America*. Baton Rouge, 1973.

Skipper, Ottis Clark. *J. D. B. De Bow, Magazinist of the Old South*. Athens, Ga., 1958.

Snay, Mitchell. *Gospel of Disunion: Religion and Separatism in the Antebellum South*. New York, 1993.

Stampp, Kenneth M. *The Peculiar Institution: Slavery in the Antebellum South*. New York, 1956.

Stanton, William. *The Leopard's Spots: Scientific Attitudes Toward Race in America, 1815–1859*. Chicago, 1960.

Stowe, Steven M. *Intimacy and Power in the Old South: Ritual in the Lives of the Planters*. Baltimore, 1987.

Sydnor, Charles. *Slavery in Mississippi*. 1933; rpr. Gloucester, 1965.

Takaki, Ronald T. *A Pro-Slavery Crusade: The Agitation to Reopen the African Slave Trade*. New York, 1971.

Taylor, George Rogers. *The Transportation Revolution, 1815–1860*. New York, 1951.

Taylor, William R. *Cavalier and Yankee: The Old South and American National Character*. New York, 1957.

Thomas, Emory M. *The Confederate Nation, 1861–1865*. New York, 1979.

Thompson, Edgar T. *Plantation Societies, Race Relations, and the South: The Regimentation of Populations*. Durham, 1975.

Tise, Larry E. *Proslavery: A History of the Defense of Slavery in America, 1701–1840*. Athens, Ga., 1987.

Tushnet, Mark V. *The American Law of Slavery, 1810–1860: Considerations of Humanity and Interest*. Princeton, 1981.

Vandiver, Frank. *Ploughshares into Swords: Josiah Gorgas and Confederate Ordnance*. Austin, 1952.

White, Deborah Gray. *Ar'n't I a Woman? Female Slaves in the Plantation South*. New York, 1985.

Woodman, Harold D. *King Cotton and His Retainers: Financing and Marketing the Cotton Crop of the South, 1800–1925*. Lexington, Ky., 1968.

Woodward, C. Vann. *American Counterpoint: Slavery and Racism in the North-South Dialogue*. Boston, 1971.

Wright, Gavin. *Old South, New South: Revolutions in the Southern Economy Since the Civil War.* New York, 1986.

———. *The Political Economy of the Cotton South: Households, Markets, and Wealth in the Nineteenth Century.* New York, 1978.

Wyatt-Brown, Bertram. *Southern Honor: Ethics and Behavior in the Old South.* New York, 1982.

———. *Yankee Saints and Southern Sinners.* Baton Rouge, 1985.

Articles

Bensel, Richard Franklin. "Southern Leviathan: The Development of Central State Authority in the Confederate States of America." In *Studies in American Political Development.* vol. II. Edited by Karen Orren and Stephen Skowronek. New Haven, 1987.

Bernard, L. L. "Henry Hughes, First American Sociologist." *Social Forces,* XV (1936), 154–74.

Brugger, Robert J. "The Mind of the Old South: New Views." *Virginia Quarterly Review,* LVI (1980), 277–95.

Clark, Christopher. "The Household Economy, Market Exchange and the Rise of Capitalism in the Connecticut Valley, 1800–1860." *Journal of Social History,* XIII (1979), 169–89.

Donald, David. "The Proslavery Argument Reconsidered." *Journal of Southern History,* XXXVII (1971), 3–18.

Faust, Drew Gilpin. "Culture, Conflict and Community: The Meaning of Power on an Antebellum Plantation." *Journal of Social History,* XIV (1980), 83–98.

———. "A Southern Stewardship: The Intellectual and the Proslavery Argument." *American Quarterly,* XXXI (1979), 63–80.

Finkelman, Paul. "Exploring Southern Legal History." *North Carolina Law Review,* LXIV (1985), 77–116.

Fox-Genovese, Elizabeth. "Antebellum Southern Households: A New Perspective on a Familiar Question." *Review,* VII (1983), 215–53.

Fox-Genovese, Elizabeth, and Eugene D. Genovese. "The Divine Sanction of Social Order: Religious Foundations of the Southern Slaveholders' World View." *Journal of the American Academy of Religion,* LV (1987), 201–23.

Genovese, Eugene D. "The Southern Slaveholders' View of the Middle Ages." In *Medievalism in American Culture: Papers of the Eighteenth Annual Conference of the Center for Medieval and Early Renaissance Studies,* edited by Bernard Rosenthal and Paul E. Szarmach. Binghamton, N.Y., 1989.

Genovese, Eugene D., and Elizabeth Fox-Genovese. "Slavery, Economic Development, and the Law: The Dilemma of the Southern Political Economists, 1800–1860." *Washington and Lee Law Review,* XLI (1984), 1–29.

———. "The Religious Ideals of Southern Slave Society." *Georgia Historical Quarterly,* LXX (1986), 1–16.

Hahn, Steven. "The 'Unmaking' of the Southern Yeomanry: The Transformation of the Georgia Upcountry, 1860–1890." In *The Countryside in the Age of Capitalist Transformation: Essays in the Social History of Rural America,* edited by Steven Hahn and Jonathan Prude. Chapel Hill, 1985.

Hesseltine, William B. "Some New Aspects of the Pro-Slavery Argument." *Journal of Negro History,* XXI (1936), 1–15.

Kolchin, Peter. "In Defense of Servitude: American Proslavery and Russian Proserfdom Arguments, 1760–1860." *American Historical Review,* LXXXV (1980), 809–27.

Luraghi, Raimondo. "The Civil War and the Modernization of American Society: Social Structure and Industrial Revolution in the Old South Before and During the War." *Civil War History,* XVIII (1972), 230–50.

Maddex, Jack P., Jr. "A Paradox of Christian Amelioration: Proslavery Ideology and Church Ministries to Slaves." In *The Southern Enigma: Essays on Race, Class, and Folk Culture,* edited by Walter J. Fraser and Winfred B. Moore, Jr. Westport, Conn., 1983.

———. "Proslavery Millennialism: Social Eschatology in Antebellum Southern Calvinism." *American Quarterly,* XXXI (1979), 46–62.

———. "'The Southern Apostasy' Revisited: The Significance of Proslavery Christianity." *Marxist Perspectives,* II (1979), 132–41.

McCurry, Stephanie. "The Politics of Yeoman Households in South Carolina." In *Divided Houses: Gender and the Civil War,* edited by Catherine Clinton and Nina Silber. New York, 1992.

Morrow, Ralph E. "The Proslavery Argument Revisited." *Mississippi Valley Historical Review,* XLVII (1961), 79–94.

O'Brien, Michael. "Biography and the Old South: A Review Essay." *Virginia Magazine of History and Biography,* XCIII (1985), 375–88.

Ramsdell, Charles W. "The Control of Manufacturing by the Confederate Government." *Mississippi Valley Historical Review,* VIII (1921), 231–49.

Rogers, Tommy Wayne. "Oakland College, 1830–1871." *Journal of Mississippi History,* XXXVI (1974), 143–60.

Snay, Mitchell. "American Thought and Southern Distinctiveness: The Southern Clergy and the Sanctification of Slavery." *Civil War History,* XXXV (1989), 311–28.

Wyatt-Brown, Bertram. "Modernizing Southern Slavery: The Proslavery Argument Reinterpreted." In *Region, Race, and Reconstruction: Essays in Honor of C. Vann Woodward,* edited by J. Morgan Kousser and James M. McPherson. New York, 1982.

———. "Proslavery and Antislavery Intellectuals: Class Concepts and Polemical

Struggle." In *Antislavery Reconsidered: New Perspectives on the Abolitionists,* edited by Lewis Perry and Michael Fellman. Baton Rouge, 1979.

Dissertations and Theses

Bruss, Melvin Kellogg. "History of Oakland College, Mississippi, 1830–1870." M.A. thesis, Louisiana State University, 1965.

Guess, Richard Malcolm. "Henry Hughes, Sociologist, 1829– 1862." M.A. thesis, University of Mississippi, 1930.

Hearn, Walter C. "Towns in Antebellum Mississippi." Ph.D. dissertation, University of Mississippi, 1969.

McCurry, Stephanie. "Defense of Their World: Gender, Class, and the Yeomanry of the South Carolina Low Country, 1820–1860." Ph.D. dissertation, State University of New York at Binghamton, 1989.

Neal, Lamar B. "'Chronicles of the Fire Eaters': A Contemporary Account of the Secession Controversy in Mississippi, 1849–1853." M.A. thesis, Mississippi State College, 1956.

Straka, Gerald Milton. "The Influence of Thomas Carlyle on the Old South, 1848–1865." M.A. thesis, University of Virginia, 1953.

INDEX

lectual influences, 74; and God, 75; and Hughes's legal training, 75; "Practical Sociology" section of, 75, 78*n*, 81, 85, 87, 115; and definition of *sociology*, 75–76, 112–13; style of, 75, 81, 140; "Theoretical Sociology" section of, 75, 78, 78*n*, 79–82, 84–85, 87, 103; and state power, 76–79, 87, 92, 96–98, 186; and United States Constitution, 80; contradictions of, 81, 104, 111–12, 137; and southern society, 81, 85, 98, 138; and human nature, 82; and warranteeism, 85–138; and labor obligation, 87; and property rights, 97, 99–100, 114; and manumission, 104–107, 109, 111; and racism, 107–12; and miscegenation, 108–109; and nonwarrantors, 110–12, 124; and free labor, 115–16, 147; and free labor households, 118, 120, 127–31; and plantation households, 118, 119, 120–27; reaction to, 139–43; and African slave trade writings, 146, 147, 149, 152, 159, 177; and science, 163. *See also* Warranteeism

Tushnet, Mark, 93, 99–100

Unfree labor: and state power, 1, 5, 188; Hughes's promotion of, 2, 67, 187, 188; Hughes's defense of, 4, 6, 168; and social organization, 5, 180; and slavery reform, 101; and racism, 107–108, 112. *See also* Slavery; Slaves; Warranteeism
United States Constitution, 80, 169

Van Dorn, Earl, 182
Vattel, Emmerich de, 95
Vertner, Mrs. S. E., 182
Virginia, 144, 184

Wages: and market, 92, 128–29, 147; and state power, 102; and plantation households, 125, 126–27; and free labor households, 129, 131–32, 134; and labor

distribution, 148. *See also* Income distribution
War of 1812, pp. 8, 9
Warranteeism: Hughes's development of, 3; and labor obligation, 5, 88, 91, 94, 105–106, 110; slavery's evolution into, 5, 85–86, 138, 168–69; and Civil War, 7; and Hughes's legal training, 75; and order, 76–77, 101, 180; and seven systems, 79; distinguished from slavery, 85–87, 94–95, 97, 99, 101, 104, 116, 168–69; and duty, 85; and state power, 87, 89–90, 92–97, 99–103, 105, 112, 114, 117, 179*n*, 187–88; and classes, 88–90, 107, 108, 110, 111; and subsistence, 94, 95, 107, 111, 126, 167; and human property, 99; and property rights, 100, 123; and hierarchy, 101; and manumission, 105–106, 111; and freedom, 106–107, 111; and free labor, 107, 115–16; and southern society, 108; and race, 109, 159, 167; and nonwarrantors, 110–12; and market, 116, 126; distinguished from free labor, 118, 124, 126, 147, 149; and plantation household, 119, 133; and families, 120, 123–24; and law, 122–23; contradictions in, 137, 167; reviews of, 141–42; and Hughes's African slave trade writings, 147–48; and United States Constitution, 169; and emancipation, 171. *See also* Slavery; Warrantees; Warrantors
Warrantees: and labor obligation, 5, 88–90; rights of, 86, 103, 125, 134; and state power, 87, 90, 92–95; and warrantors, 94, 95, 103–105, 121, 124, 135–36; and race, 109, 111; and plantation households, 121, 123–24, 132; transfer of, 136. *See also* Slaves
Warrantors: and state power, 87, 90, 92–95, 97, 99–103, 105, 114; and labor obligation, 88–91; role of, 93–95, 97–99, 106–107, 121–22; and warrantees, 94, 95, 103–105, 121, 123–24, 135–36; and